CHANCELLORSVILLE

Lee's Greatest Battle

CHANCELLORSVILLE

Lee's Greatest Battle

2nd Edition

Edward J. Stackpole

Commentary by D. Scott Hartwig
Foreword by William C. Davis

Stackpole Books

Copyright © 1988 by Stackpole Books
Copyright © 1958 by Edward J. Stackpole

Published by
STACKPOLE BOOKS
Cameron and Kelker Streets
P.O. Box 1831
Harrisburg, PA 17105

Printed in the United States of America

10   9   8   7   6   5   4   3

Cover design by Tracy Patterson.

Library of Congress Cataloging-in-Publication Data

Stackpole, Edward J. (Edward James), 1894–
    Chancellorsville : Lee's greatest battle / Edward J. Stackpole ;
commentary by D. Scott Hartwig ; foreword by William C. Davis. —
2nd ed.
        p.   cm.
    Bibliography: p.
    Includes index.
    ISBN 0-8117-2238-4
    1. Chancellorsville, Battle of, 1863.   I. Title.
E475.35.S8   1989
973.7'34 — dc19   88-29178
                                                                 CIP

DEDICATION

To the men of *my* Company M, 110th
Infantry, 28th Division, American Expeditionary Forces, World War I, of
Latrobe, Pennsylvania, who fought and
died on the battlefields of France.

FOREWORD

For a century and a quarter, the battle at Chancellorsville has remained the ultimate campaign of the Army of Northern Virginia. The army led by General Robert E. Lee, outnumbered two to one, faced by a foe better equipped and better supplied, lacking the presence of one of its two experienced corps commanders, still managed to crush and demoralize the Army of the Potomac in one of the most daring engagements in all of military history. More than any other military encounter, the battle at Chancellorsville ensured the enduring fame of Lee's great subordinate, Thomas J. "Stonewall" Jackson, just as surely as it was the battle that killed him.

It is strange that this most brilliant of Lee's battles has spawned fewer historical treatments than many of his lesser engagements. In the half century following the fight, only a few books emerged that dealt with Chancellorsville, none of them very distinguished. This changed in 1910 when John Bigelow published his massive book, *The Campaign of Chancellorsville*, a model scholarly study of a Civil War campaign. Unfortunately, it is ponderous, excessively detailed in places, and difficult to find.

Almost fifty years later, in 1958, for a new generation General E. J. Stackpole wrote a book in the popular readable style that would characterize the Civil War literature being written as the Civil War Centennial approached. *Chancellorsville: Lee's Greatest Battle* met with instant success. It was widely accepted by the general public and by Civil War buffs and praised by scholars and specialists. *Chancellorsville*, well written, blessed by battle maps that are the envy of many a Civil War book, grounded in the sound logic of a career military leader, quickly became the book of record for its time and its subject. Thirty years later, it is still often consulted.

Stackpole brought wide experience to his work. A combat infantry officer in World War I and a division commander in the next war, he was the author of four other Civil War battle studies dealing with Gettysburg, Fredericksburg, Cedar Mountain and Antietam, and the Shenandoah Valley Campaign of 1864. All are distinguished by the same clear style and the same broad acceptance.

Nevertheless, as any historian knows, history is not static. Oddly, history changes, and in the three decades since *Chancellorsville* first appeared, new scholarship and new thought have challenged some of the conclusions and interpretations made by Stackpole in 1958. A contemporary perspective doesn't invalidate his book. Rather, it further refines and illuminates it.

This second edition of *Chancellorsville* has been updated with commentary by Scott Hartwig, a longtime student of the battle. Outdated or no longer accepted conclusions have been examined. History is a fluid process in which little remains certain for long. This new edition simply continues the "flow" begun those thirty years ago.

It is testimony to the lasting value of *Chancellorsville* that, like the armies and leaders it so forcefully memorializes, it, too, lives on in the new interest of generation after generation.

William C. Davis
Editor-in-Chief,
National Historical Society

PREFACE TO FIRST EDITION

Grateful acknowledgment is made to Mr. Albert Dilla-hunty and Mr. Ralph Happel, Park Historians at the National Military Park at Fredericksburg, for their valued assistance in critically reading the manuscript and correct-ing the basic map on which many of the battle situations were plotted. Thanks are also due Mr. Roger S. Cohen, Jr., of Rockville, Maryland, for searching the manuscript for discrepancies.

The illustrations are mostly Brady photographs or con-temporary drawings, the latter mainly from *Battles and Leaders of the Civil War*. The maps are based on con-temporary maps drawn by Jed Hotchkiss, Chief Topog-rapher to General Jackson, and on several appearing in Bigelow's *Chancellorsville*. The Hotchkiss map was se-lected because, although it contains some inaccuracies especially as to stream lines, it probably portrays best the woods, the clearings, and the roads as they existed at the time of the battle. This is important in a number of in-stances, such as the fact that a clearing, extending from Hazel Grove to Fairview, permitted activities on one to be observed from the other. However, a number of mis-spelled names such as Zoan Church, Talley's, and Bullock's, have been checked by visits to the battlefield, plus infor-mation furnished by the Park Historians. Some gross errors in the course of the Rappahannock have been corrected from the modern topographical map prepared by the U. S. Army Engineers. The roads north of the Rappahannock have been sketched in from Bigelow's maps, the Hotchkiss map not extending that far. Similarly, Hotchkiss did not portray the wooded nature of the terrain north of the river nor south of the unfinished railroad, and that has been left blank also on the map drawn for this book.

The draftsmanship is by Mr. Ray Snow, Chief of the Art Department of The Telegraph Press. The research for the maps, and the plotting of the situations, was accomplished by Colonel W. S. Nye, who as editor also made significant contributions to the text.

E.J.S.

CONTENTS

LIST OF ILLUSTRATIONS

The capital letters in parentheses after most of the titles in the list refer to the
following sources from which the illustrations were taken, and to which credit is due:

(B)   *Battles and Leaders of the Civil War.* New York; The Century Company, 1884.

(F)   Edwin Forbes, a battlefield artist whose drawings appeared in several peri-
      odicals, such as *Harpers, Century,* etc.

(L)   Library of Congress.

(N)   National Archives.

(P)   National Park Service.

(R)   *Photographic History of the Civil War.* Review of Reviews, 1912.

(U)   U.S. Army Military History Institute, Carlisle, Penn.

LIST OF MAPS

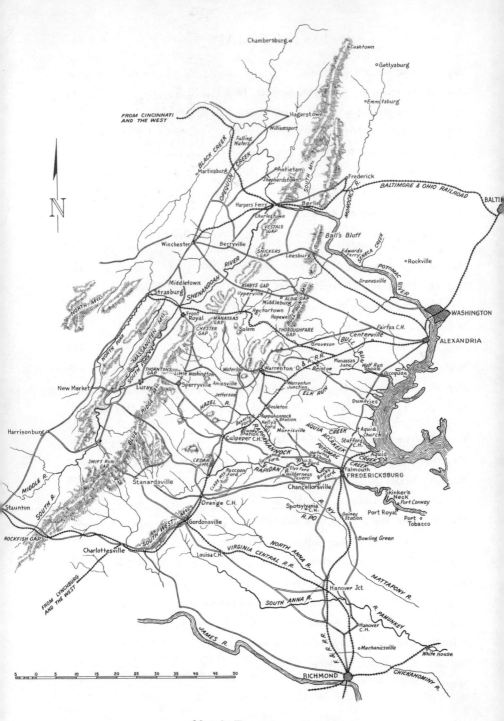

MAP 1. THEATER OF OPERATIONS

110TH PENNSYLVANIA INFANTRY AT FALMOUTH, VIRGINIA, APRIL 24, 1863

CHAPTER 1

A NEW GENERAL TAKES COMMAND

IT WAS snowing heavily on the afternoon of Saturday, April 4, 1863 as a little steamer carrying a distinguished cargo glided down the Potomac River from the Washington Navy Yard.

President Abraham Lincoln, accompanied by Mrs. Lincoln, Tad, and a small group of friends, was on his way to pay his first field visit to the Army of the Potomac under its new commander, Major General Joseph Hooker. Following Burnside's defeat at the Battle of Fredericksburg in December the army had, since Hooker assumed command on January 25, been undergoing a period of reorganization and rehabilitation in its camps near Falmouth, on the north shore of the Rappahannock River.

Poor visibility caused the steamer to put in for the night in a protected cove. The next day the journey was continued, with the snow still falling. Dropping anchor at Aquia Creek Landing, the army supply base, the party completed the trip in a gaily decorated open freight car equipped with wooden benches. Lincoln was greeted at Falmouth by Hooker's chief of staff, Major General Daniel Butterfield. Then the presidential party, snugly ensconced in two army ambulances, was escorted by a large cavalcade of mounted officers to the headquarters of the commanding general.

At the time of removing Burnside from command, the Commander-in-Chief had put aside his misgivings about Joe Hooker and had given him full responsibility for restoring that potentially powerful but badly mismanaged army to a fine edge of efficiency. This Hooker had done with considerable success, and now the army was ready for a final inspection before beginning the spring campaign.

The Presidential Review

The grand review of the Army of the Potomac that Hooker staged for the President's benefit was a succession of close order march-bys of 120,000 men that might have given the Commander-in-Chief renewed hope, had it not been for Hooker's overconfident assertion that "I am going straight to Richmond, if I live." This, the old refrain which Lincoln had heard so often, troubled him. He noted that it came from the lips of a general who on more than one occasion had been a bit too impetuous in throwing his troops prematurely into battle, and in other instances had been surprisingly slow both to think and act.

Lincoln was mounted on a horse that was too small for him, so that his long legs almost touched the ground. This awkward appearance, with his stovepipe hat towering above him, might have caused smiles from the amused soldiers had it not been for the President's haggard, worried countenance that seemed to record the heartbreaking defeats of the first two years, grief over the dead of previous battles, and the anticipated burden of other battles yet to come.

In all probability the President would have preferred to see some demonstrations of the tactical training of the troops and their individual and group proficiency with weapons in the form of simulated combat, rather than a series of parades. But that would have been too much to expect. From time immemorial and even today the practice has been to turn out the troops in their best spit-and-polish. This is the standard formula for entertaining distinguished visitors with what has come to be the military pomp and splendor that every commander, and—it must be admitted—the enlisted victims themselves, hope will result in an enthusiastic reception from and a favorable impression on the visiting dignitaries.

As usual on his visits to the army in the field, Lincoln was tireless in meeting personally as many officers and soldiers as he possibly could. He was anxious to test for himself the quality of their morale, and to find out first-hand how they were being fed and cared for, and what they thought about the war. What he learned was reassuring so far as the attitude of the soldiers was concerned. Things looked favorable, despite the President's own inner uncertainty about Hooker himself.

Hooker's Military Background

The appointment of General Hooker has been the subject of considerable speculation and widely varying reports, but there is little doubt that the final choice was Lincoln's and his alone. Secretary of War Stanton was outspokenly opposed to Hooker as was the General-in-Chief, Henry W. Halleck. Stanton's choice for Burnside's successor was Major General John F. Reynolds, who took himself out of consideration by expressing doubt that he would be allowed the necessary liberty of action as army commander. Generals Meade and Rosecrans were also supposed to have been considered, but Hooker, who wanted the job badly for himself, behind the scenes pulled all available stops in his efforts to secure the appointment. He is believed to have had friends in high places at Wash-

MAJOR GENERAL JOSEPH HOOKER

ington who were backing Secretary of the Treasury Chase to succeed Lincoln as President. These friends, sounding Hooker out to determine whether he had political ambitions of his own, were said to have been reassured on that score. They promptly made Hooker their candidate for army commander.

Hooker graduated from West Point in 1837, Halleck in 1839. Something may have occurred to arouse enmity between the upper classman and the plebe. Additionally there is a story to the effect that Halleck had uncovered some unfavorable tales about Hooker when they were both living in California as civilians in the late 1850's.

[4]

However that may be, the President went over the list of senior commanders, disregarding the strong objections of Stanton and Halleck, and chose the handsome but vainglorious forty-eight year old Hooker, despite a record of disloyalty to superiors the counterpart of which is not to be found elsewhere in American military history.

With all his faults, Hooker had proven himself to be an able fighting man. The Mexican War, in which he had won a brevet as lieutenant colonel for distinguished services, was his first combat experience. After sixteen years of service, however, following his graduation from West Point, he had resigned his commission and moved to California. Here, with little success, he undertook farming and civil engineering. At the start of the Civil War he took off for Washington, where the elderly General-in-Chief, Winfield Scott, gave him such a cool reception that he was still in civilian clothes when the first Battle of Bull Run passed into history. It seems that during the Mexican War Hooker's habit of talking out of turn and criticizing his superiors had made him permanently unpopular with General Scott, who just happened to be the General-in-Chief of the Army of the United States in 1861.

As the defeated Federals streamed back into Washington from Bull Run, it was a propitious moment for Joe Hooker to play his only remaining card. Bypassing General Scott, he secured an appointment to pay his respects to the President. At that meeting Hooker did most of the talking, informing Lincoln that he had at one time been "Lieutenant Colonel Hooker of the Regular Army," was returning to his home in California since he did not seem to be wanted in the Army, and had been an interested observer of the recent Manassas affair. Hooker closed his remarks by suggesting, with doubtful modesty, that "he was a damned sight better general than any you had on that field."

Whether Lincoln was intrigued by his handsome, ruddy

face and soldierly bearing, appraised his brash self-assurance as an evidence of confident ability, or was simply hard up for capable combat leaders is not clear. But the result was that Hooker walked out with a commission as brigadier general of volunteers. He was on his way.

Hooker's rise was rapid. He commanded a division through the Peninsular campaign and during Pope's Northern Virginia campaign and the Second Battle of Bull Run; led his corps at South Mountain and in heavy fighting on the Federal right at Antietam; and commanded the Center Grand Division of two corps under Burnside in the Fredericksburg campaign. Possibly the sobriquet "Fighting Joe" may have contributed something to his legendary fighting qualities, but he himself disliked the appellation because he probably knew, as few did, that the name had been attached to him as a result of a compositor's error in failing to place a hyphen in a dispatch from the Peninsula. The item in question should have read: " (still) fighting—Joe Hooker" but it came out in print as "Fighting Joe Hooker."

Lincoln's famous letter on the occasion of his appointment to army commander would seem to show that the President, fully aware of Hooker's weaknesses, knowingly took a calculated risk because he wanted leaders who would fight and win battles, regardless of personality, or even character deficiencies. The letter has been printed many times, but is included here as an essential part of the record:

> Executive Mansion,
> Washington, January 26, 1863.
> Major General Hooker:
> General:
> I have placed you at the head of the Army of the Potomac. Of course I have done this upon what appear to me to be sufficient reasons. And yet I think it best for you to know that there are some things, in regard to which, I am not quite satisfied with you.

I believe you to be a brave and a skilful soldier, which, or course, I like. I also believe you do not mix politics with your profession, in which you are right. You have confidence in yourself, which is a valuable, if not an indispensable quality. You are ambitious, which, within reasonable bounds, does good rather than harm. But I think that during Gen. Burnside's command of the Army you have taken counsel of your ambition, and thwarted him as much as you could, in which you did a great wrong to the country, and to a most meritorious and honorable brother officer. I have heard, in such way as to believe it, of your recently saying that both the Army and the Government needed a Dictator. Of course it was not for this, but in spite of it, that I have given you command. Only those generals who gain success can set up dictators. What I now ask of you is military success, and I will risk the dictatorship. The government will support you to the utmost of its ability, which is neither more nor less than it has done and will do for all commanders. I much fear that the spirit which you have aided to infuse into the Army, of criticising their Commander, and withholding confidence from him, will now turn upon you. I shall assist you as far as I can, to put it down. Neither you, nor Napoleon, if he were alive again, could get any good out of an army, while such a spirit prevails in it.

And now, beware of rashness—beware of rashness, but with energy, and sleepless vigilance, go forward, and give us victories.

Yours very truly
A. Lincoln

Noah Brooks, a close friend of the President, happened to be present at Hooker's headquarters when he received Lincoln's letter. Brooks has reported Hooker's reaction:

He finished reading it almost with tears in his eyes; and as he folded it and put it back in the breast of his coat, he said, "That is just such a letter as a father might write to a son. It is a beautiful letter, and although I think he was harder on me than I deserved, I will say that I love the man who wrote it."

Two Serious Defects

Hooker's two major weaknesses were his fondness for liquor and his chronic habit of criticizing his superiors and intriguing with the object of superseding them. The latter trait first showed itself at West Point, where he narrowly escaped expulsion, but managed to finish the course and was graduated.

At his first conference with Lincoln the day after his appointment, Hooker told the President bluntly that he and Halleck could not get along; he would have to bypass the General-in-Chief and report direct to Lincoln. We do not know whether Lincoln agreed to the suggestion, but by that time he had had ample opportunity to appraise Halleck and apparently raised no serious objection to Hooker's announced determination to disregard the chain of command. Hooker proceeded to do that to the point of virtually ignoring Halleck as though he did not exist.

Hooker appears to have had a congenital hostility to everyone who ranked him, which may have been a form of defensive psychology, an effort to minimize in advance possible critical attitudes on the part of his superiors. As time went on, he openly criticized even the President who, he said, was incompetent. At South Mountain, preceding the Battle of Antietam, Hooker was in command of the First Corps under Burnside as commander of the right wing. While that corps fought bravely and successfully, other corps performed equally well. Yet Hooker's report, filed late in 1862, was full of misrepresentations and downright untruths. It ignored his immediate superior, and "made a characteristic effort to grasp all the glory of the battle at the expense of truth and of dealing with his commander and his comrades."* The point was that Hooker was writing for history. Since his report was not published until the *Official Records of the Rebellion* came out in printed form several decades after the battle, those officers and units whose actions were maligned by Hooker never had the opportunity to refute his statements until long after the war was over.

His superior, General Burnside, had no opportunity to read Hooker's report until after the Battle of Fredericksburg, when he was quick to file a supplemental report on South Mountain, pointing out "gross misstatements" and adding: "General Hooker should remember that I had to order him four separate times to move his command into action, and that I had to myself order his leading division (Meade's) to start before he would go."

During the Fredericksburg campaign, where he served throughout as one of Burnside's three grand division commanders, Hooker's attitude toward Burnside had bordered on the insubordinate on several occasions. His indifferent support of the army commander's plan of action, vague and unsound though that plan may have been, left much to be desired. The combination of Hooker's South Mountain report and his attitude at Fredericksburg convinced Burnside that Hooker must go. Burnside, two days before he himself was relieved, submitted for approval to the President his now famous General Orders No. 8, dated January 23, 1863, the first paragraph of which read as follows:

> General Joseph Hooker, major-general of volunteers and brigadier general U. S. Army, having been guilty of unjust and unnecessary criticisms of the actions of his superior officers, and of the authorities, and having, by the general tone of his conversation,

---

*According to Major General Jacob R. Cox, who commanded a division in the Ninth Corps.

endeavored to create distrust in the minds of officers who have associated with him, and having, by omissions and otherwise, made reports and statements which were calculated to create incorrect impressions, and for habitually speaking in disparaging terms of other officers, is hereby dismissed the service of the United States as a man unfit to hold an important commission during a crisis like the present, when so much patience, charity, confidence, consideration, and patriotism are due from every soldier in the field. This order is issued subject to the approval of the President of the United States.

Grant's Appraisal of Hooker

Supporting Burnside's opinion, General U. S. Grant's appraisal of Hooker, in his *Memoirs,* was short and to the point:

"I regarded him as a dangerous man. He was not subordinate to his superiors. He was ambitious to the extent of caring nothing for the rights of others. His disposition was, when engaged in battle, to get detached from the main body of the army and exercise a separate command, gathering to his standard all he could of his juniors." Strangely enough, in spite of the unfavorable opinion which Grant held of Hooker, he restored him to command of two consolidated army corps in September 1863, after Lincoln had removed him from command of the Army of the Potomac just prior to the Battle of Gettysburg. As commander of the Twentieth Corps, Army of the Cumberland, Hooker staged a surprising comeback at Lookout Mountain, Missionary Ridge, and in subsequent action in the South. As a result of these actions he was brevetted a major general, U. S. Army "for gallant and meritorious services at the Battle of Chattanooga, Tennessee," and received the thanks of Congress in January 1864 "for the skill, energy and endurance which first covered Washington and Baltimore from the meditated blow of the advancing and powerful army of Rebels led by General Robert E. Lee." Thus it appears that Joe Hooker still had friends in high places in Washington despite his failure at Chancellorsville and the adverse opinion of most of his fellow-generals.

He Liked His Liquor

It was no secret that Hooker was fond of his liquor. It followed naturally that he was a consistent drinker; but it

MAJOR GENERAL DARIUS N. COUCH

was also true that only a few drinks had a marked effect on him, which perhaps served as a mild deterrent to a maximum volume of intake. His florid complexion and weak chin could have been cause and effect in reverse, the weak chin denoting a character defect and leading to a mild form of inferiority complex which he subconsciously tried to hide by going over to the offensive in his dealings with others.

The enlisted men of the army adopted a song entitled "Joe Hooker is Our Leader," an important line of which emphasized the fact that "he takes his whiskey strong." The evidence is not at all conclusive, however, that Hooker gave his drinking precedence over his responsible duties as division, corps, and army commander. His senior corps commander at the Battle of Chancellorsville, Major General Darius N. Couch, stated positively that Hooker was not drinking during that battle, but on the contrary had temporarily "gone on the wagon." Couch added that it would have been better had Hooker continued his customary drinking habits, presumably on the premise that temporary abstinence on the part of a heavy drinker is supposed to weaken his mental capabilities. For those who may choose to think so, Hooker's drinking habits may have to bear a heavy responsibility for what happened at Chancellorsville.

PARADE AT FALMOUTH
110th Pennsylvania Volunteers, part of Whipple's division, III Corps

WINTER CAMP NEAR FALMOUTH

CHAPTER 2

HOOKER REBUILDS HIS ARMY

Hooker's initial instructions from General-in-Chief Henry W. Halleck, in late January 1863, strongly implied that the Lincoln Administration would be happy to have the new army commander take the offensive against Lee as soon as possible. The patience of the Washington high command with its succession of unsuccessful field generals was obviously wearing thin.

General Hooker, who had other ideas, refused to be hurried. Washington's insistence was a bit importunate, thought Hooker, who as yet had scarcely had time to turn around and get his bearings. In spite of the continued pressure, he wisely determined to put his forces in first-class condition before undertaking a major spring operation.

The first and most important task which confronted him was to improve discipline and restore morale, both of which had deteriorated badly after the Battle of Fredericksburg, and the even more depressing "Mud March," that had resulted in Burnside's removal. The other major measures which Hooker instituted provided for better rations and more healthful and sanitary living conditions for the men, the creation of an effective intelligence system, the elimination of Burnside's grand divisions, the introduction of security measures, and the concentration of the scattered cavalry units into a single cohesive corps.

All of these improvements were initiated and pushed to completion with such energy and determination that the Administration began to breathe more freely and to feel more hopeful that the selection of "Fighting Joe" might indeed justify the faith that had prompted his selection, despite the misgivings which stemmed from his ill-advised boastfulness in the early stages of his appointment to high command.

There were sound reasons for Hooker's delay. Desertions and absence without leave had grown to scandalous proportions after Fredericksburg, occurring at the rate of some two hundred daily. Hooker's report of February 15 listed over 85,000 officers and men absent without leave—well over half the army! Recognizing that this situation constituted a grave danger to his forces, Hooker immediately adopted a remedy which proved effective. His solution was to authorize the granting of furloughs on an extremely liberal basis, at the same time assisting commanders in apprehending stragglers and deserters by prescribing a system of corps insignia, so that a man's proper unit and place of duty could easily be identified. His orders also provided that deserters returned to military custody be promptly brought before a court martial.

More than ten percent of the officers and men were

being carried on the sick rolls when Hooker assumed command. The common complaints of dysentery, typhoid fever, and a variety of respiratory diseases accounted for much of the illness, but there were also cases of scurvy, caused by diet deficiencies. Hooker cut the sick rate in half by requiring higher sanitary standards, by getting the men out of the filthy mud-and-brush dugouts in which they had been spending the winter, and by such common-sense, obvious measures as regular airing of bedding.

The ration was improved by the issue of flour or soft bread four times a week in place of the usual hardtack. Fresh onions or potatoes were issued twice a week, and the variety and palatability of the meals were upgraded by detailing trained men as regular cooks, in addition to "two undercooks of African descent" to each company.

Tobacco was issued regularly and there was even an occasional issue of whiskey, when men came off picket duty or had suffered undue exposure in line of duty. Idleness, the bane of all armies and one of the prime causes of low morale, was reduced by requiring the troops to be turned out for drill or other military instruction whenever the winter weather was not too severe. Thus the health and esprit of the army was gradually rebuilt, so that by the time of Lincoln's visit in April many qualified observers believed it to be at the peak of condition.

Military Intelligence Agency Established

McClellan's chief dependence on detective Allan Pinkerton and his civilian spies had resulted in a dismal failure to furnish reliable enemy information. Nor is there evidence that Burnside did anything to improve that situation. In the words of the Joint Committee on the Conduct of the War:*

---

* Second Session, 38th Congress, quoted in John Bigelow, Jr., *The Campaign of Chancellorsville*, p. 47. Yale University Press. New Haven, 1910.

When General Hooker assumed command of the army there was not a record or document of any kind at headquarters of the army that gave any information at all in regard to the enemy. There was no means, no organization, and no apparent effort to obtain such information. And we were almost as ignorant of the enemy in our immediate front as if they had been in China. An efficient organization for that purpose was established, by which we were soon enabled to get correct and proper information of the enemy, their strength, and their movements.

Hooker established a Military Information Bureau which at first served only the Army of the Potomac, but which increased in size and scope throughout the war until it became virtually a national agency and may be regarded as the beginning of the present Army intelligence system. The new bureau was nominally under Hooker's Provost Marshal General, Brigadier General Marsena R. Patrick, but the active chief was Colonel George H. Sharpe, commander of the 120th New York Infantry. Hooker called in Sharpe, had him appointed Deputy Provost Marshal General, and gave him almost complete freedom of action in organizing and operating the bureau, which functioned separately and reported direct to the army commander.

Colonel Sharpe initially employed a relatively small number of scouts, chosen from cavalry and infantry units on the basis of their demonstrated good judgment, powers of observation, and resourcefulness. Signalmen were also used, who from their high observation towers were generally able to observe and report dispositions and movements of enemy forces. Finally, to round out the system, civilian agents and spies were utilized, particularly in Baltimore—which since the outbreak of the war had been a chief gathering place of undercover agents of both sides, as well as a main point on the underground channel extending down through Maryland, across the Rappahannock at

Port Royal, thence to Richmond. Over this route a considerable movement of contraband, agents, newspapers, and other covert transmission of information passed back and forth throughout the entire war.

The fact is that all during the war it was found desirable by both sides to keep a route open for couriers, cotton speculators, and even spies. This route, not generally publicized, but known to those with a need to know, took advantage of the fact that Maryland was technically a "loyal" State, although lower Maryland was sympathetic to the Southern cause and the city of Baltimore required virtually an "army of occupation" to keep it in line after the riots of 1861. The balance was sufficiently delicate to moderate the heavy hand of authority, with the result that clever spies found it relatively easy to move about at will in both directions across the border and into the respective capitals.

Southern spies and couriers traveling north had no difficulty entering Washington during daylight hours unless they were known and recognized. John H. Surratt, son of Mrs. Mary E. Surratt, one of the group hanged for plotting the assassination of Lincoln, made the round trip regularly in carrying dispatches between Richmond and the Confederate group in Canada. It was by the aforementioned "underground" route that the Richmond government regularly received the New York and Washington newspapers with their valuable intelligence of Union troop movements and plans.

At the time of the Chancellorsville campaign Colonel Sharpe's scouts functioned primarily along the outpost line, although they occasionally made secret forays deep into enemy territory. The information which they gathered was military in character, and was transmitted promptly to army headquarters, where the reports were sifted, analyzed, and passed on to General Hooker. Incredible as it may seem, the Army of the Potomac now, for the first time since the beginning of the war, was given the means to effectively gather information of enemy dispositions and movements.

Hooker Plugs Information Leaks

The establishment of an intelligence-gathering agency was only part of the solution. Hooker could now expect to receive positive intelligence on the location and movement of enemy elements, but that of itself was not sufficient to prevent the enemy from continuing his own heretofore successful efforts to keep himself posted on the activities of the Union army. So Hooker took steps to plug information leaks from the Federal side by setting up a system which today would be called counterintelligence.

Security had previously been almost nonexistent in the Army of the Potomac. This condition had extended from top to bottom. Washington and Baltimore were hotbeds of spies; the Confederacy had many active agents planted in the National Capital as well as elsewhere throughout the North. These agents continually passed information to Richmond, practically at will, and for the first year of the war, at least, were allowed to come and go almost without interference. During the Fredericksburg campaign it is said that Lee even had an agent located in the military telegraph office at Aquia, who intercepted vital messages which Burnside was transmitting to Lincoln and Halleck.

On the Rappahannock, security had been lax at every point. The outpost system was particularly vulnerable. Pickets from opposing camps were in daily contact, exchanging news, supplies, and amenities. One method was by means of miniature sailboats which transported coffee and newspapers across the river to the Confederates, who sent the tiny craft back loaded with tobacco, news from Richmond, and rumors—mostly false.

Hooker proceeded to tighten the outpost system. He required a more efficient habit of inspecting sentinels and outguards by commanders, insisted that the sentries, out-posts, and officers keep their eyes on matters other than card games and newspapers, and promptly report all enemy activities observed. This novel procedure occasioned some dissatisfaction at lower levels, but had a generally whole-some effect without impairing the over-all morale of the army.

Lee's apparently uncanny foreknowledge of Federal plans in the past was in fact the result of little more than wholly ineffectual security measures on the part of the Northern generals. Confederate Intelligence did of course benefit hugely from an efficient civilian spy system in Vir-ginia and adjoining territory, in addition to the activities of an aggressive cavalry that constantly probed Union positions for information.

The Northern newspapers felt the pressure when Hooker clamped down on the free and easy access to army news sources which they had enjoyed for several years, not in-frequently at the expense of the troops. In line with his determination to prevent leaks to the enemy, he issued peremptory orders to restrict the freedom of action of the horde of newspaper correspondents who traveled with the army, and whose dispatches had been one of the most fruitful sources of Lee's information.

The correspondents were there to get stories, naturally, but the lack of judgment and self-restraint displayed by some had on a number of occasions disclosed to the Con-federates the strategic and even some of the planned tactical dispositions of Union commanders, frequently before the orders had gone down to the lower echelons. One incident which occurred during the latter part of April alone dem-onstrated the need for such censorship. When Hooker's offensive was about to be launched, the New York and Philadelphia papers carried a story about the discovery of a "hot" wire which was found to run across the Rappahan-nock River and was traced by Federal Intelligence personnel to a house within the Union lines in Falmouth. The southern terminal of the wire was presumably somewhere in Fredericksburg, within the Confederate lines. An investigation disclosed that the owner of the Falmouth house was a Rebel or at least a Rebel sympathizer, who had up to then been feeding important information to Lee's headquarters. The mere fact that that particular leak had been plugged was news which obviously should not have been divulged to the public, and thus to Lee.

Another particularly glaring example of the thoughtlessness of the Northern press was the publication, in at least one newspaper, of the complete report of the Army Medical Director showing the number of sick in the army on a specific date as 10,777. That wasn't too bad, but the report went on to point out the ratio for the entire army as 67.64 per 1000. By solving a simple equation, Lee was thus given the approximate strength of Hooker's army, which was of course information of incalculable military value.

With the full support of the War Department, and no doubt as a direct result of these serious security leaks, Hooker on April 30, 1863 issued General Orders No. 48, which required all newspaper correspondents accredited to the Army of the Potomac to publish their future correspondence and reports over their own signatures. The order stated ominously that failure to comply with the order would result in the joint exclusion of the noncomplying reporters and their journals from the lines of the army.

If there was any single principle of war to which Hooker subscribed wholeheartedly in his preparation for the Chancellorsville campaign, it was the element of surprise. Burnside had talked a lot about surprising Lee at Fredericksburg, but his actions completely belied his words. Aware of Burnside's unfortunate loquacity, Hooker decided to reverse the procedure. In so doing he went to such lengths in keeping his plans under wraps that not even members of his immediate staff, to say nothing of his corps commanders, were informed in advance beyond the point of receiving such fragments of the whole picture as would permit them to issue necessary march orders to their units, with the instructions for their future movements and combat orders to follow in due course. The only exception to this rule of Hooker's would be his directive to George Stoneman, cavalry corps commander, which had to be fairly complete because Stoneman's mission would carry him to the rear of Lee's army, out of touch with Hooker's headquarters.

At this stage Hooker was exercising sound judgment, for Lee's sources of enemy information were legion, including even the Federal pickets. As has been noted, these sentries were in the habit of freely informing their Confederate counterparts across the Rappahannock of any new bit of news. Such items included, for example, the receipt of instructions to load up with eight days' rations and extra ammunition; or the rumor that the Union cavalry was off on some adventure down Port Royal way or up by United States Mine Ford.

Hooker even insisted that a letter outlining his forthcoming plan of campaign, written on April 11 to President Lincoln (see page 92), be hand-carried by his chief of staff, General Butterfield. The latter was instructed to deliver it to the President in person, with no one present other than Lincoln and Butterfield, not even the Secretary of War or General-in-Chief Halleck. Lincoln rather liked that—it was a refreshing change—and he was prompt to send Hooker a cryptic telegram the following day, giving his approval to the plan as presented.

Federal Cavalry Reconstituted

The reorganization of the Federal cavalry was one of

Joe Hooker's most important organizational reforms, in that the effectiveness of that arm of the Union Army began with the changes he inaugurated. This long overdue move consolidated all of the cavalry into a single corps, thus bringing into an integrated command the scattered regiments which heretofore had been parceled out to the tender and unskilled mercies of the several corps and division commanders, whose utilization of their attached cavalry reflected a sad lack of understanding of the potential capabilities of the mounted arm. The cavalry had been ineffectual chiefly because of the indifference, neglect, and sheer lack of knowledge as to its proper employment displayed by the ranking generals, who dissipated the regiments in detachments for escort and messenger service and for occasional reconnaissance and picketing missions. But in the early stages nobody expected much of the horsemen, who in turn naturally failed to develop the superior combat self-assurance that made Major General J. E. B. "Jeb" Stuart's Confederate cavalry the outstanding weapon that Lee knew so well how to employ.

The attitude of the 76-year old General-in-Chief, Winfield Scott, originally set the pattern of opinion which served to retard the development of the cavalry arm until the war was half over. Scott believed that the cavalry would be ineffective against the new rifled cannon that were being manufactured, and apparently no one else questioned his judgment. General McClellan, Scott's successor for a time, was enough of a horseman to have invented the famous McClellan saddle. Better things might have been expected from him by that branch of the service. He must have understood the proper use of cavalry, but there is no evidence that he devoted his recognized organizational talents to improving its status. It therefore remained for Joseph Hooker, an artilleryman, to take the step which restored the self-respect of the horse soldiers and started the cavalry on the path to its ultimate success.

The Federal cavalry, at least the regiments recruited in the Eastern states, was sufficiently handicapped as it was, for while the North was rich in men, money, and draft horses, it was comparatively poor in riding horses, riders, and marksmen. Although many men came from farms, others were from offices, mines, and workshops; and even the farmers weren't noteworthy horsemen. The mounts were of indifferent quality, imperfectly broken and trained. Furthermore, the mounted arm in the North was neither encouraged nor supported; consequently the raw material, both human and horseflesh, compared unfavorably with that of the Confederates. The organization and training of a Federal cavalry unit was a time-consuming, uphill struggle merely to exist. Scorned by the other branches, relegated to inconsequential duties and missions, it is not surprising that its morale and effectiveness was on a low level.

The senior cavalry officers who had served in the pre-war Army were experienced, but, owing to the low esteem in which the arm was held in the North, they were often of an older group, passed over for promotion, and consequently low in morale. One bright exception was John Buford, who had already done much to improve the Federal cavalry, but who at this time was still only a brigadier, whereas his West Point contemporaries were generally corps commanders. The younger, more dashing group, such as Sheridan, Custer, Farnsworth, Merritt, Kilpatrick, Devin, Mackenzie, Wilson, Gregg, and others had not in early 1863 come to the fore.

In one respect—weapons—the Federal cavalry had the edge. Their mounted troops were generally armed with the Sharp carbine, a breech-loading single shot weapon; the Colt or other make of revolver; and the saber. About this time also the Spencer repeating carbine was beginning to appear, a seven-shot weapon which was capable of delivering vastly greater firepower than anything possessed by the Confederates.

The Confederate Cavalry

The initial superiority of the Confederate cavalry stemmed largely from the fact that horse breeding and riding was virtually indigenous among the white youth of the plantations, a fact which engendered a love for and natu-

BRIGADIER GENERAL GEORGE STONEMAN

ral aptitude in the exhilarating life of a dashing cavalier. These potential cavalrymen, even before entering the service, were generally accomplished horsemen and accustomed to the use of firearms. Initially most of them came from the best families of the South and consequently were fairly well educated, highly intelligent, and resourceful. They were imbued with a burning patriotism and high love of excitement and adventure, hence very little time and drill were required to convert the recruits into experienced and capable troopers.

The Confederate cavalry was at first mounted on well-bred horses, perfectly broken and trained. But each trooper had to supply and maintain his own mount, so that as the months went by, and the early crop of superior blooded horses was used up, the Confederates were forced to seek remounts from any source at hand. The small war carried on by Stuart's cavalry against Federal outposts, and their eager readiness to raid hostile territory for remounts and forage, was prompted by something more fundamental than a mere search for excitement.

Most Southern troops carried two or three pistols; some had muskets as well. Others possessed carbines of newer pattern, usually furnished by their opponents. But their arms were of such a variety of models and calibers that the problem of replacement, repair, and ammunition supply was always a serious one.

Stoneman in Command

The newly constituted Union cavalry corps consisted of three cavalry divisions under Pleasonton, Averell, and Gregg respectively, with a reserve brigade under Buford, adding up to about 12,000 men and 13,000 horses. All these officers were brigadier generals, as was the corps commander, Stoneman. It would appear from this that Hooker considered the reorganized cavalry to be on probation until it should prove itself, or else he was not too sure of Stoneman's capacity when he gave him the cavalry corps to command. No other explanation seems to make sense, in view of the fact that Stoneman had commanded a full infantry corps at Fredericksburg, under Hooker's immediate supervision. He now had three cavalry division commanders as his lieutenants, hence would appear to have rated the rank of major general* to put his corps on a par with the seven infantry corps of the army, all of which were commanded by generals who were wearing two stars on their shoulders.

*Stoneman was assigned as major general by War Department Order in April, 1863.

George Stoneman was a graduate of the West Point class of 1846, in which he had been a classmate of Thomas J. "Stonewall" Jackson and George E. Pickett. After graduation he was assigned to the First Dragoons, and all his service in Mexico and throughout the Civil War was with the cavalry except for the brief interlude as infantry corps commander under Burnside. Although breveted a colonel for the Fredericksburg campaign, one may wonder why the citation was awarded, since Stoneman seems to have had little to do in that battle as commander of the Third Corps, a part of Hooker's Center Grand Division. Burnside virtually ignored his grand division and corps commanders by ordering divisions into action directly rather than through the discretionary control of the intermediate headquarters. All three of Stoneman's divisions were thus fed into Franklin's attack on the left and Sumner's on the right, leaving Stoneman without a command during most of the battle.

Stoneman was a reliable, conscientious, and responsible corps commander, but entirely too cautious and conservative for the new role that he was now being called upon to fulfill. To match Jeb Stuart and his cocky troopers, what the Union Army needed but failed to get until Sheridan rode on the stage was the hell-for-leather, hard riding, calculatingly reckless type of leadership which Stoneman was not equipped to furnish. He gave his best, but that was not quite good enough, at least under the unpredictable dual-personality command of Joe Hooker.

The Artillery a Victim
of Hooker's Error of Judgment

The artillery of the Army of the Potomac had clearly demonstrated its superiority over that of the Army of Northern Virginia at Malvern Hill, Antietam, and Fredericksburg. Its efficiency was no accident, but the result of the able, concentrated, devoted zeal of one of the great artillerymen of all times, Henry J. Hunt.

A classmate of Halleck and a contemporary of Hooker during West Point cadet days in the latter half of the 1830's, Hunt had served as an artillery commander with great distinction in every battle of the Mexican War, during which he was breveted successively captain and major. In the half-dozen years immediately prior to the Civil War, he played a leading part in the untiring and highly successful efforts of a small group of officers to improve the artillery arm of the service, particularly the light artillery. To his vigor and initiative more than to any other single factor may be attributed the tactical and battle excellence of the Union artillery during the war.

The marked advantage of the industrialized North, blessed with an ample supply of skilled mechanics, over the agricultural economy of the South was another major reason for the superiority of the Federal artillery. The same genius for successful tinkering with motorized equipment would later give the American Yankees a marked advantage over many of the less favored Europeans and Asians in the wars of the twentieth century.

The majority of the field guns used by the armies on both sides were muzzle-loaders, both smoothbore and rifled pieces, the principal exception being a small number of Whitworth breechloaders which the Confederates imported from Manchester, England, in 1863. The manufacture of that type of improved gun had not yet been started in this country, despite its obvious advantages for the greater safety of the gunners.

The Federals were fortunate not only in having more artillery than the Confederates, perhaps on a ratio of at least three to two, but the proportion of rifles to smoothbores, with the greater range and accuracy of the former, was also greater in the Union armies. The effective range of the rifled guns was twice that of the smoothbores, which were limited to approximately 1,500 yards. The artillery in both armies was continuously plagued by defective shells, and in that respect at least the competition between the contenders was a standoff.

As Chief of Artillery of the Army of the Potomac under both McClellan and Burnside, a position which he retained under Hooker and on through the entire war, Hunt's experience under a variety of battle conditions made him the foremost artilleryman of his age. Never satisfied, he was continuously engaged in perfecting the organization and efficiency of his artillery. His crowning achievement was attained when at the psychological moment, from Cemetery Ridge, he hurled the devastating destruction of his 80 massed guns against Pickett's charging Confederates, and virtually swept them from the field of Gettysburg in Lee's final, convulsive effort to gain the victory.

McClellan and Burnside had the intelligence or wit to recognize Hunt's competence and allow him complete freedom of action in his command of the army artillery. Not so Joe Hooker, himself an artillery officer until he attained command of a division. When Hooker was placed at the head of the army he withdrew the command authority from Hunt, leaving him with only administrative responsibilities, although still Chief of Artillery with the rank of brigadier general. To make matters worse, artillery officers were promoted and reassigned, without adequate replacement, until only five officers of field grade remained to direct the action of almost 10,000 artillerymen manning 412 guns for the forthcoming campaign. Moreover, because of the scarcity of artillery officers of the lower grades the five field officers were left with insufficient staffs.

During the maneuvering before the Battle of Chancellorsville, Hooker for some unexplained reason kept Hunt on the north bank of the river, wasting his time and skill on administrative duties that properly belonged to a staff officer. Hooker's inexcusable failure to restore tactical control of the artillery to his Chief of Artillery until the second day of the battle not only resulted in many guns being left behind without Hunt's knowledge, but deprived the Army of the Potomac of his proven talents at a time when more effective employment of the artillery might have changed the entire complexion of the battle.

It must be concluded from the record that General Hooker, nominally at least an artilleryman, must have had a very inadequate appreciation of the value and capabilities of that arm, or in his self-complacency believed that he could employ the artillery to better advantage under his own personal control as army commander. Whatever his motives, the historic fact is that the Federal artillery was destined by his action to be severely handicapped in its operations during the Chancellorsville campaign, both from the shortage of field and staff officers and in the selection of positions from which it could employ to advantage its tactical mobility and firepower. Hooker's mismanagement of his artillery contrasted strangely with the constructive measures which he had taken to improve the status of the cavalry and restore the combat readiness of the infantry.

Other Organizational Changes

When Burnside succeeded McClellan on November 9, 1862,* he had created the three grand divisions on the premise that it would reduce the number of subordinate commanders through whom to transmit orders. This was sound enough in theory. The trouble was that Burnside did not know how to make the system work effectively. In the Fredericksburg campaign he failed to recognize the grand divisions as autonomous wings; he issued anomalous orders which confused rather than helped his principal lieutenants; he allowed them no discretionary powers what-

---

*He was appointed to command the Army of the Potomac on November 7, 1862, and assumed command on November 9.

HOOKER AND HIS STAFF

Hunt is second from the left, front row; Hooker is fourth; and Butterfield is fifth.

soever; and in the end thoroughly disgusted them all with the organizational innovation. Hooker had been one of Burnside's three grand division commanders, and he would have no more of it. On February 5 he reverted to the former organization whereby the army commander would deal directly with seven infantry corps, with the addition of one cavalry corps. Thus he eliminated one link in the chain of command and to that extent speeded up operations in the system of communications. For the best tactical results this was not a sound decision, while admittedly an administrative improvement. Hooker would have done better to have retained the wing conception to make it a permanent part of the army organization, and reduce the number of corps by consolidations, as Grant was to do in the winter of 1863-64. This would have greatly increased the strength of the infantry divisions and made them comparable to the larger Confederate divisions. At the same time it would have rendered several corps commanders surplus and probably precipitated "within the party" a situation that might have done more harm than good.

In the last analysis neither Burnside nor Hooker possessed the qualifications that make great leaders. Consequently it made little difference whether the grand division theory was in effect or not. Neither general was capable of successfully leading a huge army in combat, so it was really immaterial whether they gave orders to three, five, or seven corps or wing commanders.

Finally, to round out his organizational changes, Hooker created an inspector general's department, with inspectors for each branch, infantry, cavalry, and artillery. In addition, each brigade was given an inspector, all of whom were organized to function under the chief inspector of the army. While this system took away some of the traditional responsibility of commanders, drastic reform was clearly necessary after the army had sunk into a slough of despondency and ineffectiveness after the Battle of Fredericksburg.

Vast Federal Troop Strength

The Eleventh Corps under Major General Franz Sigel and the Twelfth Corps under Major General Henry W. Slocum, neither of whom Burnside had used in the Battle of Fredericksburg, had by this time become an integral part of Hooker's combat army. The army was now constituted as shown below. The only subsequent change before the Battle of Chancellorsville was the substitution of General Oliver O. Howard for General Sigel, the latter having requested a transfer out of pique because he claimed that he had been downgraded through having had the strength of his Eleventh Corps drastically reduced. This he regarded as a slight by reason of the fact that his lineal rank in the Regular Army was a few files further up the list than Hooker himself, as well as several of the other corps commanders with larger corps.

	Strength
Army Headquarters	60
First Corps, Maj. Gen. John F. Reynolds ...	16,908
Second Corps, Maj. Gen. Darius N. Couch .	16,893
Third Corps, Maj. Gen. Daniel E. Sickles*..	18,721
Fifth Corps, Maj. Gen. George G. Meade ..	15,824
Sixth Corps, Maj. Gen. John Sedgwick ...	23,667
Eleventh Corps, Maj. Gen. Oliver O. Howard	12,977
Twelfth Corps, Maj. Gen. Henry W. Slocum	13,450
Cavalry Corps, Maj. Gen. George Stoneman*	11,541
Reserve Artillery (400 guns), Brig. Gen. Henry J. Hunt	1,610
Engineers and Signal Corps	800
Provost Guard	2,217
Total	134,668

The organizations listed above constituted the Army of the Potomac, over 134,000 effectives including 71 batteries of artillery with 412 guns, all under the command of General Hooker. This huge army seemed to be somewhat smaller than the one which had been available to Burnside for the Fredericksburg campaign. But that was an illusion, for Hooker's army was backed up by 125,000 additional Federal troops which gave depth to the Union dispositions and provided potential strategic support should it become necessary. Heintzelman had 45,000 men defending Washington; Schenck commanded 30,000 at Harpers Ferry, Winchester, and the area protecting the Baltimore and Ohio Railroad; 35,000 under Dix protected the lines of the James and York Rivers; and Foster had 15,000 more in North Carolina.

On the face of it, it would appear that Lee's relatively small Army of Northern Virginia was hopelessly outnum-

---

*Promoted from brigadier general per G. O. No. 96, War Dept., April 15, 1863.

See the Appendix for organization, strengths, casualties, and times of arrival on battlefield, of both armies.

bered, ringed about as it was by Federal superiority that approximated a strength ratio of four to one, with a two to one ratio if the Army of the Potomac alone were considered. Hooker's mission was to keep Lee's army from threatening Northern territory and to destroy it as soon as possible. He certainly had under his immediate command all the troops that he needed for the purpose.

The fly in the ointment was that Hooker, Heintzelman, Schenck, Dix, and Foster all reported directly to General-in-Chief Halleck in Washington, yet Hooker and Halleck were barely on speaking terms. That meant an absence of harmonious relations which one may be sure would result in a lack of cooperation and coordination, with adverse effect on any combined effort which might be planned. All of which was grist to Lee's strategic mill.

Staff Deficiencies

When the Civil War started, the United States Army was living in the past so far as military staff techniques were concerned. In 1861 virtually the same staff system was in effect as at the close of the Revolutionary War, and during 1861-1865 only minor changes were effected, without significant improvement either in organization or theory. This was true despite the fact that in 1855 a trio of young officers, including Captain George B. McClellan, had been sent to Europe by Secretary of War Jefferson Davis to study developments in the art of war as practiced by the major European countries, including Prussia. But the young officers missed the most important thing, the development of the great Prussian staff system, about which nothing whatsoever appeared in their report.

When McClellan, as commanding general of the Army of the Potomac, discovered how greatly he was handicapped by the inadequacies of the existing staff system, he made at least a start in the direction of improvement by creating the post of chief of staff for the army. Had he gone one step further and mandated a similar executive position for every corps, division, brigade, and regiment in his army, the gain in operational efficiency could not have failed to be enormous. In those cases where corps commanders adopted the expedient, it was on a purely voluntary basis and reflected no credit on the War Department or the General-in-Chief.

The most surprising staff deficiency was in the field of military intelligence. While the lack of trained intelligence officers was primarily the fault of the high command in Washington, the generals in the field might have shown sufficient ingenuity to improvise a procedure for assimilating and evaluating the information that was bound to flow into headquarters, even though it was not consciously sought by positive means. Had such been tried and proven its worth, the procurement of officers with a bent for intelligence duties would not have been difficult. General Hooker's action in substituting military personnel for Pinkerton spies was a constructive move, but the time was too short for the innovation to filter down to subordinate combat organizations, with the result that no perceptible tactical benefit accrued to the Army of the Potomac during the Chancellorsville campaign.

In the absence of trained, capable general staff officers, the commanding generals of army corps and divisions of necessity directed their campaigns and fought their battles on a strictly personalized basis, more often than not through the medium of oral, and frequently incomplete, fragmentary "off the cuff" orders. The general's word was law, and it depended largely on his individual personality whether such staff as he had would be made conversant with his plans or given the opportunity to render assistance in perfecting them and putting them into effect.

There can be no doubt that the history of the Army of the Potomac would have been a very different one had the successive army commanders been able and willing to profit by the aid of trained general staffs such as those that functioned in the two most recent wars in which this country has been involved. In retrospect, the need for such staffs was even greater during the Civil War, for the reason that far more physical exertion was then necessary, mostly on horseback, and communications were primitive by today's standards. This placed a great strain on the capabilities of the commander, leaving him but little time or energy for forward thinking and planning.

The absence of staff organization and procedures is conspicuous in the *Official Records,* where the Tables of Organization for the Army of the Potomac failed to note, under General Headquarters, even the unofficial position of the Chief of Staff. The Chief of Artillery is however listed as is the Provost Marshal General, while the commanders of the engineer brigade, the signal corps, and the ordnance detachment are noted in their command status only. No record is found to indicate the presence of an adjutant general, inspector general, a chief of chaplains, a surgeon general, or even a chief quartermaster, although some at least of those positions were known to be filled, as evidenced by correspondence signed by "Assistant Adjutant General," "Acting Signal Officer," "Chief Quartermaster," et al.

Hooker knew just the man he wanted for his Chief of Staff, but the request was distinctly out of character for a general whose capacity for political intrigue had been so well developed during his rise to power. Brigadier General Charles P. Stone, professionally well qualified for the assignment, had been unfairly tagged as the sole architect of the Federal disaster at Ball's Bluff in the fall of 1861. As a result he had been cast into utter military darkness, from which Hooker wished to save him in spite of the radical Republicans who allegedly made Stone the scapegoat chiefly because he was the most likely candidate for the award.

Denied the opportunity to take Stone, Hooker turned to a nonprofessional general, Daniel Butterfield, who as a businessman at the start of the war raised troops and commanded a New York brigade under McClellan, moving up to corps commander under Burnside at Fredericksburg. Butterfield had not particularly distinguished himself as a field commander, but enjoyed rollicking parties and Hooker liked to have him around headquarters as a congenial drinking companion. This may conceivably have had something to do with his selection for the post of army chief of staff, in which position he would be in intimate daily proximity to the commanding general.

Butterfield's chief claim to fame up to this time had been as inventor of a new bugle call which would more appropriately soothe the soldiers to sleep at night. With an ear for music, the regular "lights out" call did not suit him, and his whistled rendition of what he regarded as a more suitable call was translated by an apt bugler into "Taps," which proved so acceptable that it quickly spread to other units and has remained regulation ever since.

TAPS

ADVANCE OF THE CAVALRY SKIRMISHERS

Chapter 3

PRELIMINARY CAVALRY ENGAGEMENTS

The year 1863 was to mark the emergence of the Union cavalry as a fighting arm and the corresponding decline in the Confederate cavalry's capacity to dominate every skirmish or combat in which it engaged. A balance in combat effectiveness as between the mounted forces of the opposing armies became a possibility as a result of Hooker's consolidation order. A period of trial and error was first necessary, however, in action with the enemy, for the Federal horsemen to acquire proficiency and the confidence that they could meet Stuart's experienced veterans on even terms.

Hooker's initial mission for his rehabilitated cavalry would today be known as counterreconnaissance, or screening. The corps was directed to form a ring of outposts which virtually encircled the camps of the Army of the Potomac in the Falmouth area. This line of outposts, which extended for almost one hundred miles, proved to be hopelessly ineffectual. It had the effect of immobilizing 12,000 troopers in country that was a succession of thick woods and trails that could not possibly be sealed off against the depredations of small, fast-moving bodies of enemy cavalry. The second fallacy was to deny the cavalry the opportunity for intensive training in preparation for its new combat missions. The long distances traveled by the reliefs and the fact that the horses were kept saddled for instant use served to wear down men and horses in inconsequential picketing which in reality defeated its own purpose. The great length of the line that had to be manned and the effective enemy civilian underground organization made it a simple matter for enemy cavalry to penetrate the screen almost at will.

After a bit Hooker concluded that the long outpost line wasn't such a sound idea after all, or else the stepped-up tempo of Confederate cavalry movements changed his mind, for the bars were lowered to allow the Federal cavalry to do some offensive traveling of its own. The first mission, in early February, called for a force of three regiments, with a battery of artillery and a division of infantry in support, to move up the river to destroy the Rappahannock bridge, where the Orange and Alexandria Railroad crossed the river and which the Confederates had rebuilt after its destruction in 1862. The weather was atrocious, with a mixture of snow, hail, and rain. The timbers of the wooden bridge scheduled for destruction were thoroughly soaked, and someone had neglected to furnish the troops with combustibles or incendiary material. What was worse, Wade Hampton's Confederate Brigade was found posted at the southern end of the bridge awaiting their arrival. The net result was that the combined Federal force of 16,000 men returned meekly to its camps with the score zero-zero in the initial effort of the cavalry to justify its existence.

Stepped-up Cavalry Operations

This minor adventure triggered further movements. During the months of February and March the cavalry forces of the opposing armies became more active. Stuart's troopers as usual took the initiative by crossing the Rappahannock at the middle fords and engaging in lesser skirmishes and an occasional sizable hit-and-run raid. They killed outposts and captured prisoners, and on one occasion conducted a notable reconnaissance in force. On that historic foray, elements of four regiments of Fitzhugh Lee's Brigade crossed at Kelly's Ford and penetrated to within five miles of the main camp of Hooker's army at Falmouth, in an exciting adventure known as the skirmish at Hartwood Church.

Such cavalry brushes were routine for the aggressive Confederate horsemen, but the increasing frequency of their operations indicated that with the approach of milder weather and the drying up of the muddy roads, General Lee was determined that Hooker should not make any major troop movements without his prior knowledge.

To their surprise, the Confederate cavalry did not have things all their own way. The Federal horsemen almost at once began to exhibit unaccustomed skill, strength, and boldness. The change for the better had been a long time coming. Once started, progress was rapid although somewhat painful, for the Federal cavalry could not expect to become fully successful until it had gained the benefit of time, combat experience, and aggressive leadership to match that of the incomparable Jeb Stuart and his almost equally famous brigade commanders.

The Ubiquitous Lees

Fitzhugh Lee, a nephew of R. E. Lee, and Stuart's favorite brigadier, was a major influence in making the

Confederate cavalry the devastating scourge that in the early war years contributed so greatly to the succession of victories scored by Lee's Army of Northern Virginia.

Fitzhugh Lee was a fighter who had served in the Indian Wars on the western prairies during the late 1850's after graduating from West Point. In the spring of 1859, while

BRIGADIER GENERAL FITZHUGH LEE, C.S.A.

campaigning under Van Dorn in Western Kansas, he was wounded in a fight with Comanche Indians, as a result of which he carried an arrowhead imbedded in his chest for the rest of his life. Perhaps that early souvenir was a lucky piece, for Fitzhugh Lee was involved in every major battle in the eastern theater and in dozens of minor cavalry affairs with the enemy, throughout the Civil War, but never received so much as a scratch.

In an age when heavy beards were commonplace, Lee had managed to produce a magnificent black chin adornment. His photographs indicate that his beard had an overall length of fully twelve inches, shaped like a broad-edged spade. It has been suggested by historians that the compelling reason for this oversize facial decoration was in his case a desire to conceal his youth, for he became a major general in 1863 at the tender age of 28. Thirty-five years later, during the Spanish-American War, he again

BRIGADIER GENERAL W. H. F. LEE, C.S.A.

served his country as a major general, after attaining distinction in civilian pursuits and public service, including a stint as Governor of his native State of Virginia.

Next to General Robert E. Lee, Fitzhugh was the most prominent of the Civil War Lees, although he had plenty of company. R. E. Lee's three sons, cousins of Fitzhugh, all served in the Confederate Army. William Henry Fitzhugh Lee, the second oldest, also a cavalry brigadier, was called "Rooney" to avoid the confusion of having two Fitzhughs in the mounted branch. He too became a major

[41]

general, at the age of 27, closely rivaling his cousin Fitzhugh as one of Stuart's dependable lieutenants. Wade Hampton, Stuart's second in command, was the third brigade commander who in company with Stuart and the two Lees made cavalry history in the Virginia theater of operations. Rooney Lee, a graduate of Harvard University, had gained some measure of fame in undergraduate days by rowing No. 5 on the 1857 Harvard crew, of which he was the heaviest but one of the best oarsmen. R. E. Lee's other two sons, George Washington Custis and Robert, Jr. played creditable but more modest roles in the war and were rarely in the news. Justifiably, then, the Lees ranked in the Confederacy as a family group to which the South was heavily indebted.

The Affair at Hartwood Church

As the Federal cavalry improved and became more aggressive, and Lee's sources of enemy information became increasingly difficult to tap, conflicting reports drifted in from the Richmond area which half convinced Lee that Hooker might be preparing to repeat McClellan's 1862 strategy by secretly shifting his army to a position on the Peninsula from which to attack Richmond on the east. Lee had to know for sure and apparently the only way to secure positive information was to have his cavalry penetrate the Federal screen.

Fitzhugh Lee's Brigade was selected for the purpose. He moved out from Culpeper Court House on the morning of February 24 with detachments from several different regiments of the Virginia cavalry, totaling about 400 men. Crossing the Rappahannock at Kelly's Ford, the outfit marched via Morrisville in the direction of Hartwood Church, a prominent landmark about eight miles northwest of Falmouth on the Warrenton Post Road (Pike), where a number of roads converged. The going was difficult in the heavy snow, but no opposition was offered by the Federals until Lee's scouts ran into enemy out-guards in the vicinity of Hartwood Church on the morning of February 25.

Dressed in Federal overcoats, the Confederate advance party surprised the Federal pickets, captured them without a shot being fired, and opened a hole through which Lee's troopers poured in two columns. The right column followed the Warrenton Pike leading directly to Falmouth, while the left angled off along the Ridge Road which paralleled the Pike a few hundred yards to its north.

The Third Pennsylvania Cavalry, manning the Hartwood Church sector of the Federal outpost line, was on the point of being relieved by a composite force made up of six squadrons, 600 men, detailed from a Pennsylvania regiment which had never been under fire, and a New York regiment, composed of Germans, who had acquired the reputation of being constitutionally opposed to being shot at.

The commanding officer of the relieving squadrons, hearing the yells of the charging Confederates, quickly deployed his squadrons in line. About that time the galloping Confederates of Lee's right column swept past on his left, whereupon the colonel, fearing for his rear, detached several of his squadrons to pursue the enemy. At that point Lee's left column drove directly at the three squadrons that were still in position. It was too much for the inexperienced Federals, who promptly broke for the rear, followed shortly by the detached squadrons, who ignored the colonel's order to charge and instead made what was described as "very good time in the opposite direction."

It was obvious however that the daring Confederates would soon be in real trouble if they kept boring in past the outpost supports and reserves to the positions manned by the infantry corps. Lee wisely checked the headlong

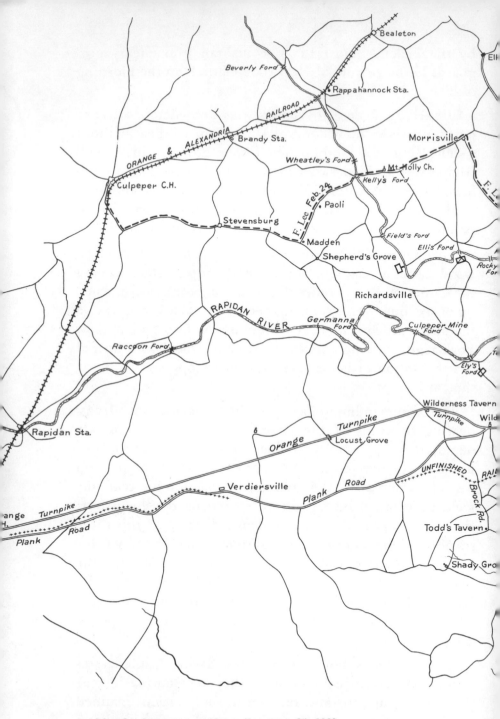

MAP 2. SITUATION AT NOON, FEBRUARY 25, 1863

Showing the locations of major units of the opposing armies, and the route taken by Fitzhugh Lee in his foray through Hartwood Church. Hood's and Pickett's Divisions of Lee's army are not shown, being in the Suffolk area.

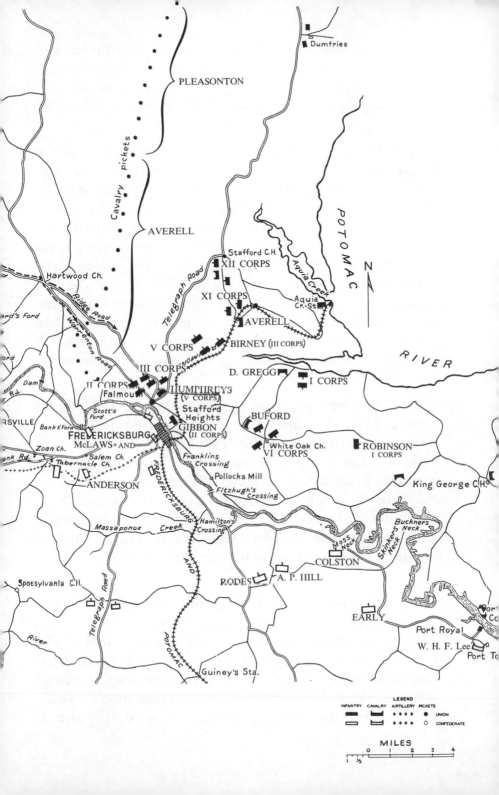

Dumfries

PLEASONTON

Cavalry pickets

POTOMAC

AVERELL

Hartwood Ch.

Ridge Road

Warrenton Road

Stafford C.H.

XII CORPS

Telegraph Road

XI CORPS

Aquia Creek

Aquia Cr. Sta.

AVERELL

V CORPS

BIRNEY (III CORPS)

III CORPS

RIVER

II CORPS

Falmouth

HUMPHREYS
(V CORPS)

D. GREGG

I CORPS

Scott's Ford

Stafford
Heights

BUFORD

Banks'Ford

FREDERICKSBURG

GIBBON
(II CORPS)

White Oak Ch.

ROBINSON
I CORPS

McLAWS = AND

VI CORPS

Zoan Ch.

Salem Ch.

Franklins
Crossing

Tabernacle Ch.

King George C.H.

ANDERSON

Pollocks Mill

Fitzhugh's
Crossing

Massaponox Creek

Hamilton's
Crossing

Moss
Neck

Buckners
Neck

Skinker's Neck

COLSTON

Spotsylvania C.H.

RODES

A. P. HILL

Telegraph Road

River

EARLY

Port Royal

W. H. F. Lee

Guiney's Sta.

N

advance and commenced his retirement in the direction of Morrisville. During the return march his men enjoyed a few spirited skirmishes and engaged in occasional counter-attacks on the ever increasing numbers of the defenders.

Dusk was approaching when Lee's small detachment headed for home. During the course of the afternoon the alarm which had been spread by the small force of Confederate cavalrymen reached Brigadier General William W. Averell, commanding the Federal cavalry division in that sector. Averell ordered his men to horse, reported the attack to Corps Commander Stoneman, and to army head-quarters, which directed him to send a brigade to Hart-wood Church to meet the threat. Meantime General Sickles, commanding the Third Infantry Corps, reported to Hooker that enemy cavalry in force had penetrated to within a few yards of his infantry sentinels, and inquired whether he should take one of his brigades out to repel the attack.

As the rumors continued to spread through the infantry camps, Lee's detachment of four hundred men mush-roomed to a strength of five regiments and then to three brigades. The exaggerated reports raised a serious question at army headquarters whether the hostile attack might not perhaps be aimed at Stafford Court House and Dum-fries, nine and seventeen miles respectively east and north-east of Hartwood Church. Averell was now ordered to assemble his entire cavalry division at Hartwood.

Nor was that all. As Lee's troopers were wending their way back to Morrisville, Hooker was wiring Heintzelman in Washington to send out from Rappahannock Station nonexistent troops to intercept the enemy. Hooker also directed the commander of the Second Corps, General Couch, to send a brigade for the same purpose. Stoneman was instructed by Hooker to alert Pleasonton's cavalry division and the reserve brigade, prepared to move at dawn. Hooker even telegraphed the situation to Secretary of War Stanton, but there is no record of anyone having wakened Lincoln from a sound sleep to inform him of the "serious threat" to the Army of the Potomac.

It was all pretty silly in retrospect, and if there weren't a lot of red faces in the Falmouth area there should have been. The Federal cavalry was certainly undergoing its baptism of fire the hard and unsuccessful way. During all the fuss, Fitzhugh Lee and his triumphant troopers, bearing in tow about one hundred and fifty Federal prisoners, calmly rode back to Morrisville. Still in enemy territory, he went into bivouac for the night, leaving behind only fourteen men killed, wounded, and missing.

As an outstanding example of how not to use cavalry, the affair at Hartwood Church, it may be hoped, was carefully studied by the officers of Stoneman's corps. Averell's division alone should have been able without much trouble to have blocked Lee's retrograde movement. From beginning to end it was a story of "too little, too late." The least that could have been expected was that Averell or Pleasonton, or both, would have thrown sizable forces across the main escape routes, in sufficient depth to assure the defeat or even the destruction of Lee's entire force, which would have had a hard time escaping had they been forced by solid opposition to move off the roads under the weather and ground conditions existing.

The Federal Cavalry Retaliates

Fitzhugh Lee had accomplished his mission with a vengeance. His successful raid satisfied his commanding general that Hooker's main body had certainly not moved to the James River. The raid was particularly galling to General Averell, commander of the Second Cavalry Division, against a part of whose outpost line Fitz Lee's raid had been executed. The genial Confederate, an old friend and classmate of Averell at West Point, had added insult to injury by leaving a written message for Averell which read:

> I wish you would put up your sword, leave my state and go home. You ride a good horse, I ride a better. Yours can beat mine running.* If you won't go home, return my visit and bring me a sack of coffee.

Averell, deciding to get back at his old pal, secured Hooker's permission to return the compliment. His plan was to cross the Rappahannock with a force of three thousand men and six pieces of artillery, attack and destroy Lee's cavalry, reported to be in the vicinity of Culpeper. Averell was dead serious in his retaliatory plan, for in getting ready for the fight he had directed his troopers to sharpen their sabers, telling them that he would see to it they were given the opportunity to use them in the forthcoming action.

Army headquarters warned him that reports had been received telling of Confederate cavalry operations involving from 250 to 1000 men near Brentsville, but that he would have to provide for his own security. Averell, who still had much to learn about the independent employment of cavalry, took the rumors too seriously, with unfortunate results the following day when his forces tangled with Fitz Lee.

Carrying four days' rations and one day's forage, the Federal force bivouacked the night of March 16 at Morrisville, which seemed to be the accepted stopover point for the cavalry of both armies. There Averell split his force to leave two regiments, about 900 men, to guard the fords and secure his return route, a dubious decision in that it reduced his strength by almost one-third, against a purely imaginary danger. In reality he had nothing to protect except a line of retreat, and there were other ways to get back if it came to that.

---

*Referring to the speed with which the Federal pickets gave way when attacked. Bigelow, *op. cit.*

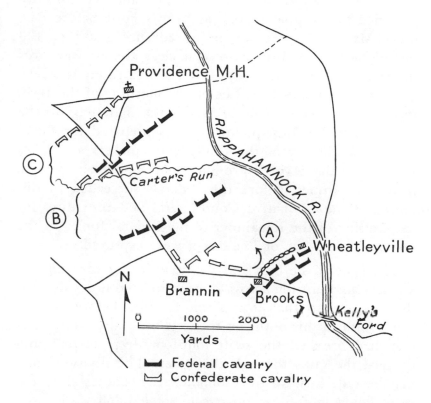

MAP 3. ENGAGEMENT AT KELLY'S FORD, MARCH 17, 1863

Phase A (shown on map as A): Averell crossed the Rappahannock at Kelly's Ford and deployed behind the stone wall running between Wheatleyville and Brooks' farm. Meanwhile Fitzhugh Lee with his brigade of five regiments was approaching in column on the road leading southeast toward Brannin. His leading regiment turned off to its left into the field and charged the Federal position; but was repulsed by heavy fire from behind the stone wall. As the other regiments started to deploy, they were charged by the Federal cavalry and withdrew north of Carter's Run.

Phase B (see B on map): During this phase, Averell pulled up facing the Confederates and waited for them to charge him, as they had customarily done. When this charge came, the Federal easily repelled it with their repeating carbines, reinforced by the fire of horse artillery. This fire broke up and badly disorganized the Confederate units, so that they no longer had a large formed body of troops on the field.

Phase C (see C on map): The fragments of Lee's Brigade made their way back to a line running generally southwest from Providence Meeting House. The situation was an invitation for Averell to make a coordinated attack, again disperse the re-forming Confederate squadrons, then pursue the remnants vigorously. Instead, he withdrew, leaving Fitzhugh Lee in possession of the field.

[49]

Averell's reduced force of 2100 men and six guns approached the Rappahannock at Kelly's Ford before daybreak March 17, preceded by an advance guard of 100 picked men, with instructions to clear the passage over the river for the main body. Fitz Lee had received a telegram from General R. E. Lee on the morning of the 16th, that a large force of Federal cavalry was marching up the Rappahannock. Consequently he was prepared for them. The strengthening of the Confederate pickets at Kelly's Ford meant that Averell promptly met opposition. A brisk little fight ensued before the Federals succeeded in disposing of the combative Confederates and providing for the crossing of the remainder of the Federal force. In the process, twenty-five of Lee's men were captured.

The fight at the ford and the necessity for carrying the artillery ammunition across by hand to keep it dry delayed the advance, so that it was midmorning before Averell could form up his outfit on the west bank after the horsemen had breasted the swift four-foot deep current and dragged the guns through the water. The division commander rode forward to reconnoiter the country side, and in so doing spotted an open field some 1,200 yards from the river, which appeared to offer promise as a good battlefield.

Fitz Lee received word at Culpeper about 7:30 A. M. that the Federal cavalry had crossed. Mounting his brigade at once, the troopers moved out at a fast trot, through Brandy Station and on towards the river. Lee could count less than 1,000 effectives and he had no idea as to the strength of the invaders. He moved rapidly, nevertheless, relying on his experienced veterans to dispose of the opposition, for whose fighting ability he had little respect.

Averell, knowing Lee's impetuous nature, advanced toward him slowly and cautiously, with detachments to front and flank watchfully preceding the main column. The first clash occurred about noon less than a mile from the ford, a dismounted fight that wa, spirited but inconclusive. Sparring for an opening, Lee launched the Third Virginia in a mounted charge that was forced by the heavy Federal fire to veer across the front of the Fourth Pennsylvania and the Fourth New York, which regiments had ranged themselves dismounted behind a protecting stone wall.

It was this charge to which Major John Pelham, Stuart's famous Chief of Artillery, had attached himself as a visitor. In the course of the skirmish, Pelham became one of the victims of the Federal carbine fire which poured out from behind the stone wall to break up the Confederate attack. General Jeb Stuart and Pelham, on court-martial duty at Culpeper, had joined Lee's Brigade on borrowed horses to watch the engagement, as soon as they got the word. Stuart contented himself with being merely an observer and made no move to interfere with or advise Lee in his conduct of the engagement. But Pelham, with less rank, who loved a fight and was always seemingly attracted to the more dangerous spots, couldn't resist the temptation to take an active part in the battle. He had been a thorn in the flesh of many a Union division and corps commander in earlier battles. Therefore his death at Kelly's Ford, with the loss to the Confederates of their most effective artilleryman, might of itself almost be said to have been complete justification for Averell's raid, inconsequential as it proved to be in other respects.

Piecemeal Confederate attacks from different directions failed to dislodge Averell's regiments, which were proving to be pretty fair scrappers themselves. It was now Averell's turn to take the initiative. The brigades of Colonel Duffie and McIntosh moved out at the gallop in a converging attack from two directions, and that did it. The outnumbered Confederates, driven from the field, retired about a mile. Lee rallied and reorganized them, behind Carter's Run. They formed in line to dispute the expected advance of the Federals. The ensuing battle, with artillery engaged on both sides, surged back and forth in mounted and dismounted charges and countercharges until the afternoon was almost spent.

Captured Confederates had reported the presence on the field of Stuart and Pelham, which caused Averell to jump to the erroneous conclusion that this meant reinforcements would soon appear. Averell also heard nearby trains in motion to the south and suspected the approach of Confederate infantry. This happy strategem had occurred to Lee, who had ordered empty trains to be shuttled up and down the line to his rear. In combination, the two factors proved a psychological deterrent to any further aggressive effort on the part of Averell, upon whose over-wrought imagination they had an important effect.

About 5:30 P.M. Averell broke off the engagement and returned unmolested by the same route over which he had advanced, having sustained less than 100 casualties and taking with him some 40 prisoners. His official report was factual and restrained; after describing the raid in detail, he stated briefly: "My horses were very much exhausted. We had been successful thus far. I deemed it proper to withdraw."

Jeb Stuart, however, described the affair in rather flamboyant language, regarding it as a great victory for the Confederates. In a published general order dated March 18, the day following the engagement, he spoke disparagingly of the Federal effort, referring to "the serious disaster inflicted on this insolent foe, in which he was driven, broken and discomfited, across the Rappahannock—leaving many of his dead and wounded on the field." There was no mention in Stuart's order of the Confederate casualties, which Lee himself later reported as one hundred and seventy, compared to less than one hundred for the Federal cavalry.

Actually it was neither a victory nor a defeat for either side, although Averell's departure from the scene left Lee in possession of the field, which gave Stuart the basis for his exaggerated claims on behalf of Lee. It was however a distinct failure on Averell's part, since he had promised his men a victory, and his mission, to destroy or rout the Confederate cavalry, remained unfulfilled.

The chief gain to the Federals was the evidence that the Northern cavalry had proven itself able to meet Stuart's vaunted Confederates in a cavalry action on enemy territory with honor to themselves. The result was a terrific boost to their morale, despite Hooker's dissatisfaction with Averell for failure to destroy Fitz Lee's cavalry, or even to score a decisive victory over the latter's disorganized and driven brigade. This should have been comparatively easy had Averell demonstrated greater aggressiveness and less timidity. Having chosen to leave the field to his opponent, but before retiring, Averell took occasion to return Fitzhugh Lee's earlier note with the laconic message: "Here's your coffee. Here's your visit. How do you like it? Averell."

This, the first purely cavalry combat of any size that had occurred to date, had a salutary effect on the Union army far in excess of the strategic fruits, which were nil. What it did prove was that the Federal cavalry could march and fight offensively. The skirmish therefore had considerable significance for the future of that arm.

What the raid failed to prove is mere speculation, that always elusive "might have been." Yet it is an intriguing thought that, with Averell's original superiority of more than three troopers to every one of Lee's, had he been more of a bulldog and less of a boxer, he might have destroyed Lee's Brigade as an effective fighting force, and for all practical purposes deprived R. E. Lee of all cavalry except Rooney Lee's Brigade. In the light of what happened at Chancellorsville six weeks later, such a finale to the battle of Kelly's Ford could have changed the whole complexion of the Chancellorsville campaign.

Averell's Background

Averell's military record does not reveal any outstanding exploits. Graduating from West Point in 1855, he served continuously in the cavalry until his resignation from the Army at the close of the Civil War. He appears to have

BRIGADIER GENERAL WILLIAM W. AVERELL

been an average combat leader, who as a young officer engaged in several prewar skirmishes with the Indians. In one of these he was severely wounded in a suprise night attack by the wily savages, resulting in a sick leave of absence from October 1859 to April 1861. He saw plenty of action during the Civil War, particularly after the Federal cavalry came into its own. His fights in the winter and spring of 1863 prior to and during the Chancellorsville

campaign found him pitted against Stuart's capable brigadiers, Fitzhugh and Rooney Lee. Averell was clearly no
match for those more aggressive generals whose superior
drive and veteran experience in cavalry action had become
a byword.

Conceivably Averell might have achieved a better score
had he been so fortunate as to serve under more aggressive
commanders, or had the cavalry arm been nourished and
encouraged to demonstrate its capabilities earlier in the
war. General Stoneman, the first cavalry corps commander,
was not the type to encourage that uninhibited cavalry
spirit of the offensive that should have been inherent in
the very conception of the cavalry role in the 1860's. The
stifling restrictions that blanketed the Federal mounted
arm in the early days undoubtedly contributed to the lack
of enterprise displayed by many of its generals during the
transition period, although there were plenty of field and
troop officers who could and would have put on more
spirited shows if their ranking officers had demonstrated
more aggressive qualities of leadership.

Averell's combat approach was a bit too conservative
for the pre-Chancellorsville requirements. He lacked the
necessary initiative and experience in the capacity of a
division commander, when Fitz Lee forced his way through
Averell's position and got away without punishment at
Hartwood Church. Again when Averell retaliated and
muffed his chance between Kelly's Ford and Culpeper,
the Federal cavalry failed to foreshadow the later successes
which greater experience and more fiery leadership were
destined to make possible. Nor did Averell show to any
better advantage during the so-called Stoneman raid in
the rear of Lee's army during the Battle of Chancellorsville, as recounted in a later chapter.

On balance, then, the Federal cavalry actions in the
winter and spring of 1863 failed in part to achieve the
results which might have been gained from the improved

conditions under which the Cavalry Corps was then operating; and the responsibility for the less than satisfactory outcome rested on the cavalry leaders far more than on General Hooker, who gave them their first opportunity.

Famous Confederate Guerrillas

The ability and readiness to improvise, to adapt the means at hand to the circumstances of the moment, has always been a refreshing facet of the American character, from early pioneer days to the present. Paradoxically, and due in large measure to the rigid pattern in which the professional army officer has traditionally been encased through the unimaginative straightjacket of regulations and strict conformity to the "approved solution" as the sine qua non of tactical maneuvers, the Regular Army until quite recently has consistently resisted pressure for modernization from civilians of vision and from advanced thinkers in the ranks of the Army itself. "What was good enough for your father is good enough for you," a pronouncement by which many a complacent adult frustrates his ambitious offspring, seemed unfortunately to be the guiding principle which dominated the restrictive outlook of entirely too many Federal officers in positions of authority at the outbreak and during the early years of the Civil War.

The Confederacy suffered far less from that sort of deadening influence. A new nation was being created, in which bureaucratic rigidity had not yet fastened itself too firmly on the body military. Any measure, however revolutionary, which might help the cause was given an opportunity to prove its worth.

In such a flexible atmosphere, the opportunity was present for great individualists like Nathan Bedford Forrest, John H. Morgan, Turner Ashby, and the youthful John Singleton Mosby, to attract and lead men of similar tastes and spirit in the excitingly successful adventures by which their bands of irregulars, partisans, and guerrillas created havoc in enemy territory.

There is reason to believe that the far-flung raids of that famous Confederate quartet caused greater material and psychological damage to the North, killed and captured more Federals, and pinned down a greater number of enemy troops than the regular cavalry. With a fraction of the manpower, the partisans are reputed to have hurt the Union on a greater scale than did the undeniably successful but more romantic and widely publicized operations of the gay cavalier, Jeb Stuart, and his regularly constituted cavalry brigades.

Mosby's activities generally coincided geographically with the operations of the Army of Northern Virginia. A lawyer by profession, he was a bantam in size, weighing only 125 pounds, but his energies and adventuresome spirit were measurable in inverse ratio to his displacement of weight. The life of a cavalryman was made to order for the young man, who enlisted as a scout and first attracted attention by guiding Stuart's troopers on their first great ride around McClellan's army in June 1862.

The Partisan Ranger Act, passed in the early days of the war by the Confederate Congress, had not only given the rangers freedom of action and independence from the orders of the regular establishment, but permitted them as well to retain whatever loot they might be able to capture from the enemy. Mosby commenced his raids with the approval of Stuart, with only nine followers in January 1863, against the outposts of Washington, D. C. Immediately he began a series of harassing attacks against the Federal pickets, usually terrorizing small troop detachments and consistently bringing in prisoners and booty.

So successful were Mosby's raids and so popular was the character of service he offered that his force quickly expanded to eight companies of cavalry and one of horse artillery. Many of these men were deserters from Stuart's own corps, anxious to share the romantic, undisciplined type of fighting for which Mosby's tactics afforded ample opportunity, and to participate in the division of the spoils which his raids invariably secured. His lightning hit-and-run surprise attacks generally resulted in turning over to General Stuart valuable enemy information, and there can be no doubt that Stuart, and in turn Lee, derived much benefit from his services, far more perhaps than either would have been willing to admit

Mosby's Amazing Exploit

One of the most amazing cavalry feats of the entire war was staged on March 8, 1863 by Captain Mosby, when he led a small mounted force of 29 rangers from Aldie, at the foot of Bull Run Mountains, to Fairfax Courthouse, in the heart of the enemy country and not over fifteen miles from Washington. Through rain and pitch darkness, with the express purpose of capturing the British adventurer, Colonel Percy Wyndham, who commanded the 5th New York Cavalry, stationed at Fairfax, Mosby led his troopers on an adventure which for sheer drama would be hard to duplicate.

Wyndham had sent a number of taunting messages to the bold raider which so got under his skin that he decided to humiliate the annoying Britisher by capturing him in his bed and sending him in as a prisoner. As the affair turned out, Wyndham was in Washington. But Brigadier General Edwin H. Stoughton, West Point 1859, and only twenty-five years of age, who was commanding an infantry brigade on Heintzelman's line of outposts protecting Washington near Centerville, was sleeping soundly in his quarters at Fairfax Courthouse. Mosby captured Stoughton, one captain, thirty enlisted men, and fifty-eight horses, all of whom he escorted safely back to the Confederate lines in spite of frantic efforts by the Federal cavalry to corral him. Stoughton himself was sent to Libby prison, from which he was soon paroled, but the ridicule he suffered at the hands of Army and public alike was so great that he resigned from the Army and died in New York a few years after the war.

Mosby himself declared in his *Memoirs* that the capture of Stoughton was his greatest exploit and that it was never again possible to duplicate the feat because the Federal cavalry had learned its lesson and become too smart to again be caught napping in such a humiliating fashion.

Both Robert E. Lee and Stuart were professional soldiers and West Pointers, and neither was particularly happy over the guerrilla exploits of the peripatetic Mosby and his men. Their attitude was understandable in face of the ease with which Mosby gained deserters from the Regular Confederate cavalry. Uniformed soldiers have a constitutional aversion to guerrillas who, while masquerading as inoffensive civilians, treacherously cut throats at night. The activities of the bushwhackers on both sides were notorious and revolting and no amount of romantic TV programs can make a partisan an honorable type of foe. In the last analysis, of course, war itself can scarcely be regarded as honorable, except by a broad interpretation of the moral code. But guerrilla warfare carried the concept far beyond the pale of ordinary decency.

By the same token, however, the high command did not wish to make too great an issue of the matter lest their opposition result in the loss of Mosby's valuable services to the Confederacy. R. E. Lee is on record in a number of letters to the War Department at Richmond in which he deplored the unwisdom of maintaining the status of the guerrillas indefinitely, on the premise that their services would achieve better results if they were linked with the chain of command. That was the last thing in the world that Mosby would endure. He went so far as to decline the first offer of a captaincy in the Partisan service if it should tie his hands. Lee insisted, and it was only after Mosby had gone over Lee's head to the Secretary of War and won his point that he would accept the appointment. He was shortly moved up another grade, and it was as a major of Partisan Rangers, untrammeled by orders or restrictions from the regular establishment, that the independent John Mosby continued his depredations until the end of the war.

Mosby's impact on events in the Chancellorsville campaign is conjectural, but there can be little doubt that his activities served a useful purpose in arousing the Federal cavalry to its own shortcomings and in accelerating its transposition to an effective counterweapon against the Confederate cavalry, regular or irregular.

Stuart's Cavalry Widely Dispersed

The attrition caused by constant activity on the part of Stuart's cavalry, on reconnaissance, raids, foraging missions, and occasional full-scale battle action, together with the growing shortage of good horses for replacements and the diminishing manpower of the South, was beginning to have an adverse effect on the Confederate cavalry. This occurred just about the time the high command of the Union Army awoke to a realization of the strategic value of good cavalry in the field operations of a large army.

In the interim between the battles of Fredericksburg and Chancellorsville, Stuart's compact cavalry, which at one time had totaled over 10,000 men, with the famous young Pelham commanding the division's small complement of fast moving field artillery until his death in action at Kelly's Ford, was spread thinly over Virginia on essential missions. This wide dispersion of force reduced Stuart's effective strength for the approaching campaign to only two brigades with their artillery, those of Fitzhugh Lee and W. H. F. Lee, about 2,500 troops in all.

During April, Fitzhugh Lee's veteran regiments were operating from Culpeper as a base, covering the long line of the Rappahannock west of Fredericksburg. W. H. F. Lee's Brigade initially covered the right of the Confederate position from the vicinity of Port Royal, seventeen miles down river from Fredericksburg. Wade Hampton's Brigade had been transferred south of the James River, on recruiting duty, while the rest of Lee's cavalry was engaged in northwestern Virginia with other troops as expeditionary forces under Generals W. E. Jones and John D. Imboden. These latter forces had been dispatched from the Shenandoah Valley early in April by General R. E. Lee on a two-pronged raid for the dual purpose of procuring supplies and recruits and inflicting as much damage as possible on the Baltimore and Ohio Railroad. But the execution of that task was so prolonged that the Battle of Chancellorsville had been fought and won by Lee's greatly depleted Army of Northern Virginia before Jones and Imboden could rejoin.

The contempt in which Stuart's cavalry held the Union cavalry, in spite of its promise of reincarnation, could not have been more clearly expressed than by this decision of Lee's to release such a large proportion of his cavalry on side missions, out of reach of the army, in the face of Hooker's vast two to one superiority directly across the Rappahannock. The reason was of course that the unenterprising character of the Federal cavalry had been demonstrated so repeatedly that the Southerners had little reason to fear a surprise crossing far from the Falmouth camps without receiving ample warning, and the time had not yet come for the Northern horsemen to prove them wrong.

FIGHTING ALONG THE TURNPIKE

CHAPTER 4

THE ARMY OF NORTHERN VIRGINIA

THE four months that elapsed between the Battle of Fredericksburg, December 13, 1862, and that of Chancellorsville on the first three days of May, 1863, constituted a period of suspended animation, a breather between rounds so to speak, while the two armies took stock of their losses, sought replacements, corrected their deficiencies, and made ready to have at one another again when the weather and condition of the roads should make it practicable to resume the contest.

While the Union defeat at Fredericksburg was a clean-cut military success for the Confederacy, it was in a sense just as barren a victory as Chancellorsville would prove to be, for Lee's army was unable to exploit either success and could ill afford the cumulative loss of manpower suffered in the two great battles.

Burnside's army had managed to extricate itself, on a night of wind and rain, from its unhappy position in and below Fredericksburg after that battle, without hindrance from or even the knowledge of the Confederates. The consequent inability of the Southerners to reap the fruits of victory was a keen disappointment; for Lee knew full well that the North could discount its losses, that his own army was still on the defensive in its own territory. He realized that sooner or later, despite a succession of victories against huge odds, the South would bleed to death unless somehow he could contrive to crack the Federal armor wide open and destroy the Union's will to fight.

The brevity of Lee's immediate report to his superiors at Richmond was perhaps an indication of his distress that the enemy had been able to withdraw from the Fredericksburg battlefield without further punishment, and to return relatively intact to his former camp sites across the Rappahannock to reorganize for another attempt.

Lee Strengthens his Fortifications

The Army of Northern Virginia, after Fredericksburg, made no major effort to molest the Army of the Potomac in its winter quarters in the Falmouth area and on the high bluffs of Stafford Heights along the north and northeast bank of the river opposite the town of Fredericksburg. Lee's victorious troops held their strong defensive positions on the ridge line, from which they had so badly battered the Federal attackers in December, and in areas to the west and south. The Battle of Fredericksburg had demonstrated the great natural strength of the position, which Lee proceeded to further fortify by the construction of trenches and other earthworks, and by extending the line along the river in both directions with the town as a pivot. Nevertheless Lee's numerical inferiority, and uncertainty as to where the Federals might next attempt to force a crossing, compelled him to maintain a defensive line that now extended for more than twenty-five miles.

As a result of hard, constant digging and construction, the defensive arc which was the Confederate line was greatly strengthened against direct attack. The line extended from Port Tobacco, a mile or so below Port Royal, to the U-shaped bend in the river at Banks' Ford. (See Map 2). This was twenty-two miles on a straight line but considerably longer if one were to follow the trace of the entrenchments and artillery emplacements constructed at appropriate intervals. The defenses on the heights west of Fredericksburg and extending to Hamilton's Crossroads were infinitely stronger than in December, when Burnside had signally failed to penetrate them. The position was also well oriented, for the Richmond, Fredericksburg and Potomac Railroad, Lee's main supply line to Richmond, roughly bisected and was at right angles to it.

The commanding general's headquarters remained on Lee's Hill two miles southwest of Fredericksburg, with an army depot and the winter quarters of the artillery at Guiney's Station,* on the line of the railroad and some twelve miles south of Fredericksburg.

Operating on interior lines, and despite the great length of his defensive position, Lee felt no concern that the enemy would be able, even with more than a two to one superiority in combat strength, to force a breakthrough at any point. Lee had so disposed his troops that he could quickly concentrate a sufficient number anywhere along the line to seal off or drive back any attack that the Federals might mount. He had done just that on many occasions, and had supreme confidence both in his own sense of timing and in the capacity of his generals to move their troops

---

*The spelling used here is that shown in Confederate reports and correspondence given in the *The Official Records of the Rebellion* as well as on a number of contemporary maps, including those of Jed Hotchkiss. According to local citizens well informed on the history of the area, the site was named for the original colonial settler, one Michael Ginney or Guinney. Today the station is known as *Guinea Station*. Bigelow, Map 2, places Lee's headquarters at Lee's Hill, but Freeman, *R. E. Lee,* II, 484, says he camped in a clearing on Mine Road.

rapidly and efficiently any reasonable distance to threatened points, by forced marches if need be.

Lee's Supply Problems

The chief concern of the Confederates, as always, was the security of Richmond, the procurement of food, forage, and horse replacements, and the addition of recruits to make good the losses suffered during the recent campaign. The shortage of food in the Army of Northern Virginia was so acute as to threaten the dissolution of the forces. General Lee, in a letter to Secretary of War Seddon, on January 26, expressed keen anxiety over the deficiency, stating that he had on hand only one week's supply of rations and four days' each of fresh beef and salt meat of the reduced ration. The surrounding country had already been thoroughly drained of its provisions. Lee saw no way to secure foodstuff locally except by impressment, which was one measure he did not care to adopt, as it would, he knew, lead to great hardship for the civilian population, already feeling the pinch of famine. The April "food riot" in Richmond indicated the temper of the populace, apparently stretched to the breaking point.

Richmond had no answer to Lee's request except to direct that the ration, already being issued on a reduced scale, be further reduced. Lee was also urged to make use of the necks and shanks of beef, which the commissary department, quite in character trying to justify its own deficiences, claimed he had not done so far.

Although the winter was comparatively mild in its early stages, a great deal of snow and rain began to fall toward the latter part of January, the snow at times reaching a depth of several feet and causing serious discomfort to the suffering soldiers. Log huts plastered with mud and covered with layers of straw and mud to keep out the wintry blasts provided cover of a sort, but with little of the comforts of home. The soldiers were miserably damp and huddled together, a condition that was somewhat improved, when the spring season arrived, by knocking out the mud for better ventilation.

The issue of clothing, when available, was insufficient in quantity and of poor quality. Trousers would last only about one month, jackets somewhat longer, perhaps two or three. Flannel cloth was virtually unobtainable, so cotton trousers were sometimes handed out even in mid-winter. They were better than nothing, to be sure, but the almost complete absence of overcoats and blankets, and the scarcity of shoes, suggests a mild—and not so mild at that— repetition of the bitter experience of Washington's shivering soldiers at Valley Forge in the winter of 1777-1778.

The transportation of equipment and supplies by rail met Lee's minimum requirements, in the absence of destructive raids by the relatively unaggressive Federal cavalry, during the period of reconstitution between campaigns. His main line of supply, the Richmond, Fredericksburg and Potomac Railroad, connected the two towns first named, with Richmond the main base. A forward supply point was established at Hanover Junction, with advance depots at Hamilton's Crossing and Guiney's Station. The Virginia Central Railroad, which crossed the theater of operations a few miles south of, parallel to, and in rear of the protective barrier of the North Anna River, linked Hanover Junction to that other vital Confederate intermediate supply point to the west, Gordonsville, on the Orange and Alexandria Railroad. This latter railroad, a logistic necessity for both armies, ran north through Culpeper to its terminal point directly across the Potomac from Washington.

Expedients in Acquiring Ordnance

The initial shortage of ordnance in the Confederate armies and the increasingly difficult problem of replacement were both reasonably well solved during 1862 by the acquisition of the huge stores of artillery, rifled muskets, and ammunition that had been taken from Federal Generals Banks, McClellan, Pope and Burnside in the course of their various defeats. These fortuitous captures supplemented the meager supplies obtainable from the works in Richmond and other Southern arsenals, together with the sporadic imports from Europe.

The United States Government authorities at Harper's Ferry, in April 1861, on receipt of information that Virginia State troops planned to seize the arsenal, had decided to destroy the building which contained 17,000 muskets before abandoning it to the enemy. The finished muskets were destroyed by the fire, but the local citizenry extinguished the blaze in time to salvage many thousands of partly-finished muskets, valuable machinery, tools, and much other vital equipment, all of which was safely removed to Richmond and Fayetteville, North Carolina. The capture of all that priceless material was a Godsend to the limited armament potential of the Confederacy and undoubtedly played a major part in advancing its capacity to wage war.

The battlefields of 1862 had made it possible for many regiments to completely replace their smoothbore muskets with rifled arms taken from the Federals, while replacements from the arsenals improved to the point where Jackson's corps alone during the winter received 10,000 muskets in addition to those already with the troops. Salvaging equipment from dead Federals and careful combing of the battlefields resulted in a huge replacement of arms, particularly in those cases where the Confederates held the field after the battle, a normal situation in that year.

Discipline and Morale

The Confederacy adopted conscription at an early date—a wise decision from every point of view. One major advantage of this to Lee's army was the reasonable assurance that his units, depleted by earlier campaigns and by attrition from other causes, would each time be rebuilt to strength. At this midpoint of the war, the Confederacy was beginning to approach but had yet to reach the bottom of its manpower barrel.

The Confederate soldier was hard put to it to devise amusements for passing the long hours when not engaged in military chores. The officers were better able and more free to locate diversion, but recreation for the enlisted men as a rule was left to their own ingenuity and initiative. Entertainment consisted principally in staging amateur theatricals, and minstrel shows, and in card games and gambling of all sorts, song fests, and frequent snowball fights between units. The latter was a popular pastime for which nature in generous measure provided the novel ingredients, which many of the soldiers from the deep South had never before seen. The organized entertainment offered by touring stars of stage and screen that brightened the outlook for war-weary veterans of our latter-day wars remained for the twentieth century to provide. Military bands in the 1860's were few and far between, doubtless because every physically fit soldier was needed for the Confederacy's fighting outfits.

The interesting pastime, previously mentioned, of exchanging gossip, newspapers, tobacco, and the like, between opposing pickets continued until Hooker clamped down and spoiled the fun for both sides.

It has been generally believed that the morale of the Southern troops was naturally high as a result of their consistent victories and superior leadership. But there were some indications to the contrary. The March 31, 1863 returns for both armies show the rate of absence without leave to be three times as great in Lee's army as in Hooker's. For this there are two possible explanations. By this time Hooker's generous furlough policy had reduced the number of disgraceful desertions in the Union army. On the other hand it had become a regular procedure for many Confederate soldiers to take French leave during the lull between storms. This did not necessarily mean an intent to desert. Often it was merely a reflection of the individuality and independent character of the country boy who was not too amenable to Army discipline. Many had learned that they could get better food and cooking at the homes of acquaintances. Others felt impelled from time to time to visit their own homes to assist in planting or harvesting crops, or to lend a needed hand for other household duties.

As a rule these men, who would have to be carried on the rolls as absent without leave, intended to join their units in time for the next battle, and mostly they did. Confederate officers, beginning to feel the manpower pinch, were doubtless so glad to get the men back that the punishment, if any, was sufficiently light not to prove a deterrent to a repetition of the offense on future occasions.

Organizational Improvements

Lee, who had thoroughly tested his organizational structure, saw no reason to modify the complexion of the larger units, which had repeatedly proven their combat efficiency. He did take steps, however, to strengthen the structure of his artillery and ordnance. In the Mexican War he had demonstrated considerable skill in the employment of artillery, and all during the Civil War took an experienced personal interest in assuring battle efficiency in the employment of all the types of artillery available to his army. Not unmindful of the greater effectiveness of the Federal guns under the able direction of General Henry J. Hunt, Lee found it advisable to regroup his batteries in an effort to improve their tactical efficiency. During the winter he directed that the individual batteries be formed into battalions, with a normal complement of four batteries each, the battalions to be assigned to the several corps. All the artillery would be under the technical supervision of and report to the army chief of artillery, General Pendleton, who would exercise control through corps chiefs of artillery. The corps chiefs were in turn made responsible for assigning the battalions to divisions and for creating corps artillery reserves from excess and otherwise unassigned batteries. There was no express provision for a general reserve of artillery, as in the case of the Federals, where the bulk of the army artillery was under the direct control of the Chief of Artillery, to be parceled out to corps and divisions only when he considered it advisable. However, a Confederate general reserve of sorts was informally provided from the batteries that were not specifically assigned to corps or to the cavalry division.

Thus the corps artillery chiefs, in the artillery chain of command, had both tactical and administrative control of the guns and were authorized at their discretion to modify the composition of divisional and corps artillery as circumstances might require. Employment of the corps artillery in battle was of course the prerogative of the corps commander, operating through his chief of artillery. But the tactical dispositions, as well as the responsibility for supply, training, and operational efficiency, remained with the chief of corps artillery rather than the division or corps commander.

The Confederate artillery was handicapped in possessing part rifled and part smoothbore cannon. It was also plagued by defective shells and could have done with many more of the British guns, the Whitworth 12-pounder and the Blakely rifled 10-pounder, had the Southerners been able to get their hands on them. The Whitworth was said to have been accurate, given good ammunition, at a range of over five miles,* while the lighter and more maneuverable

---

*Jac Weller in *Civil War History,* Journal of the State University of Iowa, June 1957.

Blakely was a favorite of the horse artillery in Stuart's cavalry division. Unfortunately for the Confederates, only a handful of those types was available, but they performed yeoman service, notably the two guns, a Blakely and a Napoleon, under Major Pelham's skillful employment on Lee's right flank at the Battle of Fredericksburg.

Minor changes with respect to ordnance officers were likewise effected. The Army of Northern Virginia had been short of such specialists not only below divisions; but even in the larger organizations their responsibilities and functions frequently included other types of staff duty. This may have been in part due to the fact that Lee himself had never served as quartermaster (in modern parlance, a G-4) and as a result showed little aptitude for overcoming the problems of supply. These problems were compounded by inadequate railroad service and the lack of understanding and cooperation on the part of the civil government in furnishing the sinews of war to the armies in the field.

This situation was improved somewhat by action of the Secretary of War, who persuaded the Confederate Congress to assign regular ordnance officers to all commands from brigades up and to provide replacements through a more scientific process of competitive examination, heretofore entirely lacking. A lieutenant of ordnance was assigned to each artillery battalion, regular inspections of ordnance supplies were inaugurated, and the matter of supply became much more systematic than heretofore. The serious waste which had existed in the past was pretty well eliminated by requiring the soldiers to pay for lost equipment such as bayonets, cartridge boxes, and ammunition. After this, the losses diminished rapidly.

Staff Organization

The Confederate Army patterned its staff system after that of the United States Army, which functioned in accordance with Army Regulations of 1861. Having the same obsolescent pre-war background, it followed naturally that Southern staffs ran into similar difficulties. In the absence of an effective basic doctrine, the authority of the several staffs was frequently questioned, leading directly to such historic feuds as the one which long existed between Jackson and A. P. Hill. Nevertheless, the evolution of the Confederacy toward the substance of a general staff system made greater progress than was the case with the armies of the North. Probably the genius of General Lee was as much responsible as any other single factor, his personality and perception in dealing with the authorities at Richmond making the difference. However that may have been, it was a fact that the Army of Northern Virginia in time functioned as though a general staff had been sanctioned by Confederate law. The effect was to provide delegation of authority, supervisory power, and reasonably efficient chanelling of staff business in an orderly manner. Nevertheless there remained a twilight zone in which the functions of general and personal staffs were never clearly defined. Although Lee made specific recommendations for improvement during the winter of 1862-63, they were not enacted into law until June 1864. Insofar as he could do so, Lee anticipated the changes that were ultimately adopted. His army staff was reorganized so that its business could be expeditiously and effectively transacted.

Lee was fully aware of the presence, on the staffs of many of his corps and division commanders, of inexperienced civilians who through political machinations or family favoritism had wangled military commissions under a law which gave the President the authority to clothe such gentry with military rank and assign them to the personal staffs of general officers. He strove to eradicate that form of favoritism, which did the army little good. But the evil persisted despite his best efforts.

So far as Lee was concerned, rigidity of mind had no place in the rapidly changing face of war. He was in the habit of using the members of his staff as he saw fit, without unduly concerning himself as to their separate assignments or official titles. Colonel R. H. Chilton of the Regular Army of the Confederacy was given the post of chief of staff to Lee immediately upon the latter's appointment in June 1862. Chilton remained in that position until the spring of 1864, when he returned to duty with the Adjutant General's Department. Other members of Lee's personal staff, who were constantly at his side and for the most part remained with him through the war, bore the familiar names of Charles S. Venable, Charles Marshall, A. L. Long, Walter H. Taylor, A. P. Mason, and T. M. R. Talcott. Whether assigned as aides or otherwise, those officers doubled in brass and functioned variously as military secretary, assistant adjutant general, engineer officer, or for whatever duties there appeared to be a current need.

The pseudo general staff was made up of chiefs of branch who became fixtures and continued in their assigned positions throughout the war—such men as Brigadier General W. N. Pendleton, Chief of Artillery; Lafayette Guild, Medical Director; Lieutenant Colonel Robert G. Cole, Chief Commissary, and others.

Composition and Strength

By the end of March the organization and strength of the Army of Northern Virginia (effectives) was approximately as shown in the following table.*

First Corps (Longstreet)		17,755 officers
(2 divisions only)		and men
Anderson's Division	8,370	
McLaws' Division	8,665	
Artillery Reserve	720	

*Army of Northern Virginia, return for March, 1863.

Second Corps (Jackson)		38,199
A. P. Hill's Division	11,751	
Rodes' Division	10,063	
Early's Division	8,596	
Trimble's (Colston's) Division	6,989	
Artillery Reserve	800	
General Artillery Reserve		480
Cavalry Division (Stuart)		4,458†
Total		60,892

Strategic Shadowboxing

Averell's cavalry raid against Fitzhugh Lee's small force at Culpeper on March 17 seems to have led R. E. Lee to believe that it was a preliminary reconnaissance in force. He felt it might be a prelude to a general advance by Hooker's entire army, even though this did not seem to make much sense as an estimate in view of the terrible condition of the roads. In any case Lee wrote Longstreet, that same night, directing the return to Fredericksburg of the two divisions commanded by Hood and Pickett. These units, aggregating over 13,000 men, some weeks earlier had been shipped off to the Suffolk area in the belief that the reported transfer of Burnside's Ninth Corps to Fort Monroe presaged the shift of Hooker's weight to the Richmond area for a campaign similar to that conducted by McClellan in the spring of 1862. Hooker had no such intention, but was quite satisfied that Lee be misled as to his intentions. The result was that Hooker had received an unexpected bonus to further increase his already great preponderance of armed strength, for Lee had thus been moved to transfer two divisions to counter what he thought to be a Richmond threat, reducing even further the number of troops available to him at Fredericksburg.

Longstreet himself had been sent off to Richmond in

---

† Includes Hampton's brigade of approximately 1,500 men, which was absent recruiting.

February and given command of a special department, with 44,000 troops at his disposal, including two of his own four divisions. His was a dual mission of interposing against the apparently major Federal threat to Richmond and gathering supplies from the relatively untouched North Carolina area, where D. H. Hill commanded one element of the new force. Longstreet took the liberty of questioning Lee's March 17 decision to return Hood and Pickett, on the premise that he could not spare the two divisions. So when Lee learned that the Federal cavalry had recrossed the Rappahannock and there was no further evidence of an infantry advance from that direction, he cancelled the order and permitted Longstreet to continue on his current mission.

Along about the end of March Lee received the news that the Ninth Federal Corps had again been transferred, this time by rail to the west. This latest shift tended to quiet his earlier fear that an offensive was to be launched in the Richmond area by the Army of the Potomac, and made it practicable for Longstreet himself to mount an attack. Lee decided however that the dire necessity of collecting food took precedence over combat for the time being. Hence Longstreet was directed merely to hold Hood and Pickett close to a railroad to be ready for a quick move to join Lee promptly when they should be needed. The result of Longstreet's evident unwillingness to accept the implications of Lee's strategy and his unhurried compliance with Lee's telegraphic instructions of April 30 was that he and his two divisions did not rejoin Lee's Army of Northern Virginia until May 9, after the Battle of Chancellorsville had been fought and won.

On April 6 Lee suggested to his chief of artillery, General Pendleton, the advisability of transferring the major portion of the Confederate artillery from its winter quarters to a central location several miles west of Guiney's

Station. The new position was about equidistant from Port Royal, Fredericksburg, and United States Mine Ford, which Lee estimated covered the line of the Rappahannock within which limits Hooker might be expected to make a crossing when he should finally launch his awaited offensive.

The Battle of Fredericksburg had proven conclusively that both armies held virtually impregnable positions for *defense*. Burnside's frontal attack against Lee's strong ridge position on December 13 had been an expensive, bloody failure. Lee had anticipated at Fredericksburg a turning movement against his right flank, which was the only practicable maneuver after Burnside closed the door to a wide turning movement by the upper fords. Now Lee was confident that Hooker would not repeat the error. But in order to be forewarned he disposed his army all the way from Banks' Ford, six miles west of Fredericksburg, to Port Royal, seventeen miles to the south, a total distance of some twenty-five miles, the effect of which was to stretch his line terribly thin.

Confederate Troop Dispositions

Jackson's Corps held the long river line on the right with headquarters at Moss Neck. That portion of Longstreet's Corps, the divisions of McLaws and Anderson, which remained in the Fredericksburg area after Hood and Pickett had been detached to Suffolk, was responsible for the left of the sector. This sector extended from the immediate vicinity of Fredericksburg, including Marye's Heights, to Bank's Ford inclusive. (See Map 2). Stuart's cavalry, or what was left of it, was active on both army flanks in pursuit of its normal mission of patrolling the river from below Port Royal to as far west as Rappahannock Station. Longstreet's original defensive line, from the Massaponax Creek below Hamilton's Crossing to the Rappahannock at Fredericksburg, was thus extended in a curve some miles to the west along the Rapahannock as protection against hostile crossings at the vital Banks' Ford and United States Mine Ford.

In conforming to Lee's instructions, before his two divisions (Pickett's and Hood's) left for Suffolk, Longstreet had moved Pickett's Division from the Fredericksburg heights to a position at Salem Church, four miles west of Fredericksburg. Pickett was ordered to construct strong points and entrenchments along the shallow ridge which crossed the turnpike and angled north across two miles of open terrain to Banks' Ford. The position was to serve as a rallying point for the outpost troops stationed at the two fords, in case they should be driven back. With the departure of Pickett and Hood, this sector became so attenuated that it would have been a practical impossibility for General Lee to block a determined movement on Hooker's part against the upper portion of his line. Furthermore, the fifty square mile strip of land between the Rappahannock and the Rapidan, west of the junction of the two rivers, was only sketchily covered by the Confederate cavalry which, after all, could hardly be expected to be everywhere at once. For the river line was a long one with innumerable fords.

Lee's hard hitting divisions had learned well the lesson of flexibility. The capabilities of his corps and division commanders were such that Lee was better able than the Federals to utilize to advantage the principle of mass, which simply means the capability to bring to bear at the right place, at the right time, the number of divisions necessary to accomplish the mission. Lee was again striving to make the best possible use of the means at hand. Despite the fact that his available troop strength of approximately 60,000 men had the task of covering a defensive front of more than twenty-five miles, his confidence in them and his repeated successes in making calculated risks pay off, satisfied him that he could safely meet the Army of the Potomac at any point. He felt assured that his operations on internal lines would allow him to shift troops as needed against any threatened point on the Rappahannock perimeter.

Lee's Leadership

There is no substitute for military leadership in the grim business of war. The other self-evident factors, such as adequate manpower, weapons, equipment, and supply, which are essential to success in campaign, are still of secondary importance compared to leadership. It goes without saying that the greatest of commanders cannot win victories without capable subordinates, the tools of war, and a reasonable measure of freedom of action at the hands of civilian superiors in the government. But in the final analysis it is the character and caliber of leadership of the top commander in the field which nine times out of ten determines the winner, even against heavy odds in manpower and materiel. The *spirit of the offensive*, to use a common military term, is far from being an empty phrase.

Joseph Hooker certainly did not personify the Army of the Potomac, nor did Robert E. Lee reflect in his person all the characteristics of the Army of Northern Virginia, strong as his influence on it may have been. Nevertheless the failure of one army and the success of the other in the Chancellorsville campaign, as at Fredericksburg, can be attributed more to the individual abilities and actions of the respective commanders than to any other single or group of factors.

The more one studies Robert E. Lee's character and leadership qualities, the greater does his stature grow. Many thoughtful, historically minded persons have rightly appraised him as the most eminent of American military commanders, collaterally according him a place in the roster of the great captains of all times. The passage of

GENERAL ROBERT E. LEE, C.S.A.

time and the advent of recent wars but serves, on a broader base of comparison, to etch his name more deeply on the record. So much has been written about Lee, and his military attainments are so well known, even to those who are only casually interested in the Civil War, that no attempt will be made here to review his record in detail. An abbreviated profile, however, may be appropriate in serving to throw into stronger contrast the inadequacies of his Federal antagonist at Chancellorsville.

It is interesting to recall that it was not until the first of June 1862, more than a year after the war started, that Lee was placed in command of the Army of Northern Virginia as successor to Joseph E. Johnston, wounded at Fair Oaks. Lee's strong hand at the helm was felt almost immediately, and with such electrifying results that in less than six months, in rapid succession, McClellan's army was forced out of the Virginia Peninsula, the powerful threat to Richmond was removed, Pope's army badly defeated, Maryland invaded, a stalemate battle fought at Antietam Creek, and Burnside's army decisively repulsed at Fredericksburg.

The great Virginian was an outstanding example of a perfectly balanced human being. In 1863, at the age of 54, he had probably reached but not passed the peak of his mental and spiritual power. His erect carriage, broad shoulders, muscular physique, and handsome features made him a striking figure afoot or on horseback. A man of deep religious faith and broad human understanding, his kindly manner towards officers and enlisted men, regardless of rank or degree of importance, reflected a sincere interest in their welfare and evoked an affection and loyalty such as few great leaders have been able to inspire or deserve.

Lee's strong physique and great endurance enabled him to function smoothly under adverse conditions in the field for long hours at a stretch. He could, for example, ride fifty miles in a day, stay up half the night or until early morning discussing plans with his corps commanders, then refresh himself completely by sleeping on the ground when better facilities were not available. On such occasions, when an ordinary man of his age and responsibilities would require time to recover his energies, Lee would awake with instant alertness if aroused from sleep by an emergency. Each morning when the army was on the march he was up early and in the saddle, galloping ahead to watch his columns pass a critical point or to be present at the front to examine the situation for himself whenever fighting developed.

Lee was a firm and decisive character, knew what he wanted, and was justifiably sure of his own judgment One criticism that has been made of him, however, is to the effect that he did not give due weight to his government's civilian manpower requirements, such as the need for railroaders, mechanics, and other skilled artisans, without whom the operation of railroads and the manufacture of war materials were forced to proceed in halting fashion. His insistence on retaining this type of trained specialists in the ranks of his army, while understandable in view of his opponents' consistently superior strength, may have intensified the imbalance in aggregate strength as between the two combatants. Of that there can be no certainty. Conversely, had he not fought strenuously to keep his army intact, he could have lost the war long before Appomattox.

The other and more obvious criticism, on the strictly military plane, portrays him as not sufficiently ruthless in dealing with laggardness or downright recalcitrancy on the part of his principal subordinates. On that point it should be noted, however, that at his level Lee had to be a coordinator as well as a commander. Political considerations were often paramount, personalities had to be dealt with, and divergencies of viewpoint could not always be handled by military rule or tradition alone. It must be concluded that his patience and forebearance with Longstreet, Jackson, and others who argued with him, so long as they did not actually oppose his will, and his patient resolving of quarrels between Longstreet and Hill and between Hill and Jackson, was a calculated policy. Lee had to use the best, the only talent that was available to him and in the light of his long record of amazing victories against unbelievable odds, who will say that his judgment can be seriously questioned!

British Field Marshal Montgomery, in conversation with another famous general named Eisenhower, reminiscing on the Gettysburg battlefield in 1957, almost started another Civil War by tossing off the jocular remark that if he had been running that show he would have "sacked" both Meade and Lee after the battle. Had Montgomery been serious in making such an evaluation, which may be doubted, he would likewise have cast aside Jackson for his tardiness and inaction during the Peninsular campaign; Longstreet for his stalling tactics at Gettysburg; Ewell for his failure to exploit his opportunity to end the Gettysburg struggle on the afternoon of the first day; Stuart for his absence on a free-wheeling raid when that same battle was fought; and both A. P. Hill and Jackson for their long-drawn out feuding which the Confederacy could ill afford. These were the best men Lee had and his patience with temperamental subordinates was not only admirable but, even more to the point, a mirror of the character that made him a great man and an incomparable leader.

The crimson thread which stands out strikingly in the woven fabric of any appraisal of Lee's leadership is unquestionably that one which denotes superior intellect. This was clearly demonstrated in all his planning (except possibly in the area of supply planning), in his decisions, and above all in his analysis of military intelligence. He was especially adept in divining the most probable line of action of his opponents and in devising countermoves best calculated to nullify those actions. It had been his practise for many years to study the character of both instructors and cadets during his tour of duty as Superintendent of the Military Academy at West Point. The result, a mental if not written dossier on the good and bad characteristics of both subordinates and opponents during the war, was a priceless adjunct to Lee's acquired ability to judge human nature with unerring accuracy.

Lee also had a capacity for quickly and accurately computing time-and-space factors and calculating the logistical data required to put his troops into proper position to meet an enemy attack or to launch one of his own. In accomplishing this, as he did repeatedly, he had little or no help from staff officers, was provided only with inaccurate and incomplete maps, and lacked the advantage of the many mechanical devices now in common use to shortcut the compilation and sorting of essential data. Apparently his mind functioned with the speed and accuracy of an electronic computer.

If Lee had a flaw, or what might pass for a flaw, it cannot be found in his character nor in his physical, mental, or spiritual attributes. It was in his attitude, superinduced by his capacity for seemingly endless patience and selflessness. Up to and including the Battle of Chancellorsville, both the offensive and defensive power of his troops were so convincingly demonstrated that—in his own words —he had come to regard them as invincible. This assumption was to serve him poorly in the first really decisive battle of the war, that of Gettysburg, which followed soon after Chancellorsville.

One of his corps commanders, Lieutenant General James Longstreet, seems to have been strongly influenced by the Battle of Fredericksburg. That easy victory of the Confederates, who from their strong defensive position administered with ease such a bloody repulse to Burnside's army, apparently convinced Longstreet of the surpassing virtue of the defensive, both strategically and tactically. Nevertheless Longstreet had always been a tower of strength to Lee in the attack, so much so that the latter affectionately referred to him as "my old war-horse." Longstreet's obsession for the defensive, after Fredericksburg (he was not present at Chancellorsville), and his efforts to bring Lee to his way of thinking, are believed by some historians to have contributed in part to the ultimate failure of Confederate arms.

CONFEDERATE FORTIFICATIONS WEST OF FREDERICKSBURG

HOOKER'S ARMY MOVING TO ENVELOP LEE

CHAPTER 5

THE STRATEGY OF THE CAMPAIGN

TWO years of war had passed when the Battle of
Chancellorsville was fought. The Army of the
Potomac had yet to win a decisive victory over the Army
of Northern Virginia, although the North had gained
strategic advantage in winning the doubtful or border
states of Tennessee and Kentucky, and in retaining Maryland and western Virginia. The Federal Navy was
throttling the South's overseas trade with its effective
blockade of the Confederate seacoast, despite merchant
marine losses at the hands of daring Confederate raiders
on the high seas. But the North had troubles in addition
to its consistent failure to win battles—the difficult problem of recruiting by short-term volunteer enlistments, the
reluctance of many citizens to discard their business-as-

[85]

usual attitude in the face of all-out war, the embarrassing machinations and harmful propaganda of the anti-war contingents, and the diplomatic tug-of-war which the South came close to winning through the early efforts of its overseas agents to bring England and France to a recognition of the Confederacy.

Clausewitz defines war as "nothing but a continuation of political intercourse with an admixture of other means." This suggests that governments, which are subject to political influences, tend to make war an instrument of national policy, the effectiveness of which depends on the "other means," such as the generals, the armies, and the industrial complex.

Briefly stated, the political objective of the South, having seceded from the Union, was to secure recognition as a permanent nation. The original objective of the North was to restore the Union, with or without slavery. The military objectives were even more clear cut: conquest of Southern arms by the North, defense of its sovereign territory by the South.

The Battle of Antietam, a strategic although not a tactical victory for the Union, afforded Lincoln the awaited opportunity to issue his Emancipation Proclamation. Although the terms of the proclamation were known in the fall of 1862, the document itself was not officially promulgated until some weeks later, effective on January 1, 1863. The line of demarcation between the proclamation's political and military implications may be a bit hazy, but its impact was tremendous. European sympathy swung strongly to the North, and the people of the Northern states came to the electrifying realization that they were fighting a crusading war. That made all the difference. Lincoln's stroke of political genius had created a favorable climate for military success if only he could find a general capable of breaking the stalemate in which the Army of the Potomac was gripped on the banks of the Rappahannock.

The important change for the better in the North's political climate imposed on the Union a compulsive responsibility for exercising the initiative and for waging a strong military offensive. Military success had become a vital essential for the Lincoln administration if the fruits of the crusade against slavery were to be gathered in, the favorable opinion of the European nations sustained, and the Northern peace party suppressed.

The South, however, did not give up hope that England and France would ultimately recognize it as an independent Confederacy. Strategic opinion was divided as to the proper military course to pursue. It seemed clear, however, that if the Northern armies could be held off long enough, and the economy of the South held together, a stalemate might result in a negotiated peace that would bring recognition from Europe, preserve the integrity of the Confederate States, and in effect result in a political if not a military victory at the end of hostilities. Anything that the South might do to buy time would be advantageous to it and correspondingly discouraging to the war party of the North. It therefore made strategic sense for the Army of Northern Virginia to remain on the defensive, and so to maneuver that the fighting would take place on battlefields of Lee's choosing, thus conserving his waning manpower through defensive tactics.

Lee Faces Hooker Across the Rappahannock

The position of the Army of the Potomac was the same that it had occupied just prior to and after the Battle of Fredericksburg, on the Stafford Heights that looked down upon the river and the town. Hooker's main supply base was at Aquia Creek Station, fifteen railroad miles northeast of Fredericksburg, to which railhead supplies from Washington were floated down the Potomac and thence transported by rail to Falmouth and other conveniently located advance depots.

The Army of Northern Virginia was standing fast on its strongly fortified natural bastion along the hills west of Fredericksburg. Lee's supply lines were still the Richmond, Fredericksburg and Potomac Railroad, which carried supplies from his main base at Hanover Junction, a few miles north of Richmond, and the Virginia Central Railroad which ran east and west across the theater of operations and served his army as a convenient advanced base upon which he could retire and procure supplies when necessary. Hanover Junction and Gordonsville were the key points which he could not afford to lose, and the security of which largely influenced his strategy.

Serious combat on a large scale was not even considered during the winter months of early 1863 because the condition of the roads precluded mass movements by either army. There were, however, occasional hit-and-run cavalry raids to secure prisoners, confirm the presence or absence of major enemy units, and maintain contact while waiting for the weather to improve, the streams to return to their banks, and the roads to harden.

Lee had elected to remain on the tactical defensive for the time being to see what his new opponent might be planning. The defensive strategy which had proven successful against Hooker's predecessors was far less expensive to the Confederacy, less able than the Union Army to take and absorb losses. So long as the pressure from Washington continued and the Federals kept on beating out their brains against Lee's strong positions, any other Confederate policy would be unnecessarily wasteful. Lee required time to study Hooker and to learn how much of his boastfulness was sheer bluff. He therefore decided to give Hooker until the first of May to show his hand. If by that date Hooker had not put his army in motion or given a clear indication of his intentions, Lee would take the offensive himself to bring matters to a head.

Hooker assumed that Lee would either remain supinely in a defensive position or withdraw when threatened by Stoneman's encircling maneuver or the main flanking attack planned for the Army of the Potomac. In this Hooker made a fatal mistake. As it turned out, Lee was, as ever, offensively-minded. Not only was he to sally out of his trenches and attack Hooker at Chancellorsville, but already, early in 1863, he was considering a new campaign into the North. It is doubtful that Lee at such an early date definitely intended to launch such a strategic offensive, but was simply making tentative plans and preparations in case opportunity should present itself. Evidence of this is seen in the fact that Captain Jed Hotchkiss, chief topographer of Jackson's Corps, was preparing a detailed map of Maryland and part of Pennsylvania, the coverage of which extended as far north as Harrisburg The following notation is attached to the original map: "Map made by Capt. Jed Hotchkiss at Moss Neck—by order of Gen. T. J. Jackson," and "Used by Gen. R. E. Lee in the famous Gettysburg campaign."* The fact that the map was made at Moss Neck shows that it was prepared before the Battle of Chancellorsville, perhaps in January. This is borne out by the title on the version of the map which is printed in the Atlas accompanying the *Official Records of the Rebellion:* "Prepared by order of Lt. General T. J. Jackson in January to April, 1863 . . ."

Further evidence of Lee's early desire, if not intention, to assume the strategic offensive, is his letter to Seddon on April 9:

> Should General Hooker's army assume the defensive, the readiest method of relieving the pressure upon

---

The Hotchkiss Map Collection, p. 37. Library of Congress pamphlet, 1951.

General Johnston and General Beauregard would be for this army to cross into Maryland . . .

In the meantime, Hooker held the initiative, so Lee had to be content with endeavoring to divine the probable course of Federal action and to shape his own plans and actions accordingly. Most of his correspondence and reports at this time indicate that he expected Hooker to advance, generally by means of a river crossing somewhere between Port Royal and United States Mine Ford.

Hooker's Mission and Strategic Concept

"Go forward and give us victories," Lincoln had written, and that in brief was Hooker's mission. The North desperately needed a tonic that only a resounding military success could provide. The Army of the Potomac had been reorganized and restored to fighting trim. It was once again full of confidence and needed only an inspired guiding hand at the helm to convert a long-range hope for a victory into an actuality.

General-in-Chief Halleck had embodied his strategic views in a letter to Burnside on January 7, following the fiasco at Fredericksburg. On January 31, only a few days after his appointment as army commander, Hooker was given a copy of the Burnside letter and told that the overall strategy remained the same as outlined therein—offensive operations to be undertaken elsewhere than at Fredericksburg. He was to keep particularly in mind the importance of covering Washington and Harpers Ferry, because the troops stationed at both places were not strong enough of themselves to withstand a heavy Confederate attack. Halleck reiterated the sensible doctrine that Hooker's objective was not Richmond, but the defeat and scattering of Lee's army. He ventured the suggestion that the objective should be "to turn the enemy's works or to threaten their wings or communications in order to keep them occupied until a favorable opportunity offered to strike a decisive blow." Specifically Halleck advised Hooker to use his cavalry and light artillery against Lee's communications in an effort to cut off his supplies.

There was an urgency about these instructions, but they failed to move Hooker to precipitate action before he believed his army to be ready. Halleck wanted Hooker to commence operations as soon as possible, and the injunction was repeated toward the end of March, when Halleck accurately pointed out that Lee's forces were pretty well scattered, foraging for supplies. If there should be undue delay in launching an offensive, he said, the favorable opportunity might be lost.

It may be doubted that Hooker had enough humility in his makeup to study the campaigns of his four principal predecessors, McDowell, McClellan, Pope, and Burnside, in order to compare their performances with that of General Lee, and to evaluate the major battles of 1861 and 1862 objectively. By so doing he might have profited by the Federal mistakes, learned something from the strategic and tactical methods of the major Confederate commanders, and applied the lessons constructively to achieve a happier result than any of the first four army commanders had been able to accomplish.

Hooker unfortunately was not the student that the present situation called for. His temperament was such that he thought he had all the answers already. Not only did he have no use for Halleck, his superior in Washington, but there is little evidence that he was even moderately impressed with Lincoln's views on how to fight the army. He does seem to have been thinking fairly straight by April, however. Some of the advice proffered by Lincoln and Halleck may have rubbed off from their letters and conferences, for on April 11 Hooker wrote the President a letter which in part transmitted his current views and foreshadowed the final program which was later polished off and refined to become the plan of operations for the Chancellorsville campaign. Pertinent extracts from the letter follow:

> I have concluded that I will have more chance of inflicting a heavier blow upon the enemy by turning his position to my right and, if practicable, to sever his communications with Richmond with my dragoon force . . . . . I am apprehensive that he will retire from before me the moment I should succed in crossing the river . . . . . I hope that when the cavalry have established themselves on the line between him and Richmond they will be able to hold him and check his retreat until I can fall on his rear. . . . . while the cavalry are moving I shall threaten the passage of the river at various points and after they have passed well to the enemy's rear, shall endeavor to effect the crossing. . . . .

Hooker Fashions a Giant Pincers

Hooker's plan of action for the entire army was beautifully simple in its basic conception, as all great plans must be. In effect the Army of the Potomac would move in on the Army of Northern Virginia from two directions, like a giant pincers closing its jaws, while the army cavalry closed the escape route. This would militarily be called a double envelopment, with half the army advancing from the west, the other half from the east (either wing of equal strength to Lee's whole army), to meet in the open country a mile or so from Chancellorsville. Together they would put the finishing touches on Lee's presumably cringing Confederates, if indeed the latter had not by that time become so petrified with fear of what Joe Hooker might do to them that they had already fled in panic from the scene of their intended destruction. In the latter event Stoneman's cavalry would be Johnny-on-the-spot to "cut off large slices from his column," as Hooker confidently phrased that possibility in his directive. In Hooker's mind's-

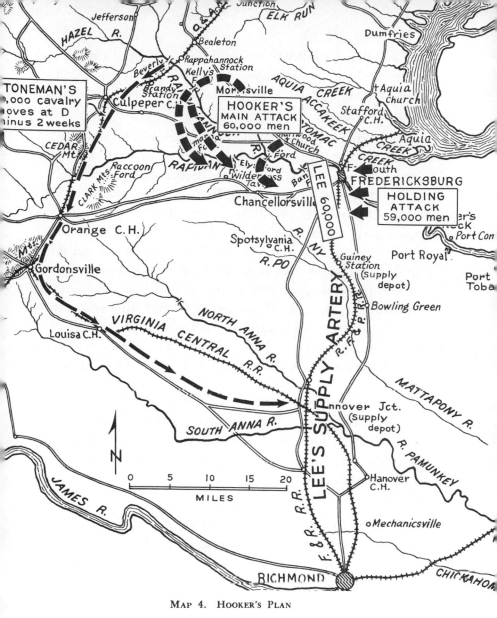

MAP 4. HOOKER'S PLAN

Superficially this plan appears to be masterly in concept. But it had at least two serious flaws, quite apart from the way in which it was executed. First, Sedgwick's secondary attack below Fredericksburg was labeled "a strong demonstration," a type of action that rarely succeeds in deceiving an opponent as canny as Lee. It should have been ordered as an all-out attack. Second, the timing of the grand cavalry raid was poor. The Federal cavalry had not yet proved that it was capable of operating so far from the protection of the main army, certainly not for two weeks. Stoneman would have had to do more than ride around the Confederate army to interrupt its line of communication for an appreciable time.

[93]

eye Lee's army would be trapped like a fox, with dog packs hemming him in on three sides and the Rappahannock River serving as a Federal ally to close the only remaining avenue of escape.

The plan in general had been soundly conceived, conformed to the fundamental principles of war, and gave every reason to hope that it would succeed handsomely if the logistics of time and space should prove valid, and the unpredictable Lee would stay put. There was only one serious flaw in Hooker's line of reasoning. That was his confident assurance that Lee would withdraw toward Richmond or Gordonsville as soon as he should discover that Hooker had unexpectedly outflanked his left and at the same time crossed the Rappahannock and attacked him at Fredericksburg. An additionally disturbing fact to Lee would be that a large body of Federal cavalry would be loose between him and the capital. Hooker knew perfectly well what he would do if the positions were reversed. He apparently could not conceive of his opponent outguessing him when unexpectedly confronted with the successful execution of that magnificent turning movement, which could not fail to give Lee the surprise of his life and leave him no alternative but "to ingloriously fly," as Hooker was to phrase it a few days later.

We do not know the thoughts that passed through Lee's mind as he sized Hooker up and evolved his own tactical concepts to counter the forthcoming Union offensive. It is quite probable that Hooker's overconfident boasts to his officers, indicating what he intended to do to Lee, had filtered into Lee's intelligence nets, and were duly evaluated as the premature mouthings of one of the generals who had shared repeatedly in the defeats which Lee had consistently inflicted on the Army of the Potomac. Robert E. Lee was a keen judge of character and so far had not encountered a high ranking opponent whose probable course of action under a given set of circumstances had been too difficult to predict. In Lee's experience the loudly boastful character had usually been found to have certain weaknesses which he would attempt to conceal even from himself by putting up a bold front. Lee may already have evaluated Hooker's overconfidence as in reality a form of inferiority complex which would result in the pendulum swinging him to the other extreme of overcautiousness if events failed to work out exactly according to schedule.

Hooker had not made any secret of his satisfaction with his winter's effort to put his army in fighting trim and his boasts had undoubtedly reached Lee's ears. Such remarks for example as "if the enemy doesn't run, God help them;" and again, "I have the finest army the sun ever shone on. My plans are perfect, and when I start to carry them out, may God have mercy on General Lee, for I will have none!" Possibly Hooker was whistling in the dark, or felt that to raise the morale of the army after Fredericksburg and concurrently assure it that the nickname "Fighting Joe" was no misnomer, he had to give forth with a few such aphorisms. Time would tell, and soon, what effect his attitude would have on the canny Lee, who was not given to developing obsessions and had managed pretty successfully in the past to weather heavy winds generated by Union army commanders whose military gray matter and strength of character under the stress of battle never seemed to come even close to matching his own.

Hooker's Plan in Detail

Meade's Fifth Corps, Howard's Eleventh, and Slocum's Twelfth, constituting the right wing of the army under the temporary command of Major General Henry W. Slocum, would make a wide turning movement, cross the Rappahannock at Kelly's Ford, above the mouth of the Rapidan and about twenty-one miles west of Falmouth. This force would turn southeastward and cross the Rapidan at Germanna and Ely's Fords, then follow the south bank of the Rappahannock below its junction with the Rapidan to uncover United States Mine Ford and Banks Ford for the crossing of Couch's Second Corps (less Gibbon's division), which latter corps would meanwhile take position prepared to cross at the first-named ford. These four corps, after a forced march of over forty miles for three of them, would then assemble at Chancellorsville with a strength of 60,000 men, as many as Lee had on the field in his entire army. At that point Hooker would take command in person.

Sedgwick with his own Sixth Corps, Reynolds' First, Sickles' Third, and Gibbon's division of the Second Corps, was concurrently directed to cross the Rappahannock below Fredericksburg at the same time and make strong demonstrations with a view to persuading Lee that this was to be the main effort. Sedgwick's specific mission was spelled out in detail. He would first show his 59,000-man, three-corps wing along the high ground opposite Fredericksburg, south of the town at Franklin's Crossing and Pollock's Mill. Then on April 29 engineer General Benham would throw four pontoon bridges over the river; Sedgwick's wing would cross and either pin Lee's army in its present lines or induce him to withdraw to the south. The principal object of Sedgwick's maneuvers would be to prevent Lee from spoiling Hooker's strategy by blocking the principal effort of the right wing and interfering with the surprise outflanking march on Chancellorsville. In the paraphrased words of the late General George S. Patton, Sedgwick would hold Lee by his nose while Hooker kicked him in the pants. If Lee stood fast at Fredericksburg Sedgwick was to attack. If Lee retired on Richmond, Sedgwick would pursue him; if he moved a considerable part of his force towards Chancellorsville, Sedgwick would "carry the works at all hazards, and establish his force on the Telegraph Road." In the latter case, a full-fledged advance by Sedgwick's wing on Chancellorsville, to attack Lee's flank and rear, would have to await Hooker's arrival at that point and his estimate of the situation as of that time. The record suggests that Hooker's move in that event would be to hold the right wing on the defensive and let Sedgwick make the principal attack.

Stoneman's cavalry corps was scheduled to make its sweep around Lee's army two weeks ahead of the movement of the infantry, to cut Lee's communications with Richmond and, in Hooker's mind, so disrupt the Confederate army as to cause Lee to hastily evacuate his present defensive position in a retreat to the south, with Hooker's infantry in hot pursuit. Stoneman's route was to be generally along the line of the Virginia Central Railroad, destroying everything along that road; he would then select strong positions on the roads paralleling the Richmond and Fredericksburg Railroad, prepared to harass Lee's columns as they retired on the Capital. Hooker's theory was that Stoneman would be able to pin Lee in place while the Army of the Potomac assailed him from the direction of the Rappahannock.

As later events were to prove, Hooker was as inexperienced in the proper employment of cavalry as were most of the Union generals. Otherwise he would have been less profligate in sending the bulk of it beyond hope of recall, and retaining only one small brigade of five regiments, about 1,000 troops, under General Pleasonton, for such vital missions as battle reconnaissance, army flank security, and close-in exploitation of local successes. Stoneman would take with him 10,000 men, while the rest of the cavalry, about 1,500, were to be held in reserve to guard the camps and communications north of the river, where their fate would be to play no part in the battle.

Hooker's conception of the role of his cavalry corps was in effect a Civil War forerunner of the "vertical envelopment" of World War II, in which paratroopers, followed by airborne units, were dropped far behind hostile lines to seize and deny to the enemy strategic positions from which to harass them in rear. The fallacy of Hooker's plan lay in the fact that it was a premature use of the horse cavalry before, rather than as collateral to, or following the action of the main army in forcing the enemy into a retrograde movement. In other words, it was imprudently uneconomic and impracticable to attempt to exploit a success in advance of its achievement.

Surprise the Key Factor

The planned river crossing by three full-size ·infantry corps, preceded by Pleasonton's small brigade of cavalry as advance guard, had much to recommend it on the side of surprise. True, it would involve crossing two rivers, the Rappahannock and the Rapidan, as well as the troublesome no-man's land between the rivers and west of the fork. But the crossing places selected were miles above the left anchor of Lee's defensive line at Banks' Ford. And the march would be subjected to little or possibly no interference whatever from Stuart's reduced cavalry force, which had present only a fraction of its full strength and had been stretched to cover a very long segment of the upper river. Most important of all, the element of surprise would be quite likely to catch Lee napping. This was on the logical premise that such an exhausting round-about approach march by infantry, involving the passage of two rivers and the tangle of unmaneuverable forest known as the Wilderness, would be the last thing Lee would expect Hooker to undertake.

Chancellorsville Terrain

The character of the Chancellorsville theater of operations was almost a "forest primeval," if we are to take literally the official report of Brigadier General Gouverneur K. Warren, U. S. Army Chief of Topographical

PART OF THE WILDERNESS ALONG LEWIS CREEK

Engineers, filed a week after the Battle of Chancellorsville. Here are a few pertinent extracts:

> . . . . . the entire region from the Potomac to the James River, and from the Blue Ridge to the Chesapeake, is a region whose characteristic is a dense forest of oak or pine, with occasional clearings, rarely extensive enough to prevent the riflemen concealed in one border from shooting across to the other side; a forest which, with but few exceptions, required the axemen to precede the artillery from the slashings in front of the fortifications in Washington to those of Richmond, ... battles that had to be fought out hand to hand in forests where artillery and cavalry could play no part; where the troops could not be seen by those controlling their movements; where the echoes and reverberations of sound from tree to tree were enough to appall the strongest hearts engaged, and yet the noise would often scarcely be heard beyond the immediate scene of strife.

The Wilderness

The Wilderness fully deserved its name. It is even today, as it was in 1863, an almost impassable second growth of heavy timber and dense underbrush, with thorny brush and an irregular surface over which lateral vines reached out to trap the unwary and slow his progress by winding streams and marsh-bordered brooks. With practically no side roads worthy of the name, other than the lateral wagon roads leading from the several fords, there were only two east-west highways, known as the Orange Turnpike, which ran from Orange Court House on the Orange and Alexandria Railroad to Fredericksburg, and the Plank Road, which between Wilderness Church and Chancellorsville coincides with the Turnpike. (See Map 10).

The following description of the two historic roads is taken from Gough's book on the Battles of Fredericksburg and Chancellorsville*, based on information furnished Colonel Gough in 1912 by the U.S. Army War College:

> *The turnpike* was not a metalled road, but a graded dirt road, top-dressed with gravel, and corduroyed in the swampy bottoms which abound in that region. The corduroyed sections were graded and ditched and the road bed was then covered with corduroy or poles, varying from 3 to 8 inches in diameter and sixteen feet long, laid transversely and covered with sand, gravel, and clay to a depth of 3 or 4 inches.
>
> *The Plank road* was in fact a road covered with planks about two inches thick and sixteen feet long, laid transversely and spiked to two longitudinal sleepers buried in the prepared road bed.
>
> At the time of the war this road had fallen into bad repair and was full of holes, where planks had broken through, exposing the soft clay bed beneath. These plank roads were primarily constructed for the hauling of tobacco to market. The tobacco was packed

---

*Fredericksburg and Chancellorsville, a Study of the Federal Operations, by Colonel J. E. Gough, V.C., C.M.G., published in 1913 by Hugh Rees, Ltd., London.

in huge hogsheads, through which an axle was placed. By attaching draught animals to the axle ends, the hogsheads were rolled to market along the plank roads, and arrived in much better condition than when rolled over ordinary dirt roads, and with the expenditure of less power than was necessary on poorer roads.

Two miles beyond Wilderness Church, going east, the Turnpike passed Chancellorsville, which was eight miles west of Lee's fortified Fredericksburg line; two or three miles further along the road emerged from the Wilderness and ran through four or five miles of broken but more open country; and finally cut through Lee's lines to wind up its course in the streets of Fredericksburg. With only an occasional small clearing that boasted little more than a deserted barn and one or two dilapilated houses to mark the area as a hopeless place in which to make a living, the Wilderness extended for some twelve to fourteen miles along the south bank of the Rapidan and Rappahannock Rivers, and eight to ten miles from north to south, embracing in all a vast area of more than 100 square miles. It was a major hazard for organized dismounted troops to traverse, to say nothing of actual fighting. Visibility was virtually zero, reference points practically nonexistent, artillery roadbound, while cavalry could force its horses through the tangled underbrush only with great difficulty. Birds and small game were the only inhabitants to divert the attention of the soldiers whose misfortune it might be to have to enter the jungle-like waste! No general with a knowledge of the conditions that his troops would encounter in the Wilderness could ever select it as a battleground, for infantry could make headway only with difficulty off the main roadways.

Union General A. S. Webb described the Wilderness in 1864 as: "Uneven, with woods, thickets and ravines right and left. Tangled thickets of pine, scrub oak and cedar prevented our seeing the enemy and prevented anyone in command of a large force from determining accurately the position of the troops he was ordering to and fro. At times our lines while firing could not see the array of the enemy, not fifty yards distant."

This then was one of the major hazards which Hooker had imposed on three of his corps; the other was the burden for the individual soldier of lugging sixty pounds or more of equipment, rations, ammunition, and extra clothing. Soldiering under Joe Hooker fell somewhat short of being a sinecure.

Hooker had planned well and apparently overlooked nothing in the logistic sense. Pack mules would replace the cumbersome ration and ammunition wagons, officers would dispense with their comfortable wall tents and strip down to bare essentials. Whatever griping might be forthcoming from the enlisted men because of their heavy loads and the long, forced march, would be more than compensated for by their natural elation at having achieved something far beyond any previous accomplishment of the Army of the Potomac—outguessing and outmaneuvering the vaunted Army of Northern Virginia. Finally there would be pontoon bridges in place and *on time,* if the rivers had not safely subsided to permit fording. With luck the feat might even be accomplished without the necessity of fighting to gain the advantage of a position which Hooker was sure would serve to force Lee into ignominious retreat. At least that was the way the supremely confident Hooker reasoned.

HOOKER'S INFANTRY LEAVING THE FALMOUTH AREA

CHAPTER 6

HOOKER'S PLAN UNFOLDS

The months of preparation were over. the roads drying rapidly, and the Army of the Potomac, sharpened to a keen cutting edge, was poised and waiting only for the word from Joe Hooker that would release the pent-up energy of a long winter in the form of a new thunderbolt of destruction against the battle-hardened but gradually weakening Army of Northern Virginia on the other side of the Rappahannock; or so Hooker figured.

Even as Lincoln wired his approval of Hooker's plan on April 12, orders were going forward to Stoneman's cavalry to be in readiness to move at daylight Monday, April 13. Each trooper was to carry on his horse not less than three days' rations and grain, with at least forty rounds of ammunition for his carbine and twenty for his pistol. The pack and supply trains were to be loaded and ready to roll with additional rations, grain, and forage to subsist men and horses for an additional period of eight days.

[103]

The invaders would not have to live off the country in order to survive, at least not for the first eleven days—assuming that all went well and the trains kept up to avoid capture or destruction. But the extra load would be a heavy burden for the individual trooper's mount, averaging between 250 and 300 pounds, depending on the variable weight of the soldier himself; there was no doubt that Stoneman's cavalry horses were greatly overloaded for the ambitious undertaking.

The cavalry commander was given written instructions in the form of sealed orders which directed him to march with his entire corps less one brigade, about 10,000 strong, at 7 A.M. on April 13: "for the purpose of turning the enemy's position on his left, throwing the cavalry between him and Richmond, isolating him from his supplies, checking his retreat, and inflicting on him every possible injury which will tend to his discomfiture and defeat."

The directive was wordy and in great detail, telling Stoneman just where to go, the precise strength of the enemy detachments he would encounter and where they would be found, and stressing the ease with which he would be able to overcome all obstacles. A few additional missions were thrown in, such as the destruction of depots, bridges, ferries, and rail facilities. In grandiloquent terms it laid upon the hapless Stoneman the injunction to let his watchword be "fight, fight, fight, bearing in mind that time is as valuable to the general (Hooker) as the Rebel carcasses." Stoneman was assured that "you may rely on the general being in connection with you before your supplies are exhausted," but the directive neglected to say how or where Hooker expected to reach him miles away to the south on the opposite side of Lee's army. The order finally concluded with the statement that it devolved on Stoneman "to take the initiative in the forward movement of this grand army; on you and your noble command must depend in a great measure the extent and brilliancy of our success."

The Union cavalry had long wanted a man-sized mission to prove its competence. Now it had it and with a vengeance. It was a broad and imaginative conception, couched in sweeping terms, but a rather more ambitious project than the recently reorganized cavalry corps was as yet capable of carrying out. Hooker, in company with virtually all of the high ranking generals of the line who were without cavalry experience, was unfamiliar with the capabilities and limitations of that arm except in a very general way. He and they seemed to think that because a horse could travel at a rate of six to ten miles an hour for hours on end, there was no limit to the capacity of a mounted organization to range widely over enemy territory and perform a myriad of concurrent missions. Nobody, however, and least of all Hooker himself, took the trouble to explain how only 10,-000 men and 22 guns could keep Lee's army of 60,000 from exercising an initiative of its own, or how it could be driven into the hands of the Army of the Potomac simply by trotting around the countryside between the Confederates and Richmond. Nevertheless the opportunity was afforded for the Federal cavalry to cause Lee considerable embarrassment and, if Stoneman's force should prove to be sufficiently enterprising and aggressive to cut the Confederate supply line, to offer a serious handicap to the Army of Northern Virginia.

Hooker, no doubt recalling the two occasions when Jeb Stuart boldly led his cavalry brigades on wide sweeps around McClellan's army, figured the Stoneman raid as a shrewd opening gambit for his forthcoming spring offensive. What he overlooked, in drawing premature conclusions on the sure success of this project, was the fact that it was Lee and not McClellan who was the intended victim. And it was Stoneman, not Stuart or Sheridan, who would spark-plug the raid with a still unproven cavalry corps that had yet to cut its eyeteeth on such a grandiose adventure.

Stoneman and his 10,000 cavalrymen moved out April 13 on schedule and headed for the upper fords. It was his purpose to plant for Confederate consumption the rumor that he was after Jones' Confederate cavalry operating in the Shenandoah Valley. Actually he intended to turn sharply south across the river above the Rappahannock bridge and at Beverly Ford, dash across the Rapidan at Raccoon Ford or other nearby crossings, and then split his force, as directed by Hooker. One element under Averell would aim for Louisa Court House to cut and destroy as much as possible of the Virginia Central Railroad, after disposing of Fitzhugh Lee's cavalry at Culpeper. The other and larger element, under Stoneman's personal command, would follow the road through Gordonsville to Lee's main supply base which was believed to be at Hanover Junction, a few miles north of Richmond, with the primary object of cutting the railroad, destroying all possible communications, and fulfilling the major function of the raid as conceived and spelled out in Hooker's directive.

The leading brigade of the corps was under the command of an aggressive colonel by the name of Benjamin F. Davis, who had first gained prominence as a cavalry commander when he refused to be bottled up with the rest of the Union forces at the time Stonewall Jackson took Harpers Ferry prior to the Battle of Antietam. Davis on that occasion had chosen to make a dash for it across the pontoon bridge to the Maryland shore, which he accomplished with distinction to himself and his cavalry troopers, and was rewarded by capturing some of Longstreet's trains a few hours later. Davis' brigade was now sent ahead by Stoneman to cross the Rappahannock and clear the area on the south bank for the rest of the corps to cross without hindrance. This mission he achieved without much opposition. On the south bank, after driving away the Confederate detachment guarding the ford, he waited for the main body to come across and get on with the war. But for some unjustifiable reason, possibly because his columns contained too many wheeled vehicles, Stoneman was unconscionably slow in getting started. While he dallied, a heavy rain started and kept falling until the wooden Rappahannock bridge was tugging at its shaky foundations, as the river rose rapidly and almost submerged it. Thereupon Stoneman decided he had better wait a bit, which he did to the unconcealed disgust of the aggressive Davis, who finally swam his horses back to the north side of the river to keep from being permanently cut off from the rest of the corps.

It was an inauspicious start for the cavalry's great adventure. With a little more dash and energy, such as Davis had demonstrated, the entire outfit could have been across both rivers and on their way to Richmond before the streams had risen to the danger point. Obviously their return by the same route would have been cut off for the time being. But that was of little moment since they were headed away from the fords anyway and had a long journey ahead of them to get in position behind Lee's army by the time Hooker's schedule called for the infantry corps' to close on Chancellorsville.

Hooker, as yet uninformed of the delay, sent off a confident letter on April 15 to Lincoln, in which he advised the President that Stoneman's cavalry had already crossed the river and was on its way, having had two days of good weather before the rains started. Later that day Hooker was forced to telegraph the President that the cavalry was still north of the river. So far as its strategic value was concerned, it would not be surprising if both Lincoln and Hooker had by now written off the projected Stoneman raid as a loss, if we may judge from Lincoln's letter to Hooker, written immediately after receipt of the disappointing telegram:

It is now 10:15 P.M. An hour ago I received your

letter of this morning and a few minutes later your dispatch of this evening. The latter gives me considerable uneasiness. The rain and mud were, of course, to be calculated upon. General S is not moving rapidly enough to make the expedition come to anything. He has now been out three days, two of which were unusually fair weather, and all three without hindrance from the enemy, and yet he is not 25 miles from where he started. To reach his point (Richmond area) he still has 60 miles to go, another river to cross, and will be hindered by the enemy. By arithmetic, how many days will it take him to do it? I do not know that any better can be done, but I greatly fear it is another failure already. Write me often; I am very anxious.

A. Lincoln

Hooker's Final Plan

Hooker was enraged. After giving the cavalry the chance to demonstrate its capabilities, Stoneman's timidity had compromised the opportunity and forced the army commander, whose march schedule for the main body was already set, to revise his program. The cavalry was now immobilized near Warrenton Junction, 13 miles northeast of the Rappahannock. It remained there for practically two weeks, held up by the heavy rain and the resulting high water and muddy roads. Hooker decided on the next round he would not depend on Stoneman's cavalry, but would make their activities secondary to the infantry. If the cavalry could still show its mettle, well and good, but the main dependence would have to be placed on the foot soldiers to flank Lee out of his fortified lines.

Hooker's original plan had been to cross the Rappahannock below Fredericksburg and move against Lee's right and rear. If successfully accomplished this would place the Federal army squarely across Lee's communication and supply lines to Richmond. The second plan, which Lincoln approved, shifted the Federal turning movement to Hooker's right and Lee's left, and gave Stoneman's cavalry the mission of getting around Lee to cut his communications and prevent him from withdrawing to the south before Hooker could administer the anticipated coup de grace. The third and final plan differed from the second solely in placing on the infantry rather than the cavalry the responsibility of leading the great flanking maneuver across two rivers to put the army on the left rear of Lee's cohorts at Fredericksburg.

In line with his determination to prevent any leak to the enemy and thus reveal his intentions, Hooker kept his plans so secret that Stoneman and Sedgwick were the only corps commanders who received written instructions which went further than the initial objective. Nothing was said, even to them, about Hooker's complete plan for the main army. Hence Stoneman was to be cut loose on his ambitious undertaking without a hint as to what the Army of the Potomac was going to do, other than what he himself might deduce from the character of his own assignment.

Stoneman's Raid

On April 28, from his advanced headquarters at Morrisville, Hooker had sent brief supplemental orders to Stoneman which amended the original April 12 directive in several particulars. The cavalry commander was told that the operations of that portion of his command which would move on Louisa Court House and the line of the Orange and Alexandria Railroad were intended to mask the main column, which would "move by forced marches to strike and destroy the line of the Aquia and Richmond Railroad." The order recommended that the point selected for the two columns to unite be on the Pamunkey (a few miles north and east of Richmond), and directed that the entire force be across the Rappahannock by no later than eight o'clock on the morning of April 29.

[109]

The adventures of the Federal cavalry during the succeeding week, while interesting and no doubt instructive to the participants, made little impression on the Confederate army and had no direct effect on the Battle of Chancellorsville. Indirectly, however, the Stoneman raid was important, and to the disadvantage of Hooker's army. There is little disagreement among historians that Hooker's decision to detach the major portion of his large cavalry corps for an independent mission was a strategic error. The raid failed to excite Lee, who virtually ignored Stoneman's maneuvering in his rear and avoided making the same mistake as Hooker by allowing his own depleted cavalry to harry and pursue the Federal cavalry.

It can only be conjectured as to what the outcome of the Battle of Chancellorsville might have been, had Hooker retained Stoneman's 10,000 troopers to cover his flanks. It is reasonable to conclude that Stonewall Jackson could never have sprung his historic surprise if the Federal cavalry had been on that flank to reconnoiter widely and reach well out, before the battle, along the roads leading from Chancellorsville.

The Confederates were not aware of the planned Stoneman raid until the movement was actually under way. By means of feints and planted messages that were allowed to fall into Confederate hands, Lee and Stuart were persuaded that the objective of the Federal cavalry was the Shenandoah Valley. This was confirmed by a dispatch from Lee to Stuart as late as April 25, and nothing that transpired subsequently appears to have modified their expectation, until Stoneman's divisions were across the rivers and headed toward Gordonsville and Richmond.

Stoneman's corps finally got moving. It was across the river on April 30, about the same time that the advance elements of Hooker's three infantry corps reached Chancellorsville. The only opposition encountered were the small cavalry brigades of Fitzhugh and W. H. F. Lee,

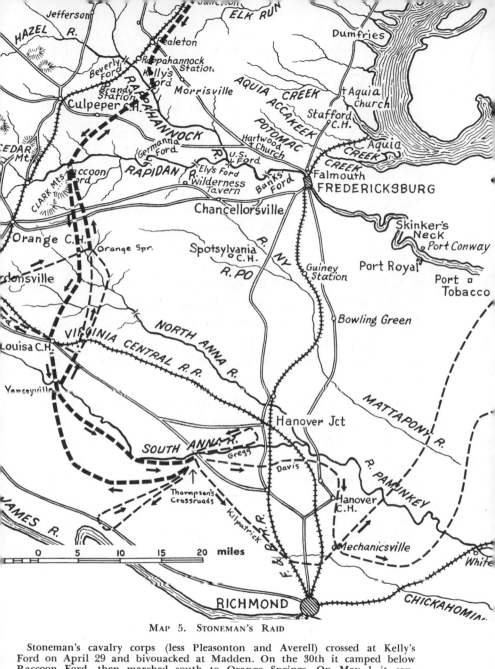

MAP 5. STONEMAN'S RAID

Stoneman's cavalry corps (less Pleasonton and Averell) crossed at Kelly's Ford on April 29 and bivouacked at Madden. On the 30th it camped below Raccoon Ford, then marched south to Orange Springs. On May 1 it continued through Louisa Court House and Yanceyville to Thompson's Crossroads, where the headquarters unit remained during the 2d and 3d. From this point the regiments of Kilpatrick, Wyndham, and Davis, and Gregg's brigade made forays as shown on the map. On the 4th Stoneman marched back through Yanceyville and the vicinity of Louisa Court House to the Orange Springs area. While near Louisa Court House, Buford's brigade rode toward Gordonville then northeast and joined the main body. The remainder of the return trip was made over the same route as followed in going south. Kilpatrick and Davis, after raiding north of Richmond, made their way back to within the Union lines near Yorktown.

totalling between them about 3,000 troopers whose attention had to be divided between the Federal cavalry and Hooker's right wing. A few minor skirmishes occurred, and some prisoners were captured, but there was no effective opposition to the far-ranging Federal cavalry, which proceeded to carry out its mission of tearing up railroad tracks and causing as much rear area damage as possible.

While the Battle of Chancellorsville was being fought, the main column under Stoneman's personal command continued on its way, but Averell's division of 3,400 sabers was held up at Rapidan Station mainly because of the exaggerated fears of its commander that he was heavily opposed. Averell marked time in the vicinity of Rapidan Station so long that his division was recalled by General Hooker on May 2 and spent the rest of the campaign north of the Rapidan. (Map 11). Averell himself was relieved of command and his division placed under General Pleasonton. (See also pp. 267-8).

Gregg's division and Buford's reserve brigade, with Stoneman's column, proved more effective in the course of their depredations, but without achieving any practical result beyond the temporary destruction of property, bridges, depots, and other war material. Colonel Judson Kilpatrick's regiment penetrated within two miles of Richmond, traveled 200 miles and captured substantial enemy detachments. Colonel Hasbrouck Davis' regiment had almost as arduous a march, but there was practically no resistance and therefore little glory to be derived from the raid. All the columns except Kilpatrick's and Davis' safely returned to the Union lines by May 11, with men and horses pretty well jaded, but with more experience back of them than most of the cavalry troops had previously been allowed to acquire. Kilpatrick and Davis ended their marches within the Union lines near Yorktown. (Map 5)

The Army Moves Into Position

Hooker's April 26 orders for the movement of his seven infantry corps from their winter camp near Falmouth to the jumpoff positions along the Rappahannock were brief and concise. The following table summarizes his march orders for the two-day development on April 27 and 28:

Organization	Objective	Start	Arrive
Right Wing			
11th Corps (Howard)	As near Kelly's Ford as practicable	Sunrise April 27	By 4 P. M. April 28
12th Corps (Slocum)	In rear of 11th Corps	Sunrise April 27	By 4 P. M. April 28
5th Corps (Meade)	In rear of 12th Corps	A. M. Apr. 27	By 4 P. M. April 28
Center			
2nd Corps (Couch) (Less 2nd Div.)	Near U.S. Mine Ford and Banks' Ford	Sunrise April 28	Same day
2nd Div., 2nd Corps (Gibbon)	Remain at Falmouth		
Left Wing			
6th Corps (Sedgwick)	Franklin's Crossing		By 3:30 A. M. April 29
1st Corps (Reynolds)	1½ mi. below Franklin's Crossing		By 3:30 A. M. April 29
3rd Corps (Sickles)	In support of 1st & 6th Corps		By 3:30 A. M. April 29

The instructions prescribed secrecy for the right wing. No fires would be permitted and special precautions would be taken to keep the men from approaching the river after their arrival at the fords. Not so for the divisions of Couch's Second Corps, however, since Hooker wanted Lee to believe that a major crossing would be made at United States Mine Ford and Banks' Ford. The three corps under Sedgwick, whose orders directed them to be in position before daylight April 29, were cautioned not to expose their initial movements, but to be prepared to make an open demonstration in full force on the morning of the 29th. By these various devices, all of which were calculated to preserve the secrecy of the projected crossing at

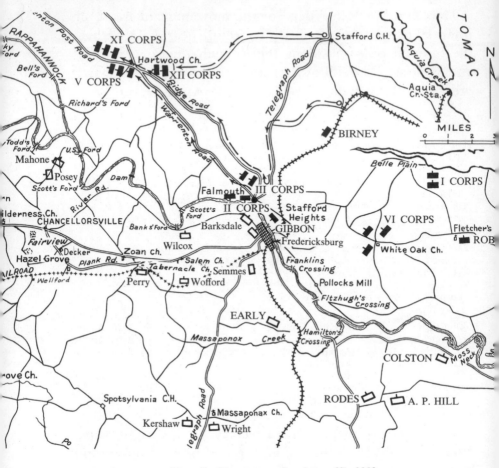

MAP 6. MOVEMENTS ON APRIL 27, 1863

Hooker's right wing commenced moving into position for the jumpoff. The XI, XII, and V Corps marched to Hartwood Church, where they bivouacked for the night. The other units, except for Stoneman's cavalry corps, remained in their winter camps. Stoneman, after his failure to start the encircling movement two weeks earlier, had gone into camp at Warrenton Junction, 8 miles northeast of Bealeton (Map 1).

Early has moved from Rappahannock Academy to his old position along Mine Road west of Hamilton's Crossing.

Kelly's Ford, Hooker hoped that Lee would misjudge his real intentions and conclude that the troops seen at Banks' and United States Mine Ford, and opposite Fredericksburg, presaged a turning movement via the aforementioned fords, in conjunction with a main attack against Fredericksburg.

One brigade of Howard's Eleventh Corps had been sent to Kelly's Ford several weeks ahead of the main body as an advance guard, and to secure the north bank at that point. The remainder of the right wing, after a short march on April 27, bivouacked in the vicinity of Hartwood Church, no farther than a three hour hike from the base camp, and approximately 15 miles short of Kelly's Ford. For the first day's march, apparently, a shakedown was considered desirable, as a mild prelude to the tough days ahead.

Sickles' Third Corps received special instructions. Hooker earmarked it as a sort of army reserve, to be employed wherever the developing situation might require, either with Sedgwick at Fredericksburg, as support to Couch at Banks' Ford, or to strengthen the right wing at Chancellorsville. Sickles was told, however, to hold his command in readiness to move early April 28, with eight days' rations and ammunition (as prescribed for the right wing), which suggests that Hooker had already practically made up his mind to use the Third Corps at Chancellorsville.

FEDERAL RIGHT WING CROSSING THE RAPPAHANNOCK AT KELLY'S FORD

CHAPTER 7

THE JUGGERNAUT ROLLS SWIFTLY

BY TWILIGHT on Tuesday evening, April 28, Hooker's army was poised on the designated positions at the several crossings of the Rappahannock. His three-corps right wing was massed north of Kelly's Ford. Stoneman's cavalry corps, two weeks behind schedule, was bivouacked near Warrenton Junction on the Orange and Alexandria Railroad. Cavalry detachments were out front, engaged in screening the infantry until the last minute before the actual crossing, to prevent Stuart's alert scouts from determining what was behind the Federal cavalry.

Couch's Second Corps, minus one division, had arrived opposite Banks' Ford, with advance detachments out towards United States Mine Ford, while Sedgwick's three-corps left wing was moving into position on the east bank of the Rappahannock opposite the lower end of Fredericksburg.

[116]

One pontoon bridge only had been ordered laid at Kelly's Ford, although the Rappahannock at that point, about 300 feet wide, was too deep and swift for the men to ford and was difficult even for horses. This bridge was completed by 7:45 P.M. April 28 without opposition from the Confederates, and everything was now in readiness for the second phase, the crossing of the two rivers and the advance on Chancellorsville.

The army commander, with his staff, established an advance command post at Morrisville, five miles east of Kelly's Ford, on the morning of April 28, leaving his Chief of Staff, General Butterfield, at Falmouth to coordinate the activities of the troops under Sedgwick and Couch, to keep Hooker currently posted on developments in that area, and to expedite communication between the two wings.

Except for the abort by the cavalry corps everything had gone smoothly, according to plan, and in good time. The curtain was now about to rise on "Operation Movement," to give it a twentieth century flavor. The morale of the Army of the Potomac rose perceptibly.

The Federal Concentration at Chancellorsville

The Eleventh, Twelfth, and Fifth Corps, the first two under Slocum's temporary command, commenced the crossing of the Rappahannock on the night of April 28, in accordance with instructions issued to Slocum and Meade during the afternoon. Preceded by elements of Pleasonton's cavalry, which Hooker had broken up for assignment to the respective corps, one regiment to each, Howard's Eleventh Corps crossed first and then halted to cover the corps of Slocum and Meade, which, in that order, marched across the swaying pontoons commencing at daylight April 29. All three corps were under instructions to then move rapidly across the neck of land between the two rivers, the Twelfth and Eleventh Corps in one column

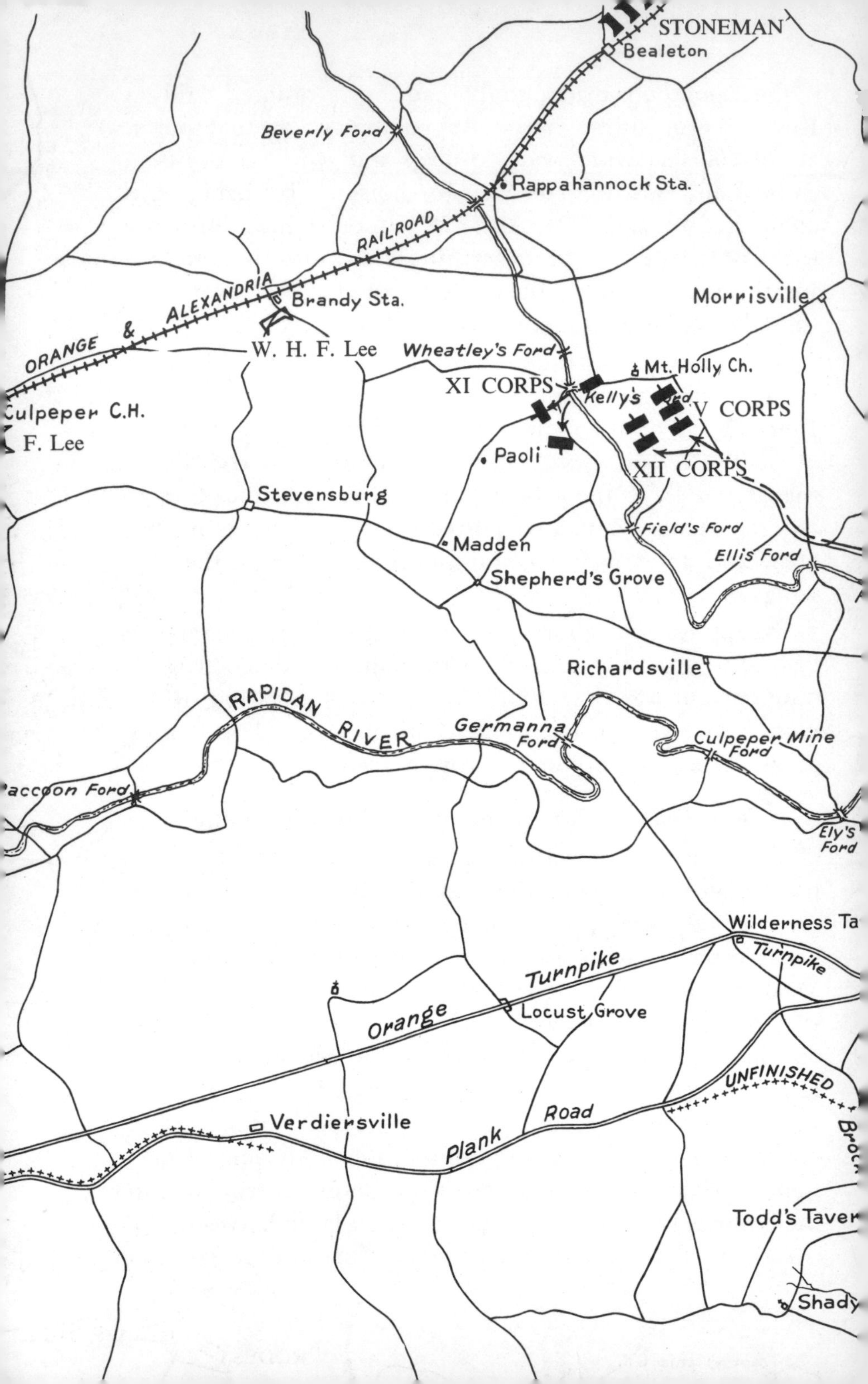
STONEMAN
Bealeton
Beverly Ford
Rappahannock Sta.
RAILROAD
ORANGE & ALEXANDRIA
Brandy Sta.
W. H. F. Lee
Wheatley's Ford
Morrisville
Mt. Holly Ch.
XI CORPS
Kelly's Ford
V CORPS
Culpeper C.H.
F. Lee
Paoli
XII CORPS
Stevensburg
Field's Ford
Madden
Ellis Ford
Shepherd's Grove
Richardsville
RAPIDAN RIVER
Germanna Ford
Culpeper Mine Ford
Raccoon Ford
Ely's Ford
Wilderness Ta
Turnpike
Orange Turnpike
Locust Grove
UNFINISHED
Verdiersville
Plank Road
Brock
Todd's Taver
Shady

MAP 7. MOVEMENTS ON APRIL 28, 1863

Howard's XI Corps left its bivouac at Hartwood Church before daylight and marched to Kelly's Ford, closing there at 4 P.M. It started crossing the Rappahannock at 10 P.M., as soon as the pontoon bridge was completed. By midnight two divisions were across and in positions covering the bridge; the third division was waiting its turn to cross. The XII and V Corps had moved to Mt. Holly Ch. Two divisions of Couch's II Corps marched from Falmouth to Banks' Ford, throwing out Carroll's brigade and outposts to U.S. Ford. Gibbon's division of this corps remained opposite Fredericksburg. The I and VI Corps moved down from their camps to their assigned places opposite where they were to cross the river. In the afternoon Sickles' III Corps moved down between, and a little in rear of these two corps.

There was no material change in the Confederate dispositions on this day. Kershaw's and Wright's Brigades are still at Massaponax Church (Map 6).

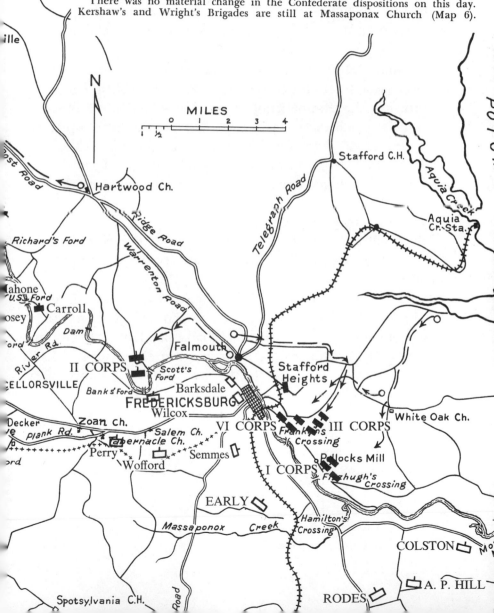

on the Germanna Ford road, while the Fifth Corps would take the shorter road through Richardsville to Ely's Ford. The advance cavalry meanwhile trotted ahead to seize the Rapidan fords. The two columns were instructed to maintain contact and, should Meade's corps meet opposition at the Rapidan crossing, Slocum was to send one of his corps along the south bank, after crossing, to disperse the enemy and clear the way for Meade's corps to cross. All three corps would then resume the advance on Chancellorsville.

Under Hooker's revised plan, Stoneman's cavalry had been scheduled to precede Howard's Eleventh Corps in crossing the Rappahannock on April 28. But Stoneman did not reach the river until 8 A.M. on the 29th, fourteen hours later than Hooker expected. By that time the Eleventh Corps had already crossed and the Twelfth was using the bridge. The cavalry was thus forced to mark time some hours longer until Slocum and Meade with their respective corps had gotten across. The cavalry was, however, allowed to cut in ahead of Humphrey's rear division of Meade's corps, which division as a result was the last to reach Chancellorsville.

In extenuation of his failure to cross according to Hooker's time schedule, Stoneman claimed, with considerable justice, that the army staff had miscalculated the time required for him to assemble his scattered corps, put it on the road, and march the intervening distance over muddy roads. It was 13 miles from Warrenton Junction to the crossing, and many of Stoneman's patrols were operating another dozen miles from his bivouac area. The weight of evidence favors Stoneman's contention. There was reason to believe that Hooker himself, who had not taken his own staff into his confidence, purposely delayed notifying Stoneman until the very last minute, in the interest of secrecy, and that he miscalculated badly on the logistics of the situation. However that may have been, the Federal

GERMANNA FORD A YEAR AFTER THE BATTLE

All early photos and drawings show that the banks of the Rappahannock and the Rapidan were clear of trees at the fords. Today these crossing sites are heavily wooded and relatively inaccessible, except where bridges exist.

cavalry was placed in the position of having been relegated to a secondary role, with two strikes against it.

Had Hooker been a more quick-thinking and less inflexible army commander, he would have been better advised to make a virtue of necessity at this stage, cancel the raid, and give the cavalry a new mission that would have kept the corps at hand and under his control to cover the army right flank in the advance against the Confederate army. The thought does not seem to have even crossed Hooker's mind. If it had, the Battle of Chancellorsville could have been quite a different story. In spite of the delay, Stoneman's original orders remained virtually unchanged, presumably in the belief, or at least the hope, that the greater mobility of the cavalry would permit it to make up the

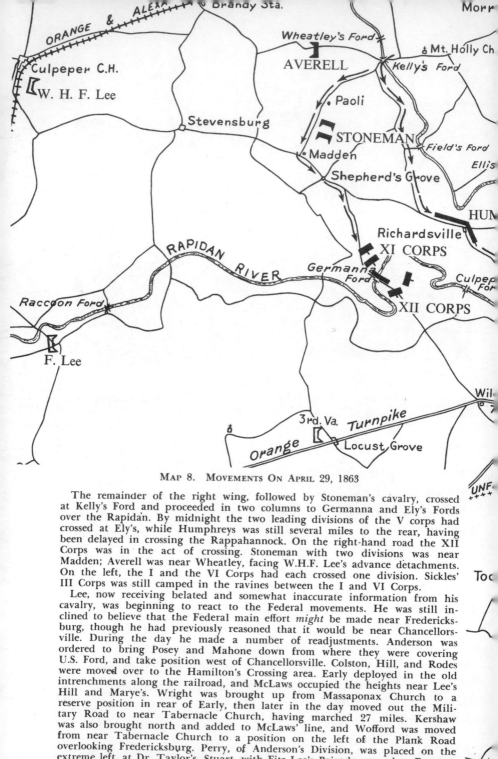

MAP 8. MOVEMENTS ON APRIL 29, 1863

The remainder of the right wing, followed by Stoneman's cavalry, crossed at Kelly's Ford and proceeded in two columns to Germanna and Ely's Fords over the Rapidan. By midnight the two leading divisions of the V corps had crossed at Ely's, while Humphreys was still several miles to the rear, having been delayed in crossing the Rappahannock. On the right-hand road the XII Corps was in the act of crossing. Stoneman with two divisions was near Madden; Averell was near Wheatley, facing W.H.F. Lee's advance detachments. On the left, the I and the VI Corps had each crossed one division. Sickles' III Corps was still camped in the ravines between the I and VI Corps.

Lee, now receiving belated and somewhat inaccurate information from his cavalry, was beginning to react to the Federal movements. He was still inclined to believe that the Federal main effort *might* be made near Fredericksburg, though he had previously reasoned that it would be near Chancellorsville. During the day he made a number of readjustments. Anderson was ordered to bring Posey and Mahone down from where they were covering U.S. Ford, and take position west of Chancellorsville. Colston, Hill, and Rodes were moved over to the Hamilton's Crossing area. Early deployed in the old intrenchments along the railroad, and McLaws occupied the heights near Lee's Hill and Marye's. Wright was brought up from Massaponax Church to a reserve position in rear of Early, then later in the day moved out the Military Road to near Tabernacle Church, having marched 27 miles. Kershaw was also brought north and added to McLaws' line, and Wofford was moved from near Tabernacle Church to a position on the left of the Plank Road overlooking Fredericksburg. Perry, of Anderson's Division, was placed on the extreme left, at Dr. Taylor's. Stuart, with Fitz Lee's Brigade, moved to Raccoon Ford; three squadrons of the 3d Virginia were pushed forward to Locust Grove.

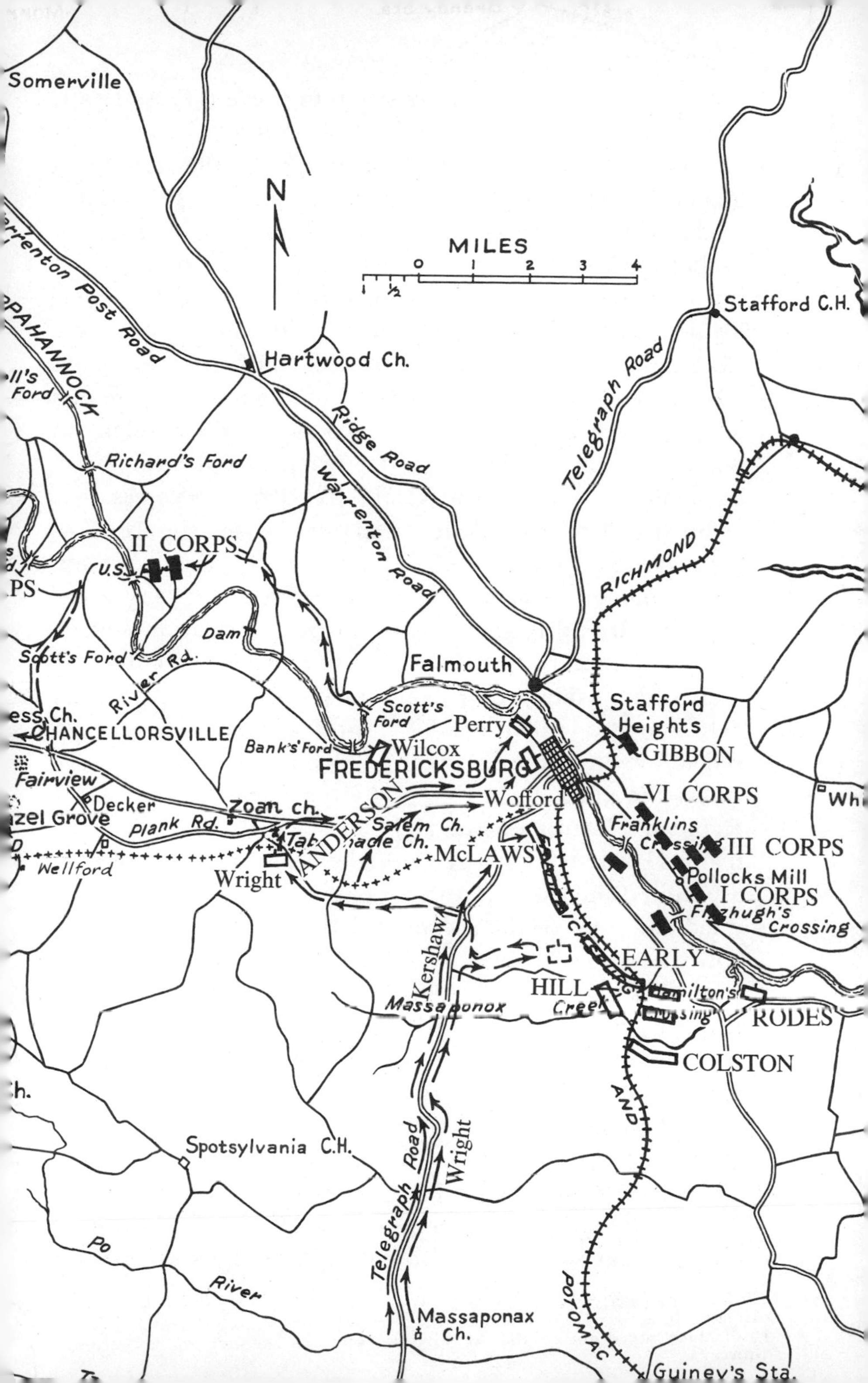

Somerville
N
MILES
0 1 2 3 4
1/2
Stafford C.H.
Warrenton Post Road
RAPPAHANNOCK
Hartwood Ch.
Ford
Ridge Road
Telegraph Road
Richard's Ford
Warrenton Road
RICHMOND
II CORPS
U.S.
Dam
Scott's Ford
River Rd.
Falmouth
Scott's Ford
Stafford Heights
Perry
Bank's Ford
Wilcox
GIBBON
CHANCELLORSVILLE
FREDERICKSBURG
Fairview
ANDERSON
Wofford
VI CORPS
Decker
Zoan ch.
Salem Ch.
Franklins
Plank Rd.
III CORPS
McLAWS
Pollocks Mill
Wellford
Wright
I CORPS
Crossing
Kershaw
EARLY
HILL
Hamilton's
Massaponax
Creek
RODES
COLSTON
AND
Spotsylvania C.H.
Wright
Telegraph Road
Po
River
POTOMAC
Massaponax
Ch.
Guiney's Sta.

lost time and still arrive in position to prevent Lee's escape when confronted by the Army of the Potomac.

The crossing of the Rappahannock on the 29th took longer than expected because it started to rain. The muddy roads made marching difficult for the heavily laden foot soldiers, many of whom felt no compunction about throwing away overcoats and other impedimenta to lighten their loads, which exceeded 53 pounds without counting the clothing they wore. Historically the soldier in the ranks takes little heed for the needs of tomorrow until he has learned from bitter campaign experience the wisdom of holding on to his blanket and other essential equipment, burdensome as the extra weight frequently becomes.

Small bodies of Confederate cavalry caused the flanks of the marching columns some annoyance, but they were not strong enough to make any real impression. In any event Stuart's job at this stage was to secure information and relay it to General Lee rather than to engage in combat.

Brushing aside Stuart's pickets and other small cavalry detachments, 42,000 men of the three Federal corps, preceded by Pleasonton's cavalry, plodded steadily forward across the pontoon bridge at Kelly's Ford and on to the Rapidan. Slocum, on the right, reached that river at Germanna Ford at 3 P.M. A Confederate detachment of over a hundred men were on the opposite bank, but were subdued and most of them captured by leading Federal units which waded the river. The Confederates had collected timbers to construct a bridge. This work was at once undertaken by Slocum's pioneers, so that the remainder of his corps and all of Howard's was able to cross the river dryshod. Slocum's men were on the south bank and in bivouac by 9 P.M. Howard started across in the moonlight at 11 P.M., completing his movement by 4 A.M. on the 30th.

On the left, Meade's Fifth Corps reached the Rapidan at Ely's Ford at 5 P.M. There was no bridge, and no bridging material. So the weary soldiers plunged into the stream,

APPROACH TO ELY'S FORD

This dirt road, leading east to the site of Ely's Ford, is the route taken by Meade's V Corps in May, 1863. Today a paved road parallels the old track and crosses over a bridge.

CROSSING AT ELY'S FORD

which was up to their armpits, cold, and running swiftly. The two leading divisions continued fording the river, completing the movement by midnight. Humphreys' division, which had been held up at Kelly's Ford by the passage of Stoneman's cavalry, did not reach the Rapidan until 1 A.M. April 30. Humphreys continued marching until he reached Hunting Creek.

Meade reached the initial phase line at Chancellorsville at 11 A.M., April 30, three hours ahead of Slocum's Twelfth Corps. He must have made a faster march, for he did not get across the Rappahannock at Kelley's Ford until after Slocum, and he did not have the benefit of a bridge at the Rapidan crossing. However, in fairness to Slocum it must be pointed out that Meade had the shorter route, and that Slocum was delayed briefly near Wilderness Church by Jeb Stuart's flank demonstration.

Initial Action on Sedgwick's Front

Pursuant to Hooker's orders, Sedgwick's Sixth Corps, Reynolds' First, and Sickle's Third, all under "Uncle John" Sedgwick's temporary command, broke camp early on April 28 and quietly moved into position on Stafford Heights below Fredericksburg, prepared to demonstrate openly the next day in the hope of persuading Lee that the main effort would be made there. Meanwhile the right wing was circling Lee's left and driving for Chancellorsville.

Bridge Laying by the Federal Engineers

Four pontoon bridges were laid by the engineers, under cover of a heavy fog, by early morning April 29, two at Deep Run (another was added later), where Franklin's Grand Division had crossed in December for the first Battle of Fredericksburg; and two more at Pollock's Mill (Fitzhugh's Crossing) further down river. Following the troop demonstration during the morning, bridgehead troops of Reynolds' and Sedgwick's Corps crossed with but

COMPLETION OF SEDGWICK'S BRIDGE AT FRANKLIN'S OLD CROSSING SITE

token resistance from the Confederates. Having crossed, they bivouacked on the plain close to the river bank, while Sickles' Third Corps remained in a position of readiness as the main body of the First and Sixth Corps, also on the east shore, awaited orders to cross.

Brigadier General Henry W. Benham, West Point 1837, in command of the engineer brigade of the Army of the Potomac, was a veteran of the Mexican War who had spent most of his years in the army constructing and repairing seawalls, forts, and harbor defenses. An earnest and efficient engineer officer, Benham made his preparations so carefully that the placement of all the pontoon bridges would have been effected smoothly and on schedule had he been given the troop help that he requested and was promised. Not if Benham could avoid it would the engineers be blamed, as they were by Burnside at Fredericksburg the previous November, for fouling up the army attack by arriving late with their clumsy pontoons.

Fifteen bridges in all were to be thrown across the Rappahannock and removed between April 28, when the first was laid at Kelly's Ford, and May 4, when the rear guard of Hooker's army had recrossed at United States Mine Ford after the battle. Actually only ten bridges were used, of which five were taken up and relaid at different points. The bridges at United States Mine Ford and Banks' Ford will be covered later.

Nine bridges were used for the advance and six for the retreat. Benham's engineers rendered valiant service throughout the campaign. They met all of Hooker's demands in spite of several unfortunate delays caused either by misunderstandings or reluctance on the part of two or three generals to make available the troops needed to assist the engineers in hauling the pontoons to the river bank.

Lee Reacts Cautiously

The first intimation Lee received that Hooker was stirring came in a message from Stuart on the evening of April 28. This message merely stated that a Federal force of all arms was moving up the Rappahannock in the direction of Kelly's Ford.

The next day, April 29, Stuart telegraphed that a crossing of the Rappahannock was in progress and that three Federal infantry corps had been identified. Lee also received courier reports from Germanna and Ely's Fords that enemy cavalry had crossed the Rapidan about two o'clock in the afternoon, but their strength had not been determined and the reports were vague on the subject of enemy infantry.

Hooker's precautionary measures to enforce secrecy on the march of his right wing had paid off handsomely. Lee *was* surprised on this occasion, despite the best efforts of the Confederate cavalry to pierce the Federal screen and develop the strength and dispositions of the large enemy force seen moving west on the 28th. Stuart's available brigades were greatly reduced in strength. His horses, many of them inferior replacements and not in the best condition at that, could not function as effectively as they had once been able to do. The real reason for Lee's surprise, however, was that for once Federal security and counter-reconnaissance measures were being efficiently handled.

Lee's information on April 28 and 29 was not sufficiently complete to enable him to fully evaluate Hooker's strategy, although the messages did tell him that a possible threat to his left was in the making. Stuart's cavalry, after the Federal crossing at Kelly's Ford, had managed to pick off enough Union soldiers to identify the Eleventh, Twelfth, and Fifth Corps, but the information was not sufficiently positive to convince Lee that all three corps were present at full strength. He knew only that "a large body of infantry and some cavalry" had crossed the Rappahannock and was headed for the Rapidan. This at least served to satisfy him that the threat was not directed at Culpeper and Gordonsville. Still he had to know much more before he could decide in his own mind the extent to which Hooker may have committed his army to a definite line of action.

In point of fact, Stuart's message identifying the Federal corps estimated their numbers as "14,000 infantry and some cavalry," an under-estimate by about 28,000, which was a bit misleading as a basis upon which to make important decisions. On that occasion Stuart made a premature guess which turned out to be only one-third correct.

The dispatches of April 29 came into Lee's hands *after* Hooker's right wing had crossed the Rappahannock and the intervening strip of land between the two rivers, and was on the point of effecting a night crossing of the Rapidan. Germanna and Ely's Fords are only ten and five miles, respectively, west of Chancellorsville, and the courier messages that Federal cavalry had crossed the Rapidan at 2 P. M., could have indicated several possibilities, all of which would have been mere guesses as to Hooker's main body.

It is doing Lee a disservice to claim that he was not surprised by Hooker's success in getting three corps on his flank so neatly, without opposition from the Confederates. This writer for one does not believe that Lee ever claimed to know exactly where Hooker's troops were and what they were up to from the time the Federal army broke camp on April 27 and fanned out from Falmouth, as claimed by Major General R. E. Colston, one of Jackson's division commanders at the Battle of Chancellorsville. Colston subsequently wrote that Lee had information every day of Hooker's movements and that a letter which Lee wrote Jackson on April 23 was proof of the fact that he expected Hooker to cross the Rappahannock above and not below Fredericksburg. These assertions by Colston were in fact only half-truths. The letter referred to had merely warned Jackson not to send more troops than necessary to meet the expected crossing at Port Royal (Hooker's feint), because he, Lee, thought Hooker's purpose at Port Royal was to draw the Confederate troops in that direction and that the actual crossing would be *above* Fredericksburg. However, Lee did not say *how far* above Fredericksburg it would be attempted, and his defense line, terminating at Banks' Ford, obviously indicated that he did not expect a crossing so far west.

Further evidence may be found in Lee's expressed annoyance in a message to Anderson (in command of a division near Chancellorsville) that he had not been informed of the situation sooner. Lee was on record as having stated an earlier opinion that, if the crossing were made above Fredericksburg, as he expected it would, the probable limits would be within the line Port Royal—Banks' Ford, inclusive. These points he thereupon established as the right and left flank respectively of his defensive line, which he directed his subordinates to fortify and man, with outpost troops at United States Mine Ford, a short march north of the Chancellorsville crossroads.

It was probably after receipt of Stuart's second report, on the afternoon of April 29, that Lee's thoughts turned to Longstreet in the Suffolk area with the divisions of Pickett and Hood. He had prepared Longstreet for this very moment, so at Lee's request Secretary Seddon sent a telegram immediately to Longstreet, advising that the Union army had crossed the Rappahannock and that it was time for him to rejoin Lee with his two divisions. As has been noted in Chapter 4, Longstreet did not comply.

To those who attribute to Longstreet as much as to any one factor Lee's defeat at Gettysburg two months later, his lack of wholehearted cooperation and subordination to his commanding general at the time of the Battle of Chancellorsville was in sharp contrast to the attitude of Jackson, Stuart, and most of Lee's other generals. Longstreet's propensity for placing his own views ahead of Lee's in spite of the fact that he was operating under orders, provides material for an interesting study of personalities and character.

Lee—A Mental Hazard to his Opponents

The history of 1862, second year of the war, in the eastern theater of operations, affords indisputable evidence that Lee and the Army of Northern Virginia had succeeded in keeping the Army of the Potomac, under its succession of commanders, in a continuous state of uncertainty as they struggled to exploit the North's superior strength and weapons in offensive operations. The combination of Lee and his principal lieutenants, Jackson, Longstreet, and Stuart, had proven so effective that, although Lee normally chose the defensive when the armies met on the battlefield, he succeeded in retaining the initiative for the Confederates throughout. As a rule he managed to maneuver so that the battles were fought on fields of his own choosing, with the advantage of terrain in his favor.

Lee much preferred the offensive, however, and always in the back of his mind was the hope that a favorable opportunity would present itself for his army to carry the fight to the Union on its own territory and away from his beloved Virginia. He had tried the strategic offensive once in 1862, and by all the rules of warfare should have paid the penalty of trying to beat the Army of the Potomac with half or less than half its strength. But Lee was superior to McClellan, Pope, and Burnside in character, military sagacity, judgment, and doggedness of purpose. Consequently his first invasion of the North in September 1862 had resulted in a tactical stalemate at Antietam, whereas it should have been a resounding victory for the Federals.

General Lee's almost invariably successful campaign plans, in preparation for the many victories that he won on battlefield after battlefield, prior to the loss of his first great battle at Gettysburg in July 1863, were a judicious compound of the strategic offensive and the tactical defensive. His Federal opponents were usually induced to maneuver, or at least strongly encouraged to do so, by his troop dispositions and rapid shift of divisions, notably through the fast marching and aggressive combat tactics of Stonewall Jackson and Jeb Stuart. These tactics accomplished the effect which Lee was seeking; the result more often than not was that the Federals attacked him on positions where the defense possessed marked advantages over the offense.

Lee's readiness to take a calculated risk, and the great faith that he placed in the ability of his men and officers to do the seemingly impossible with inferior means, came by repetition to be almost routine in his estimates of the situation. The truth was that he had an uncanny knack, which many regarded as intuition, of anticipating just about how his opponents would react under varying conditions.

Lee Meets a Crisis Calmly

One of Lee's most admirable traits, among many, was the calm, unhurried way in which he met critical military situations. This characteristic, the mark of a strong character and superior field general, was never better demonstrated than at Chancellorsville. He never permitted himself to be unduly hurried in making his estimate of the situation, but once having made up his mind, his actions were swift and sure.

Captain James Power Smith, a member of Jackson's staff, was awakened at daylight April 29, in his tent near Hamilton's Crossing, with the news that Federal troops were crossing the Rappahannock within a few miles of Jackson's headquarters, just below Fredericksburg. At Jackson's direction, Smith rode quickly to Lee's headquarters, where the general was still sleeping. Entering Lee's tent, he gently awoke him to break the news. Lee swung his feet out of bed and sat sidewise on his cot with the typical remark: "Well, I thought I heard firing, and was beginning to think it was time some of you young fellows were coming to tell me what it was all about. Tell your good general that I am sure he knows what to do. I will meet him at the front very soon."*

This was the situation that confronted him on the evening of April 29. Hooker's army had more than a two to one advantage in numbers. Only half of Longstreet's corps was on hand. His own cavalry had less than half its normal strength, while an entire corps of enemy cavalry, 10,000 strong and more aggressive than usual, was cutting in on the rear of his army and posing a threat to his com-

---

*Taken from "Stonewall Jackson's Last Battle", by Rev. James Power Smith, Captain and Assistant Adjutant General on Jackson's Staff. *Battle and Leaders of the Civil War.*

munication line to Richmond, his main source of food, forage, ammunition, and supplies. His opponent had just sprung a surprise on him by a concealed march of three army corps in a wide swing, miles to the west of the fords where Lee had anticipated a crossing. This enemy was now on his left rear with a large force of infantry, artillery, and cavalry, the actual size of which remained to be disclosed. Other Federal troops had shown themselves at United States Mine Ford and Banks' Ford, the left anchor of Lee's long defense line, while another large troop concentration was threatening Fredericksburg and even now had thrown two bridges and established bridgeheads on the west bank of the river below the town.

Would the main effort of Hooker's army be made from Chancellorsville or was the flank march a feint to draw Lee back from Fredericksburg so that it could be taken by assault from the east, as Burnside had tried to do in December? Was the Fredericksburg maneuver a feint that would enable Hooker to move in on Lee from the rear with overwhelming strength? Or might Hooker, dividing his army into two equal parts, either one of which would be as strong as Lee's entire army, have decided to attack simultaneously from two directions to crush Lee between the strong jaws of the pincers?

Lee himself had ridden out from Hamilton's Crossing that morning and discovered that the Federals, under cover of an early fog, had crossed in boats, driven back the Confederate outposts, and completed the bridges over which an undetermined number of divisions had already crossed and halted. Lee could himself see other large masses of troops on the far bank awaiting instructions to cross.

The information received from Stuart on the 29th, that elements of the Federal Fifth, Eleventh, and Twelfth Corps had crossed at Kelly's Ford and were headed for the Rapidan, provided Lee with the basis for some preliminary orders. He sent word to Stuart to rejoin the left wing of the army at once, taking care not to be cut off by the Federals, while at the same time protecting public property along the Orange and Alexandria Railroad and delaying the march of Hooker's divisions. (See Chapter 8). Later in the day he ordered R. H. Anderson to change the disposition of two of his brigades from the vicinity of United States Mine Ford to Chancellorsville, to delay the Federal advance. Jackson's Corps of four divisions was held in place for the time being, south of Fredericksburg, prepared to block any major attack from that direction.

Neither Hooker's earlier feint at Port Royal nor Sedgwick's present demonstration at Fredericksburg persuaded Lee to jump to premature conclusions. When Sedgwick paraded his divisions on Stafford Heights, but before he crossed the river in full strength, Jackson's first impulse was to prepare to attack him as soon as he should get across and occupy the plain south of the town. Lee disagreed, telling his lieutenant that it was just as impracticable now as it would have been at the first battle of Fredericksburg, because of Federal artillery superiority and the devasting fire its guns could pour into the attackers from the heights on the east bank. After Jackson had looked the ground over again he deferred to Lee's judgment and concurred in the undesirability of attacking.

HOOKER'S HEADQUARTERS AT CHANCELLORSVILLE

CHAPTER 8

HOOKER BEGINS TO SLIP

THE Army of the Potomac was on the march, gaining momentum as its right wing swept like a fast-moving glacier over the Rappahannock and Rapidan Rivers, through the forbidding depths of the Wilderness, and on to Chancellorsville, its first objective.

General George Gordon Meade, in command of the Fifth Corps, was the first high-ranking officer to reach the Chancellor House, a spacious manor house set back a few yards from the crossroads that marked the reference point designated on the map as Chancellorsville. Meade arrived about mid-day on Thursday, April 30, and within a few hours the entire right wing of three corps, eight divisions, had come up, the men resting on their arms while Slocum and Meade went into conference to discuss the next move.

Hooker's second-phase march orders to his three corps commanders, Slocum, Howard, and Meade, issued from

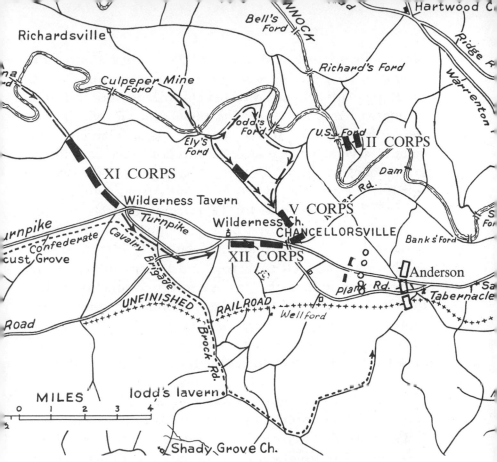

MAP 9. FEDERAL CONCENTRATION NEAR CHANCELLORSVILLE—
MOVEMENTS UP TO 2 P.M., APRIL 30

Meade's V Corps started the march from Ely's Ford at daylight, with Sykes' and Griffin's divisions, Sykes in the lead. Humphreys' division was still on the march between Kelly's Ford and Ely's. Almost at once Meade got word from the cavalry out in front that some of Anderson's division, thought to be a brigade, were covering U.S. Ford. Actually only a small detachment of Confederates remained in that area, but Meade diverted Sykes off toward U. S. Ford to clear up the situation, meanwhile continuing toward Chancellorsville with Griffin's division. He arrived there about 11 A M, and recalled Sykes.

Slocum left Germanna Ford before 7 A.M. with his own XII Corps, followed at about an hour's march by Howard's XI Corps. As he passed Wilderness Tavern one of Slocum's flank units was attacked by Stuart who came up the Orange Turnpike from the southwest. The Federal infantry brushed this small cavalry force aside and continued on the Plank Road toward Chancellorsville. The head of the column arrived at 2 P.M., to be greeted by Meade, jubilant that Hooker had succeeded in maneuvering a powerful force to Lee's left and rear. Slocum threw cold water in Meade's face with the announcement that a fresh order just received from Hooker directed that they proceed no farther, but take up a defensive position.

Anderson has three brigades astride the Turnpike in the vicinity of Tabernacle Church; his covering forces are facing a Federal cavalry regiment and an infantry brigade across Mott Run.

Morrisville about 2 P.M. on April 28, as they awaited the commanding general's word to start the columns across the Rappahannock, had directed an uninterrupted advance through Chancellorsville. The phase line on which they were instructed to march was in open, maneuverable country several miles east of Chancellorsville, beyond the grim woods of the Wilderness. The objective was an imaginary line running north and south from Banks' Ford on the Rappahannock to Tabernacle Church, located about two miles southwest of Salem Church on the Plank Road, terrain features that could be easily identified.

The plan was well conceived and was in the course of being efficiently executed. It was a foregone conclusion that the Confederates would have to relinquish United States Mine Ford as the Federal right wing advanced. Anderson's Confederate Division promptly and wisely pulled back from Chancellorsville as the leading Federal elements came up, but the Southerners were unhurried in their withdrawal as Pleasonton's advance cavalry ran into enemy rear guard opposition and pressed forward more cautiously.

The business of crossing large military forces over river obstacles by fording sounds easy, but the difficulties encountered in crossing the Rappahannock west of Fredericksburg must be seen to be appreciated. Above Falmouth, where the high bluffs rise at some points as much as 100 feet above the water line, they are close to the river, with slopes that are steep, wooded, and deeply cut by ravines.

The first feasible crossing was at Banks' Ford, some six road miles from Fredericksburg, a position of such importance that the Confederates guarded it with extreme care. There they had erected a series of earthen parapets in three successive lines on the south side, with traverses to protect the defenders against hostile artillery fire from the opposite bank. Each line was a higher slope than the one in front, permitting the riflemen to fire over the heads of the men in the forward trenches. Clearly it would be an expensive operation to reduce the defenses other than by outflanking.

Seven miles further to the west was the next practicable crossing point at United States Mine Ford, where the Confederates had also constructed strong entrenchments. Hooker's plan had taken these defenses into consideration and contemplated forcing a voluntary withdrawal of the Confederates by the process of uncovering them by maneuver, which he was well on the way to accomplishing until he changed his mind.

With the uncovering of United States Mine Ford, Benham's engineers quickly threw two bridges at that point. The two divisions of Couch's Second Corps, under Generals Hancock and French, crossed during the afternoon and went into bivouac at Chancellorsville on the night of April 30. The right wing now had a strength of four corps, ten divisions totaling about 54,000 men.

As Slocum and Meade understood Hooker's directive, there would be only a temporary pause at Chancellorsville to allow the right wing to regroup after its fast march. Meantime the cavalry would push ahead to uncover Banks' Ford and exploit the advantage already gained by the flanking maneuver. The specific instructions were that part of one corps would follow the road which parallels the Rappahannock and in close proximity to the river as it follows its meandering course past Banks' Ford and on to Fredericksburg. This would be Meade's job. The balance of his corps and Slocum's Twelfth would proceed in two columns, one along the Turnpike, the other on the Plank Road, until they reached the second phase line: Banks' Ford—Tabernacle Church, when the two corps would develop from march column into extended order to form a connected front across the three roads, the left flank anchored firmly on the river.

At that point, with everything nicely tidied up and in

order, the right wing would be drawn up in battle formation, Slocum's Twelfth and Meade's Fifth Corps abreast, Howard's Eleventh Corps in support, and Couch's Second Corps in reserve, all prepared to open the engagement in coordinated fashion, under the direction of General Hooker, who at this point would ride up and assume personal command. That is, if Lee's army were still there, which Hooker's plan did not really anticipate.

There were several sentences in Hooker's initial instructions to Slocum which did not seem particularly significant when read in context, but which may have provided a clue to the commanding general's intentions:

> . . . If your Cavalry is well advanced from Chancellorsville, you will be able to ascertain whether or not the enemy is detaching forces from behind Fredericksburg to resist your advance. If not in any considerable force, the general desires that you will endeavor to advance at all hazards, securing a position on the Plank Road, and uncovering Banks' Ford, which is also defended by a brigade of the rebel infantry and a battery. If the enemy should be greatly reenforced you will then select a strong position, and compel him to attack you on your ground. . .

In the light of subsequent events, the implications are unmistakable. Reduced to its simplest terms, the order meant that, if Lee should decline to flee and choose instead to oppose Hooker with force, the latter intended to go over from the offensive to the defensive. That in turn would mean that he would yield the initiative to his opponent and risk the loss of all that his army had just gained by surprise and maneuver.

General Meade was an excellent corps commander, experienced in combat, aggressive, and possessed of other soldierly traits which ranked him as one of the more dependable leaders in the Army of the Potomac. Anxious to put the Wilderness back of his corps, he lost no time in directing his cavalry forward from Chancellorsville to follow the River Road, establish contact with the enemy, and get on with the important business of uncovering Banks' Ford. In support of the cavalry he sent forward an infantry brigade of Griffin's division. The cavalry unfortunately took the Turnpike instead of the River Road, the infantry ran into a superior Confederate force, two brigades of Anderson's Division, and neither Federal detachment was able to make any progress.

The Captured Diary

Preceding Slocum's Twelfth Corps to the Rapidan on April 29, to sweep the roads clear of enemy detachments, the horse regiment attached to that column had operated in the cavalry tradition with speed, dash, and enterprising ingenuity. Arriving at Germanna Ford, the advance guard was confronted on the opposite bank by a party of Confederates who showed a disposition to contest the crossing. A small party of Federals promptly moved down river a few hundred yards, found a stray boat and rapidly crossed a sizable detachment. This force moved on the surprised Confederates from the rear and took as prisoners half a hundred of Stuart's cavalry, among them an engineer staff officer of General Stuart's with an interesting diary on his person.

The next afternoon, Pleasonton's cavalry surprised and captured near Chancellorsville a Confederate courier bearing a dispatch from General Lee, dated at Fredericksburg, April 30, and addressed to Division Commander McLaws. It stated that he had just been told, at noon that day, of a strong Federal concentration at Chancellorsville. The letter expressed surprise that he had not been informed sooner, and ended by summoning McLaws immediately to his headquarters.

It may be presumed, from the fact that the courier was seeking McLaws, whose division on the Fredericksburg defense line had been alerted to the possibility that it might be needed to support Anderson's withdrawn position south of Banks' Ford, that McLaws had gone forward to make a personal reconnaissance, and that the courier had not yet caught up with him. But the captured message serves to confirm the fact that the rapidity of Hooker's successful flank march had indeed taken Lee by surprise.

Pleasonton's account, written sometime later, stated that he met Hooker at Chancellorsville at two o'clock on the afternoon of April 30 and turned over to him Lee's captured message and the diary which had been taken from Stuart's staff officer. Most reports however place Hooker's arrival on the field as having occurred during the evening, some hours later than Pleasonton indicates. This partly nullifies the timeliness of what the cavalry general regarded as vital enemy intelligence that should have drastically altered the situation from the Federal viewpoint, had Hooker acted promptly. Pleasonton's account of what transpired at that time, whether completely accurate or not, is an interesting commentary on the preliminary aspects of the campaign that was now beginning to take shape.

The captured Confederate officer had kept his diary all through the war. Pleasonton, intrigued by the thought that he might find something of importance in the voluminous document, stayed up most of the night of April 29 reading it from cover to cover. His patience had been rewarded, he told Hooker, when he came across an account of a council of war held at Stuart's headquarters in March, about six weeks earlier, which had been attended by Generals Jackson, A. P. Hill, Ewell, and Stuart. The conference, which had lasted five hours, reached the unanimous conclusion that the next battle would be fought at or near Chancellorsville.

This to Pleasonton was information of the greatest significance. He called Hooker's attention to the opinion which had been expressed by Lee's high-ranking lieutenants, emphasizing the fact that the tables had now been turned and Hooker's army was already on the battlefield the Confederates had selected. He pointed out that Lee had by this time received the news of Hooker's arrival at Chancellorsville and urged that the advantage of surprise would be lost to Hooker if the Chancellorsville locale were not promptly changed in order to negate such tactical plans as Lee may already have worked out in conformity with the expressed views of Jackson and the other generals. Pleasonton then strongly recommended that the advance of the right wing be hastened, to enable the three corps to clear the Wilderness and move into the open country to the east, where maneuver would be possible. The troops could there see what they were doing, and artillery could be used to advantage. An additional advantage, he said, would be the uncovering of Banks' Ford, thus shortening by a substantial number of miles the line of communication with Sedgwick's wing at Fredericksburg. In effect, Hooker's cavalry commander was repeating the identical instructions that Hooker had given to Slocum in the original order directing the circuitous march on Chancellorsville.

Pleasonton Gets an Unpleasant Shock

Pleasonton's account stated that Hooker's apathetic reaction to his recommendations greatly shocked him, in that the commanding general could see no reason for haste, expressing the opinion that the next morning would be plenty of time to move on toward Fredericksburg and Lee's army.

The captured diary had evidently failed to disclose Lee's attitude and reactions when the conclusions of the council were reported to him, as they surely must have been. But it is almost a certainty that the combat powerhouse represented in the persons of the four major participants, and the length of time that had been devoted to the discussions, were guarantee enough that their views would be important elements in Lee's subsequent strategy.

That Hooker was opinionated, self-centered, and lacking many of the essential character traits that are basic in great leaders, military and non-military alike, is borne out by the historic facts. That he intended to rely wholly on his own judgment and disregard that of his principal subordinates, however, was not fully revealed to them until the evening of April 30. Hooker had had excellent reasons for not divulging his strategic plans to his corps commanders or even to his own staff until the very last minute. But there were obvious dangers in that policy, such as the slow transmission of tactical instructions based on the overall strategy, or staff miscalculations on the time element required for preparing and distributing contingent orders down through corps, division, brigade, and lower units. It would not be the first or the last time in the history of armies that weak links in the command and staff chain would disrupt an otherwise perfect conception. The most capable and experienced military leaders however, from the top down, make a practice of allowing a reasonable margin for human error and do not mistakenly attribute infallibility to all subordinates in the chain.

Hooker Applies the Brakes

Enthusiasm was running high as division after division of the marching Federal columns moved into the area about Chancellorsville, removed their packs and settled down to relax and swap stories while their generals went into a huddle preparatory to getting on with the war.

Meade was in high spirits as Slocum rode up to the Chancellor House. The two generals shook hands as the usually taciturn Meade greeted his friend with unaccustomed gaiety: "This is splendid, Slocum; hurrah for old Joe! We are on Lee's flank and he doesn't know it. You take the Plank Road toward Fredericksburg, and I will take the

MAJOR GENERAL HENRY W. SLOCUM

Pike, or vice versa, if you prefer, and we will get out of this Wilderness."

Evidently the enthusiastic Meade had not yet received his copy of the dispatch which Chief of Staff Butterfield had signed at 2:15 P.M., by Hooker's order. This is what it said:

> The General directs that no advance be made from Chancellorsville until the columns (II, III, V, XI and XII Corps) are concentrated. He expects to be at Chancellorsville tonight.

When Slocum showed Meade his copy of the delaying order, the wind quickly went out of Meade's sails, and as the word leaked out to the troops, Hooker's halt order had the effect of changing optimistic enthusiasm to a feeling of bitter disappointment. Officers and men alike realized instinctively that the golden opportunity to exploit the advantage already gained was being jeopardized by faulty judgment.

It would seem that Hooker's thoughts that afternoon of

April 30 were still centered exclusively on the thrilling outcome of his first large-scale operation, as he sat in his command post at Morrisville and penned the congratulatory General Order which he planned to publish with a symbolic flourish to his troops that evening. Doubtless he was planning what he would say to his men when Pleasonton interrupted his pleasant train of thoughts with the urgent exhortation to hustle the right wing on toward Fredericksburg to get the jump on Lee.

Perhaps Slocum and Meade had moved faster than Hooker had expected and were getting ahead of his timetable. It may still have been a map problem for Hooker, but it was high time that he transfer his attention from paper to the actual field of operations, where events were moving fast. It was clear enough, however, that he was not ready to clash with Lee until he could reenforce the three leading corps, already at Chancellorsville, with the additional strength to be added by Couch's Second and Sickles' Third Corps, which between them would add over 30,000 men to the 42,000 of the right wing. Then Hooker would have a force of 72,000 from which he felt sure that Lee would "ingloriously fly," to quote in advance from the order which was read to the troops at Chancellorsville that evening:

GENERAL ORDER NO. 47

Headquarters, Army of the Potomac,
Camp near Falmouth, Va.
April 30, 1863.

It is with heart-felt satisfaction the Commanding General announces to the Army that the operations of the last three days have determined that our enemy must either ingloriously fly or come out from behind his intrenchments and give us battle on our own ground, where certain destruction awaits him.

The operations of the V, XI, and XII Corps have been a succession of splendid achievements.

By Order of Major-General Hooker,

S. Williams, A.A.G.

As if that boastful general order were not enough, upon his arrival at Chancellorsville, Hooker saw fit to add a foolishly gratuitous insult to the Lord with the comment that "God Almighty will not be able to prevent the destruction of the rebel army!" One may be sure that such blasphemy must have had only the most depressing effect on thousands of God-fearing soldiers in his magnificent army, superimposed as it was on other unfortunate utterances, such as: "the rebel army is now the legitimate property of the Army of the Potomac. They may as well pack up their haversacks and make for Richmond. I shall be after them;" and "God have mercy on General Lee, for I shall have none."

Hooker's Fatal Delay

As the army commander marked time mentally and physically, the Second Corps moved across the river and went into bivouac while Sickles' Third Corps, lately detached by Hooker's instructions from Sedgwick's wing, moved up from Fredericksburg. Sickles made good time the night of April 30, crossed at United States Mine Ford and went into bivouac Friday morning, May 1, in the vicinity of Bullock's (Chandler's), a mile north of the Chancellors ville crossroads where the Ely's Ford road crosses the Mineral Springs Road.

Pending Hooker's arrival at Chancellorsville, Slocum, as senior corps commander until Couch should come on the field, was responsible for making the necessary tactical decisions, within the framework of Hooker's directive.

The latest message, jerking the machine to a numbing, frustrating, "in place, halt," flatly contradicted the earlier order which said that "the right wing, if not strongly resisted," would advance at all hazards and secure a position uncovering Banks' Ford. In the event the Confederates were found to be in force near Chancellorsville, the right wing was to select a strong position and await attack on its own ground, while Sedgwick would come up from Fredericksburg to assail the enemy in flank and rear, although the Sedgwick move was not divulged at that time.

The key words in the order are found in the phrase "if not strongly resisted." Surely a bit of rear guard skirmishing by a small force of retiring Confederates or even a brigade in position at Banks' Ford would not be construed as strong resistance against an advancing force of 40,000 troops. The fact of the matter was that Hooker intended from the very beginning that Sedgwick should pound Lee against the hard rock of Hooker's main force in a defensive position at Chancellorsville, if his strategic maneuvering should fail to drive the Confederate army to the south without giving battle. In such event, Lee was expected to take the same punishment that he had administered to Burnside at the first battle of Fredericksburg.

Hooker's real intentions had not been revealed to his corps commanders, however, so all of them naturally thought he meant what he had said in his march orders. He later gave out that his reason for suspending the advance on April 30 was to gain time for Couch's Second and Sickles' Third Corps to augment the large mass of troops already on the ground. But the truth was that he had, cravenly in the opinion of his subordinates and most historical critics of his revised strategy, chosen to let Sedgwick carry the burden of the attack with only his own Sixth Corps. For it was not long before Hooker also pulled Reynolds' First Corps away from the left wing to join the main body at Chancellorsville, leaving Sedgwick to figure out for himself what Hooker really expected of him.

Clearly something had happened to Joe Hooker that gave off ominous overtones. Here was a general who had brilliantly executed an amazing military feat and then proceeded, inexplicably, to nullify the advantage gained just at the moment of the payoff battle with an opponent facing almost insuperable odds. Had the mysterious power implicit in the very name of Robert E. Lee paralyzed Joe Hooker as soon as the test of battle impended? Had abstinence from his customary drinking muddled his thinking apparatus? Or had his initial success so gone to his head that he felt he had only to wait patiently for Lee to reveal his intentions, concede that Hooker held all the aces, and solve the problem by pulling out for Richmond?

What is probably nearer the truth is that Hooker could scarcely believe his plan had succeeded so admirably, had not thought much ahead of the present moment, and was as a result uncertain just what his next move should be. For the action of the first three days he had planned superbly, but when it came to prompt, decisive action in which he was face to face with his able opponent, he seems to have become the unfortunate victim of self-hypnosis. It was indeed not self-intoxication, for we have Couch's word for it that Hooker was not drinking at Chancellorsville. Yet Couch, his second-in-command, was far from being one of Hooker's admirers; so far in fact that after the battle of Chancellorsville he refused to serve further under Hooker and was transferred to the Department of the Susquehanna.

There in the clearing around and south of the Chancellor House, within a few yards of the key crossroads from which radiated a network of improved and unimproved roads, the hopes and aspirations of the long-suffering but spirited Army of the Potomac received another shattering setback. And it was not from Robert E. Lee this time, except perhaps indirectly through the medium of thought waves, but at the hands of Joseph Hooker himself, the architect of the offensive campaign. Hooker administered the fatal blow to his army, by remote control from a town on the other side of the Rappahannock. For the twenty-hour delay in the forward movement of his right wing was destined to be a decisive factor in giving to the Army of Northern Virginia the necessary time to concentrate. He played directly into the hands of General Lee, who desperately wanted to keep Hooker penned up in the dense woods of the Wilderness. Hooker's volte-face thus served to yield the initiative to Lee, always ready to seize it, and at the same time to paralyze the movements of his own army while the Confederates gathered their forces along the high ground between Old Mine Road and the Banks' Ford—Tabernacle Church line some six miles to the east in open country.

Having been halted where they were, still in the Wilderness, Slocum and Meade held a conference about 2:30 P.M. April 30, and decided the only thing to do was to halt their advance and forego for the time being what would have been the easy task of uncovering Banks' Ford and occupying their second phase line in maneuverable country. This was a painful decision for two good generals to have to make, impatient as they were to exploit their initial success by maintaining the offensive with its real promise of a decisive victory. Both were angered as well as disheartened by Hooker's switch to a defensive psychology, however temporary it might seem at the moment. They at least were aware of the importance of keeping moving on that Thursday afternoon, and could see no benefit in postponing the fight, if that should be Lee's purpose.

But orders were orders, so the advance brigade of Griffin's division was told to pull back to Chancellorsville, while Slocum and Meade concocted a revised plan which called for the advance to be resumed the next morning,

Friday, May 1. The order of march would be in three columns as follows: two of Meade's divisions, commanded by Griffin and Humphreys, to take the River Road; the third division of the Fifth Corps, Sykes', the Orange Turnpike; Slocum's two divisions of the Twelfth Corps would march on the Plank Road; and Howard's Eleventh Corps would follow in support of the two leading corps. All three columns were instructed to keep in touch with one another during the advance.

As night fell, the four Federal corps occupied a line extending in an easterly direction, with Howard's Eleventh Corps on the Turnpike from a point about three miles west of Chancellorsville, the right flank refused a short distance to the north, and the left flank connecting with the right of Slocum's Twelfth Corps, which formed an arc that ran south and east and enclosed the open country around Fairview. Slocum's left rested on the Plank Road a half mile south of the Chancellorsville crossroads Meade's Fifth Corps, with the exception of Humphreys' division, which came up the next morning, remained in a position of readiness in the vicinity of the crossroads, while Couch's Second Corps went into bivouac about a mile north of Chancellorsville. (Map 10).

Confederate Countermeasures

As stated in Chapter 7, General Anderson had been ordered by Lee, late on April 29, to withdraw Mahone's and Posey's Brigades from United States Mine Ford to Chancellorsville. On his arrival at Chancellorsville about midnight that day Anderson found that the movement had already started. The withdrawal continued, under Federal pressure, during the morning of the 30th, the two brigades taking up a defensive line from Zoan Church to Tabernacle Church. In falling back, one of the brigades lost some men to the fast-moving cavalry preceding the Federal corps, but

MAP 10. THE SITUATION AT MIDNIGHT, APRIL 30, 1863

The positions of the Federal I, III, and VI Corps are not shown on this map. The I and VI Corps are as shown on Map 7. Sickles' III Corps moved northwest during the afternoon on its way to U.S. Ford, and camped at Hamet, about two miles southeast of Hartwood Church.

The Confederate dispositions have not changed materially. Anderson's brigades in the vicinity of Tabernacle Church and Zoan Church are intrenching.

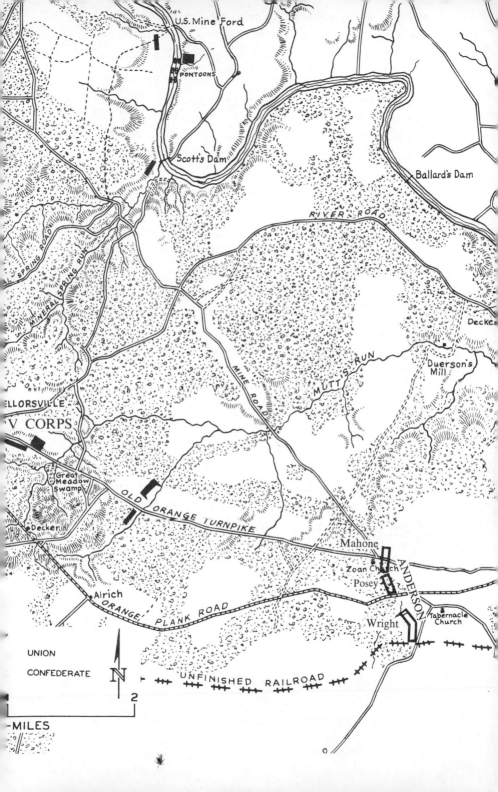

U.S. Mine Ford

PONTOONS

Scott's Dam

Ballard's Dam

RIVER ROAD

Decker

Duerson's Mill

MUTT'S RUN

SPRING ROAD

MINERAL SPRING RUN

MINE ROAD

ELLORSVILLE

V CORPS

Great Meadow Swamp

Decker

OLD ORANGE TURNPIKE

Mahone

Zoan Church

Posey

ANDERSO

Alrich

ORANGE PLANK ROAD

Wright

Tabernacle Church

UNION

CONFEDERATE

N

2

UNFINISHED RAILROAD

MILES

the enemy advance was retarded sufficiently to permit Anderson to pull back his brigades intact.

Lee now directed Anderson to form and strengthen a line of defense east of and facing Chancellorsville, at right angles to the river. He was told to rest his right on the river to cover Banks' Ford, and to anchor his left somewhat south of the Plank Road in such a position as would serve temporarily to cover the roads to Lee's left flank until more troops could be brought up. McLaw's Division, the only other one of Longstreet's Corps with Lee, was told to prepare to move the next day from the Fredericksburg position to support Anderson, if needed.

Anderson's Division spent the rest of the day in digging trenches and throwing up breastworks, under the supervision of Lee's Chief Engineer, Colonel W. P. Smith, sent out for the purpose. The position ran from below the unfinished railroad, on the left, to a point three-quarters of a mile north of the Turnpike, then curved back along Colin Run. It was extended further north as far as the vicinity of Banks' Ford by a line of rifle pits. While the work was progressing, Anderson waited for McLaws' Division to come up to support and strengthen his defense.

Toward evening Lee received a message from Stuart that four and a half hours earlier, or about 2 P.M., three Federal Corps had crossed the Rapidan at Germanna and Ely's Fords, headed southeast. Stuart probably meant that the reported corps had *completed* the crossing; if Lee so interpreted the message, he would know that the heads of their columns had reached Chancellorsville early in the afternoon, if not sooner. No more time was to be lost. Lee's decision was to attack, and the orders to put his army into position were quickly made ready.

Lee now knew for a positive fact that Hooker had divided his army, where most of its elements were, their objectives (in part), and approximate strength (also in part). It was

MAJOR GENERAL RICHARD H. ANDERSON, C.S.A.

at that point that he had decided once more to take another
of his famous calculated risks and leave Jubal Early with
10,000 men, his own division reenforced by Barksdale's
Brigade of McLaw's Division, on the Fredericksburg
heights to oppose Sedgwick's vastly superior force; reverse
Anderson's direction to move on Chancellorsville; send Mc-
Laws at once to Anderson's support at Salem Church; and
start Jackson's Corps (less Early's Division) of 30,000 men
on the march to Chancellorsville, to reenforce Anderson
and McLaws; and take command of the battle.

Lee's decision was a courageous one, in the Lee tradition.
His army had already been divided by the detachment of
one corps commander and two divisions to Suffolk. It was
further potentially divided by the danger that Stuart's
cavalry might be cut off by Hooker's right wing. Who but
Robert E. Lee would have had the strategic insight and
moral courage to assume the heavy risk of further dividing

his forces? On the other hand, who but he had such perfect confidence in his officers and men and such calm assurance that with God's blessing all would be well?

With unerring instinct, despite the fully recognized and seemingly overpowering threat to his left rear, Lee chose the offensive and elected to attack in the direction of the greater danger, while he turned his back on Sedgwick's threat without the slightest trace of panic or sense of being cornered. Nor is it deprecatory to the reputation of other great army commanders to remark that not one out of ten would have had the courage or wisdom to make the same decision under similar circumstances.

Never had Lee's exquisite skill and sense of timing been better demonstrated than on this occasion. His ability to utilize to his own advantage and the discomfiture of his opponent the time, space, and psychological factors that are so essential in planning and executing the movements of large military forces, was again to be revealed in what many historians have proclaimed to be his greatest victory —the Battle of Chancellorsville.

His strategy was simple and easily understood. He would hold Banks' Ford to keep Hooker's army divided, entertain Sedgwick with a small holding force, and move to attack the main threat by bearding the larger part of the Union army in the Wilderness den.

Stuart Rejoins Lee

Lee need not have worried overly, when he directed Stuart to rejoin the main army, about Stuart's ability to do so. But the cavalry leader's task would have been more difficult, if not impossible, had it not been for Stoneman's apathy. After crossing the Rappahannock on April 29, Stoneman's corps had bivouacked in two areas: Averell's division a few miles west of Kelly's Ford in the direction of Brandy Station; Stoneman's column at Madden, five miles northwest of Germanna Ford. Before splitting into two columns, Stoneman had called all his commanders together to give them final instructions, which caused further delay and should have been thoroughly understood before the corps left Warrenton Junction. Stoneman still had much to learn if he wished to compete with the fast-thinking, fast-moving Jeb Stuart and the two Lees.

Stuart's mission was a complicated one. Lee had directed

MAJOR GENERAL J. E. B. STUART, C.S.A.

him to take the greatest care not to be cut off by Hooker's advancing divisions in his effort to return to the army. At the same time he was told to protect public property, presumably against Stoneman's raid, and concurrently, as he marched to rejoin, to impede the progress of the Federal column crossing at Germanna Ford. This was a large order for such a small cavalry force as Stuart had under him, but his energetic actions did cause some annoyance without actually interfering with the progress of Slocum's column.

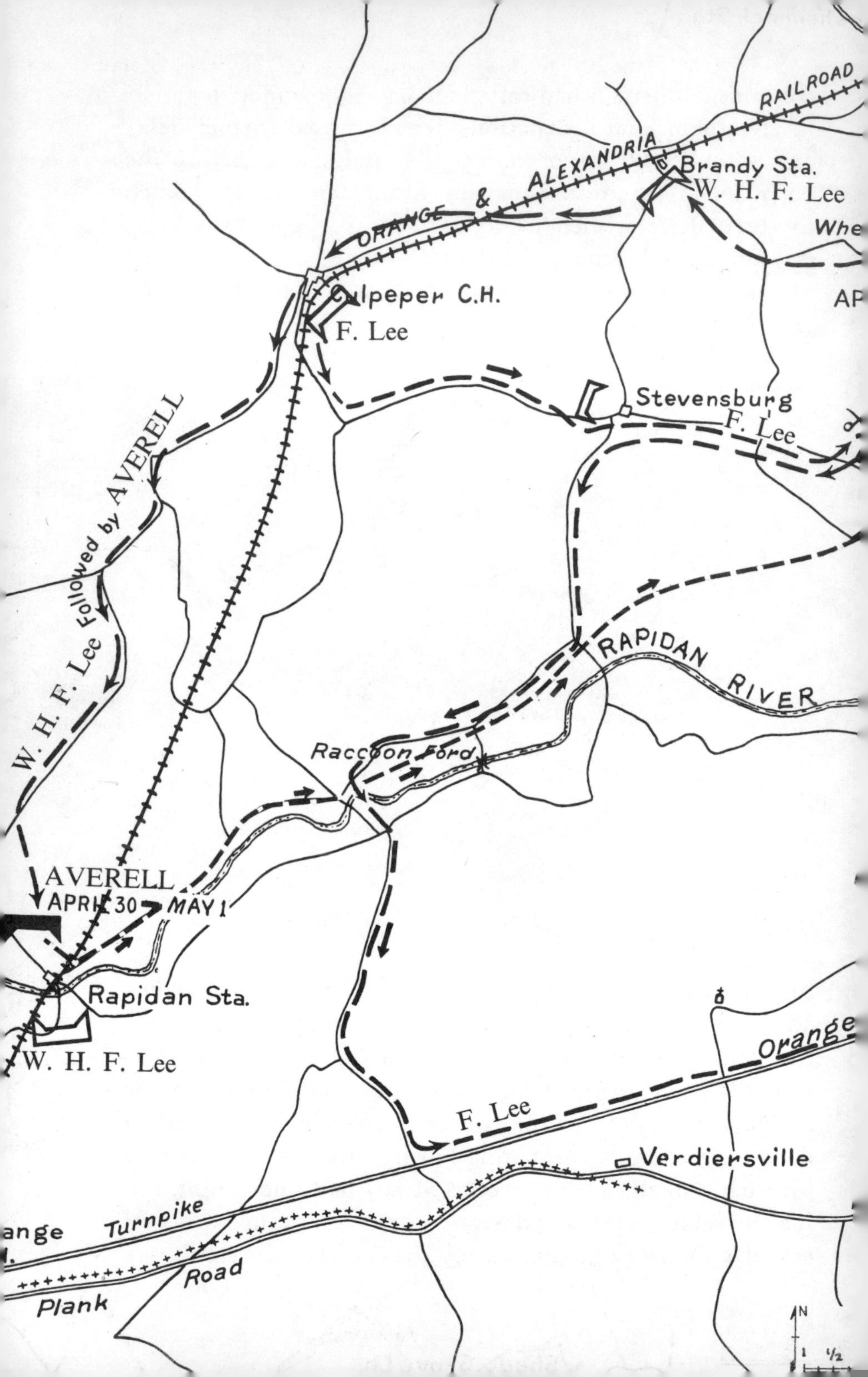

RAILROAD

ORANGE & ALEXANDRIA

Brandy Sta.
W. H. F. Lee

Whe

AP

Culpeper C.H.
F. Lee

Stevensburg
F. Lee

W. H. F. Lee Followed by AVERELL

RAPIDAN RIVER

Raccoon Ford

AVERELL
APRIL 30 — MAY 1

Rapidan Sta.

W. H. F. Lee

Orange

F. Lee

Verdiersville

Orange   Turnpike

Plank   Road

N

1   ½

MAP 11. MOVEMENTS OF CONFEDERATE CAVALRY, APRIL 29-MAY 1, 1863

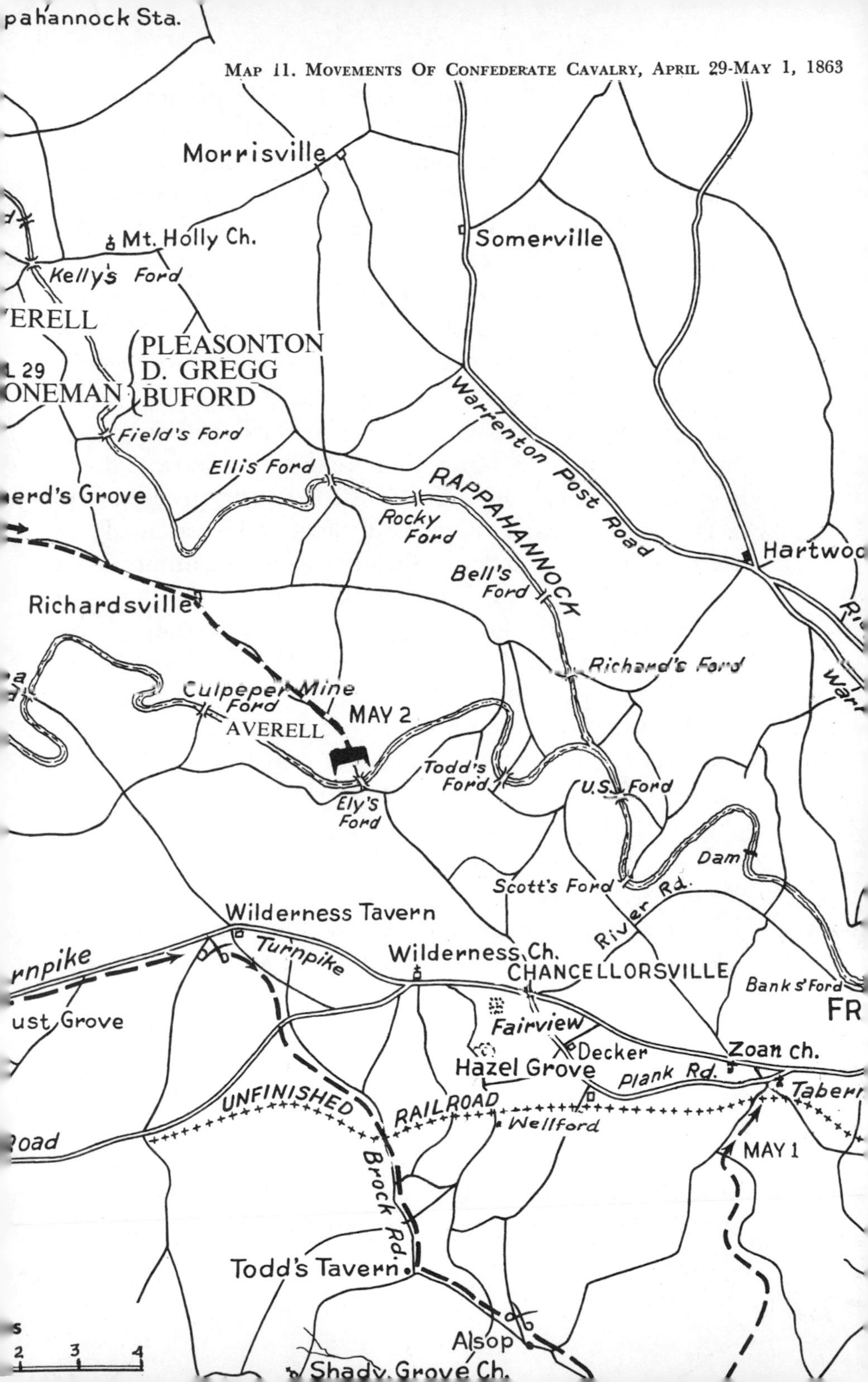

Morrisville

Somerville

Mt. Holly Ch.

Kelly's Ford

ERELL

L 29

ONEMAN

PLEASONTON
D. GREGG
BUFORD

Field's Ford

Ellis Ford

Warrenton Post Road

RAPPAHANNOCK

erd's Grove

Rocky Ford

Bell's Ford

Hartwoo

Richardsville

Richard's Ford

Culpeper Mine Ford

AVERELL

MAY 2

Todd's Ford

U.S. Ford

Ely's Ford

Dam

Scott's Ford

River Rd.

Wilderness Tavern

Turnpike

Wilderness Ch.

CHANCELLORSVILLE

Banks' Ford

FR

rnpike

ust Grove

Fairview

Decker

Hazel Grove

Plank Rd.

Zoan ch.

Taberr

UNFINISHED

RAILROAD

Wellford

MAY 1

oad

Brock Rd.

Todd's Tavern

Alsop

Shady Grove Ch.

s

2   3   4

Stuart assigned to Rooney Lee's Brigade the mission of covering Gordonsville and, to the extent practicable, of protecting the Orange and Alexandria Railroad, which would probably involve him with at least a part of Stoneman's cavalry. General R. E. Lee, at the time he directed Stuart's return, still feared that Hooker's purpose was to strike for Gordonsville, which led him to wire repeated messages to Richmond urging the dispatch of any force that might be available from that point to Gordonsville.

Stuart himself, with Fitzhugh Lee's Brigade, would march at once to the Rapidan, cross at Raccoon Ford, delay the Federal infantry, and then rejoin Lee's army. Lee's Brigade crossed on the night of April 29 and proceeded to carry out its mission. One real effort only was made in strength to effect a delay of Slocum's Federal column. That was when Fitz Lee's Brigade blocked the road with a part of his cavalry and attacked the Federals as they passed Wilderness Tavern, but Slocum detached a couple of regiments to dispose of the Confederates and kept going. Learning about that time that Meade's corps had already reached Chancellorsville Stuart directed Lee's small detached holding force to fall back on Anderson's infantry at Salem Church while he, with the main portion of Lee's Brigade, took a round-about route via Todd's Tavern and Spotsylvania Court House on his way to join up with the army.

It was bright moonlight when the brigade reached Todd's Tavern, where at Stuart's suggestion the troops went into bivouac for the night while he and his staff rode on to report to army headquarters. Stuart's party had traveled only a short distance when they ran into the Sixth New York Cavalry, 350 strong, under Lieutenant Colonel Duncan McVicar, sent by General Pleasonton on a night reconnaissance to learn what they could of the enemy dispositions, and on the off chance they might be able to destroy Confederate supplies believed to be stored at Spotsylvania Court House.

While Jeb Stuart and his staff galloped back to Lee's Brigade to rouse them to action, the Federal regiment pulled off the road and drew up in line in Hugh Alsop's field. The Fifth Virginia Cavalry came pelting down the road to find them, and as the Confederates passed, Mc-Vicar's troopers charged them in the rear, firing from the saddle, captured some prisoners, and moved on to the road junction to protect their return route. Here they were charged in turn by the Third Virginia Cavalry and there occurred a lively little fight, with Federal and Confederate units hopelessly intermingled in the shadows caused by the woods along the side of the road. Finally unscrambling themselves, the several regiments pulled apart to reorganize. The Sixth New York, minus its commander, who was killed in the charge, and their prisoners who had managed to escape in the confusion, made their way back to Chancellorsville. With a number of killed and wounded in each outfit the honors were even, and in due course Fitz Lee's Brigade continued on its way to rejoin the main army.

Major von Borcke, the big Prussian who was a member of Stuart's staff and very outspoken, was with Stuart on this adventure and frankly described the confusion that the charge of the New York cavalry caused in the Confederate ranks. He said that for once Stuart's troopers refused to obey their officers and galloped wildly off in all directions. As to the value of the Federal reconnaissance, the regiment was able to report only that it had driven through a body of enemy cavalry without being able to state whether the troops were alone or part of a larger force, for the prisoners had all made good their escape. The information turned in was therefore inconclusive, but may have had the effect of making Hooker even more cautious, if that were possible.

A Lull in the Fighting

Chapter 9

WEIGHED IN THE BALANCE

HOOKER KEPT his plans so secret that even his chief signal officer was not told what would be expected of him and could therefore take no precautions to spot the necessary material to keep his wire communications open in case of damage from artillery fire. Truly the Chancellorsville campaign, for the Federals, was a case of the right hand not knowing what the left was doing, and vice versa. Under such uncertain circumstances, whatever instructions the signal officer may have issued to his signal personnel must have lacked both clarity and conviction. All that the observers could do was to report what they saw, when the fog and rain would permit, with little idea of its importance or significance. The inevitable result, human nature being what it is, would be apathetic execution of orders that probably appeared routine to the men.

Great pains had been taken by the Federal Signal Corps to install flag signal stations on their side of the Rappahannock, and there is evidence that these were used to advantage, although perhaps not as extensively as they might have been. The field telegraph line between Butterfield's headquarters at Falmouth and United States Mine Ford rendered efficient service except for delays in restoring the line when it failed; and Professor Lowe's two captive balloons opposite Fredericksburg were up and down like jumping jacks on April 29 and 30, sending in frequent items of accurate intelligence with what the aeronauts messaged as from "Balloon in the Air."

The most portentous news came from "Hill and Brooks," at Sedgwick's headquarters dated April 29, 1863—3:30 P.M., addressed to Captain Cushing, Chief Signal Officer. The message from these signal men stated that "about 8,000 or 10,000 infantry and four batteries, followed by an ammunition train and ambulances, have just passed along in the direction of Fredericksburg, opposite this point." That would be part of Jackson's Corps, probably Early's Division, but it is impossible to determine how Hooker evaluated the information or whether it had an influence on his action in summoning Sickles' corps on April 30 and Reynolds' corps the following day, from Sedgwick's wing to Chancellorsville to augment the growing force that Hooker was concentrating at the latter point.

Visibility on April 29 had been good all through the afternoon, with the result that at Fredericksburg both the balloon observers and signal stations kept Butterfield informed of enemy movements, as the Confederates reacted to Sedgwick's demonstration and partial crossing of the river. Professor Lowe reported such interesting happenings as the movement of enemy wagon trains to the rear; the apparent strength of the units that were visible; the forward movement of two infantry regiments from the Fredericksburg heights into the rifle pits opposite Sedgwick's bridgehead troops; and other information of solid value to Sedgwick and Hooker, if correctly evaluated and utilized.

The following orders had issued from Hooker's headquarters on the afternoon of April 30:

To Benham: to secretly take up two bridges, at Franklin's and Fitzhugh's Crossings respectively, during the night and move them to Banks' Ford before daylight. This order was consistent with the initial instructions to the right wing to advance beyond Chancellorsville for the purpose of uncovering Banks' Ford, but which had not yet been accomplished.

To Sickles (12:30 P.M.): to march to United States Mine Ford and cross by 7:00 A.M. May 1. Two additional pontoon bridges had already been laid for the use of his Third Corps.

To Sedgwick: if the enemy should expose a weak point, attack and destroy him; if he appears to be falling back, pursue him by the Bowling Green and Telegraph roads.

To Gibbon: be ready to move at daylight to rejoin his corps (Couch's).

To further confuse the situation for Sedgwick, Chief-of-Staff Butterfield in a letter to Sedgwick quoted Hooker as having told him that when he (Hooker) left Chancellorsville (presumably on the morning of May 1), he expected, if there should be no serious opposition, to reach the heights west of Fredericksburg by noon or shortly after; if opposed strongly, then by nightfall.

That certainly sounded as though the Army Commander intended to act on the offensive, but the letter is a direct contradiction of Hooker's well-advertised attitude of defense in his latest instructions to the corps commanders of the right wing.

[164]

An Exciting Chess Game

For serious students of military strategy who are equally thoughtful chess players, an interesting analogy comes readily to mind. The game at Chancellorsville between Lee and Hooker started with quite a few of Lee's chessmen missing, for example a bishop, a knight, and half of his pawns. The disparity may be accounted for by the absence of Longstreet and half his corps, Stuart's reduced strength, and the manpower and supply handicaps under which the Army of Northern Virginia suffered by comparison with its opponent, which already enjoyed a greater than two to one ratio of infantry, artillery, and cavalry strength and a vastly greater replacement potential in all categories. In turn this meant that Hooker could anticipate men and equipment fillers at a faster rate than Lee. The kings, queens, and rooks may be considered intact for both contestants for the purpose of the game, which would thus narrow down to a test of the skill and abilities of the two players

In the early stages of this symbolic test of skill the champion, who had consistently bested or stalemated a whole series of challengers since the series started, suddenly discovered that his latest opponent had succeeded in maneuvering his own chessmen into a very advantageous position. Despite the fact that neither player had as yet taken any of his opponent's men, the champion was in imminent danger of being checkmated in a few more moves. It was a tense situation in an exciting game, and the champ had rarely found himself so close to defeat as at that moment. But moments of crisis were no novelty to Lee, whose level headwork and calm refusal to be mentally stampeded again stood him in good stead at this nerve-wracking stage of the contest.

Lee Makes a Bold Decision

On April 30 Lee was faced with a critical situation in which almost half of Hooker's large army was on his left rear, the Wilderness the only real obstacle at its back. The other half was either at Fredericksburg, part of it having already crossed to threaten his main position; at the lower fords; en route to augment the Chancellorsville wing; or ranging about the country in rear of him (Stoneman's cavalry). Depending on mobile reinforcements, either of the threats to his right and left could conceivably be as strong in men and guns as Lee's entire army, for Hooker had sufficient manpower to divide his army with impunity, at least against an ordinary opponent. Lee's problem was to evolve a plan that would neutralize the almost overwhelming odds that confronted him!

Lee's estimate, made deliberately, was prophetic of the historic announcement of Marshal Ferdinand Foch, Commander of the French Army and later Generalissimo of the Allied Armies in World War I, when in 1918 he calmly informed his colleagues: "My right has been crushed; my left has been driven in; I shall attack with my center!"

An anachronous paraphrasing of the Foch gem might have put thoughts such as these in Lee's mind: "My left has been turned; my right faces destruction from a powerful Union force; my communications are threatened by an enemy cavalry corps; I shall attack!"

Of course it wasn't that desperate for Lee at Chancellorsville on April 30, 1863, because neither his right nor his left had fired more than a few musket shots in anger. But the strategic result of Hooker's flank march had already foreshadowed for the Union army, without bloodshed, an infinitely greater potential gain than Burnside's disastrous and costly rushes at Fredericksburg. The sad fact, for the North, that all of the advantages initially gained were to be thrown away by Hooker's amazing reversal, detracts no whit from his early achievement.

It is a remarkable tribute to Lee's strong character that his equanimity was not even ruffled when confronted with a fait accompli at the hands of a hostile army that outnumbered his own more than two to one. The enemy had just surprised him by a masterly flank march, that, with early reinforcements, had succeeded in placing a huge body of troops on the left rear of his 60,000, wedging him into an area not over ten miles long and three to four miles wide, with powerful forces on his front and rear. While at this stage Lee had not been able to determine the exact position of all seven of Hooker's infantry corps, he was fully aware that Hooker was short of close-in cavalry and, despite the ticklish position in which he found himself, probably reasoned that Hooker knew less about him than he did about Hooker.

Comparing Lee and Hooker

In comparing Robert E. Lee and Joseph Hooker at Chancellorsville, it matters little that one had been an army commander for a much longer period than the other. Both were graduates of West Point and professional officers in the pre-Civil War Regular Army. Both had served creditably in the War with Mexico and the rise of both to positions of responsibility in the opposing armies was a matter of public record. The outcome of the test between them at Chancellorsville would turn on the character of the two men. Either might have won that battle if the result had depended solely on strategic or tactical ability, the competence of corps and division commanders, the morale and fighting ability of the men in the ranks, and on other military factors or combinations of factors. Nevertheless, in the final analysis Chancellorsville was a battle of wits between the two commanders, and all else pales into insignificance when the events of late April and early May 1863 are studied. The conclusion is inescapable. Hooker lost his nerve!

The sense of urgency that animated Hooker during the first three days of the campaign had strangely given way to a spate of cautious second thoughts. If he suddenly had a foreboding it was with considerable justification. He may have recalled memories of Second Manassas, Antietam, and Fredericksburg, with their well-etched impressions of the manner in which, on those three eventful occasions, Lee had seemingly done the impossible and fought the stronger Army of the Potomac to defeat or a standoff.

So far as Hooker could tell there was yet no indication that Lee had decided to retreat, as he had so confidently predicted. The conditions for the enemy's flight had now been fulfilled, but instead of conforming the Confederates had shown no such indication in their deliberate withdrawal before the advancing Federal hordes at Chancellorsville.

Compounding Hooker's lack of information, the Confederates had learned how to make practical use of concealment and night marches. The early morning fog on May 1, together with the fact that the march of Jackson's Corps and McLaw's Division was partly made under cover of darkness, combined to effect a major tactical change that shifted Lee's center of balance from Fredericksburg to Tabernacle Church, without the Federals knowing what was transpiring.

If there is such a thing in military experience as strategic agoraphobia, Hooker displayed the symptoms by his unaccountable disposition to keep his right wing in the Wilderness, despite the overwhelming desire of his corps commanders to get their troops onto maneuverable terrain as quickly as they could. Perhaps Hooker reasoned that if he couldn't maneuver in the thick woods neither could Lee; hence he would revert to the defensive, occupy a strong position under cover, and encourage Lee to attack him on the ground that he had chosen, "where certain destruction awaits him." The evidence seems to bear out that assumption. It is even possible that Hooker's halfhearted advance from the Wilderness late on the morning of May 1 was more for the record than a bona fide offensive gesture.

Thus Hooker was willing to allow Lee the doubtful

alternative of committing suicide, but what he really expected was that his outmaneuvered opponent would adopt the logical course and retire posthaste to the line of the North Anna River.

It would appear that Hooker never learned that command of an army involved the capacity and wisdom to delegate authority to a limited number of subordinates and to give them their heads within the framework of the army plan. Once committed, the army commander can do little to influence the outcome of the battle other than by use of his reserves at the appropriate time.

In the Confederate army, a different situation existed. One of Lee's most characteristic and, to his several lieutenants, endearing traits, was a generous, self-restrained readiness to permit a large measure of discretion and self-determination to his corps commanders, even to the extent of giving their views far more latitude and influence than was good for either Lee or themselves. By contrast, Hooker apparently did not trust anyone but himself, and even that self-confidence was to fail him when confronted with his big decision at Chancellorsville, as he frankly admitted to a friend some years after the war.

Hooker mistakenly felt that he must hold all the reins tightly in his own hands. Advice from his corps commanders was neither sought nor welcomed when offered, as in Pleasonton's case. In fact he played his cards so closely to his chest that no one, not even his own staff, was given any more information on his over-all plan than was absolutely necessary, and that only in grudging, fragmentary form that made it difficult for the corps commanders to interpret simply and accurately. Even his second-in-command, General Couch, who would have the responsibility of carrying out the plan if anything should happen to Hooker, was not advised of his intentions until the last moment, and then only because he had to be told and not for the purpose of securing coordination of effort.

A combined order to all wing and corps commanders would seem to have been the natural and wise thing to do, but that was not in the Hooker character. Instead, Slocum (and Meade), Couch, Sedgwick, and Stoneman were each given separate instructions, none knowing the mission of the others. More battles have been lost than won because cooperation between friendly elements was lacking; it would be so at Chancellorsville, as at Gettysburg two months later, although the beneficiaries would not be the same army in both cases.

No one who has ever been under fire during combat, whether on land, sea, or in the air, will deny that at such times a soldier's true character is revealed. Then it is that the men are separated from the boys, in a positive way that cannot be misunderstood by their fellow soldiers. There is no time to dissemble or play a part; death may strike at any moment, and under such tense conditions a man's soul is bared and his true character nakedly revealed by what he says and does or does not do.

The principal difference between the man in the ranks and the general of the army at such times is the extent to which the individual's attitude and actions influence and have impact on the lives and fortunes of others. The cowardly soldier who dares not face death, but chooses to drop into a convenient shell hole while his companions go forward in the face of enemy fire, may or may not influence the course of the battle. But the captain, or colonel, or general, who is deficient in moral or physical courage, bears the awful responsibility of the lives of hundreds of thousands of his fellowmen who depend on him and are sworn to obey his orders.

In Hooker's case, it was not the fear of battle that made him pause, for he had seen plenty of combat, but a psychological roadblock that he probably could not explain even to himself. When the critical moment arrived to put everything to the test by going the last mile, his courage failed him as he timidly holed up in the Wilderness and mentally shifted the responsibility for the major effort to Sedgwick's corps, the only troops that he had allowed to remain at Fredericksburg.

Hooker Greatly Overrated

Enough has been said in pointing out Hooker's shortcomings and deficiencies. One incident only may be added from the testimony of a distinguished Federal cavalry general, James H. Wilson, which raised a serious question as to the quality of Hooker's moral and personal courage. This went far beyond the established fact that his character left much to be desired and that it had been his practice to try to advance his own fortunes by belittling fellow generals and organizations other than his own.

The story told by General Wilson illustrated an inferior sense of loyalty to the best interests of the cause for which Hooker was fighting. It had to do with the occasion at the Battle of Antietam when Hooker was wounded. Wilson wrote that Hooker's corps on the Federal right flank was being roughly handled by the Confederates when Hooker received a slight wound in the sole of one foot. Going to the rear, the corps commander was urged by his associates to return to the front in an ambulance or, better yet, on a stretcher for the purpose of restoring the shattered morale of his troops and encouraging them to renewed efforts. Hooker's answer, wrote Wilson, was that he was too badly wounded for that. Yet ten days later he was seen walking on the wounded foot in Washington. The implication was obvious.

Hooker was not charged with a lack of physical courage, only moral courage. His fighting reputation had been built on his record as a division and corps commander. The aggressive traits he displayed early in the war were still apparent when he planned and carried into successful execution the magnificent turning movement which placed three corps on Lee's left rear at Chancellorsville. What happened at that stage was to prove the turning point in the campaign, the decisive factor in all that followed, and was to give Lee the opportunity to fight and win his greatest victory. Hooker lost his nerve. It was as simple as that.

IN THE VAN—CONFEDERATE CAVALRY

LEE-JACKSON COUNCIL, NIGHT OF MAY 1

CHAPTER 10

THE ARMIES MEET HEAD ON

VITAL time was slipping away for the Federals on the morning of Friday, May 1 as Hooker continued, hour after hour, to mark time in the Wilderness while Lee concentrated his army at Tabernacle Church to meet the Federal threat. Every minute counted, but Hooker had made up his mind not to advance until Sickles' corps should arrive, despite the fact that he had already massed 54,000 men at Chancellorsville and, when Sickles' three divisions would come up, at any moment, his strength would exceed 70,000.

May 1 had dawned clear and cool as the men of the right wing of the Army of the Potomac pulled themselves up from the hard ground and gathered around their campfires to absorb some heat in their chilled bodies. Hooker's army was still resting in the woods and clearings around Chancellorsville, while the generals of corps and divisions waited impatiently for their commanding general to give them the signal to get started on the road to Fredericksburg and out of the dense wilderness that imprisoned them and hampered their movements.

It would be only a question of a few hours until the opposing forces would clash somewhere between Chancellorsville and Fredericksburg. Confederate division commander McLaws had marched at midnight April 30 to Anderson's support on the Tabernacle Church ridge, while Jackson's Corps (less Early's Division) left their bivouacs during the night and were well on their way towards Chancellorsville before daylight.

By this time Lee was pretty well informed as to the strength and dispositions of the divided Federal army. His cavalry had functioned with its usual energy and resourcefulness, so that he knew at least the outline of the positions occupied by the enemy at Chancellorsville. Hooker, on the other hand, having dissipated his major means of mounted reconnaissance, was only vaguely aware of what was in front of him. The reports that had reached him the preceding day from Sedgwick had proven somewhat contradictory, but gave the impression that Lee's main body was still within its established lines west of Fredericksburg, as in fact it was.

There was even the possibility that Lee had been reenforced at Fredericksburg, if Hooker believed the rumor that Sedgwick had passed along, to the effect that Longstreet's two missing divisions had arrived from Suffolk. It seems that several Confederate "deserters" (doubtless under instructions from Jackson) had voluntarily entered the Federal lines below Fredericksburg and given out the information, to which some credence was given by the heavy movement of Confederate troops and trains that had been observed during the afternoon of April 30 by the Federal balloons and signal stations.

Hooker was clearly failing to give proper consideration to the seriousness of Lee's critical position between Hooker's own strong troop buildup at Chancellorsville and Sedgwick's large concentration at Fredericksburg. He seemed strangely reluctant to exploit the important advantage accruing from the favorable fact that his pincers had already closed the gap between his two wings from forty to not more than ten miles. Somewhere between the pincer's jaws were Lee and his 60,000 men, the potential victims of a crushing pressure from front and rear if only Hooker would shake off his odd lethargy and move confidently to finish what had been so beautifully initiated and executed up to the time of his halt order in the Wilderness.

Lee's intentions, as distinct from his actions, were apparently beyond Hooker's capacity to fathom, for the latter was still vacillating on the morning of May 1. He had received telegraphic reports from the Signal Corps that large enemy troop columns were observed about 9 A.M., moving rapidly west from Fredericksburg. The early morning fog had thinned sufficiently by that time to permit occasional balloon observations, but a light rain had started to fall, which reduced visibility for a time until the sun came out later in the morning, after Jackson's Corps had pretty well completed its night march. Coupled with the planted rumor that Longstreet's two missing divisions had arrived, the additional intelligence seems to have added to Hooker's indecision, for he delayed ordering the advance until about 11 o'clock, by which time more precious hours had been wasted and Jackson given time to unite his corps with the divisions of Anderson and McLaws at Tabernacle Church.

Finally, at 11 A.M., Hooker released to his corps commanders a circular which directed a regrouping of troops to put them on two of the three roads leading to Fredericksburg, essentially as planned by Slocum and Meade the evening before, with this exception: Hooker's circular was static, whereas the corps commanders were thinking dynamically:

The Fifth Corps on the River Road, with its head midway between Mott's Run and Colin Run*, movement to be completed by 2 P.M.

The Twelfth Corps to be massed below the Plank Road, head resting near Tabernacle Church and masked from the view of the enemy by small advanced parties; the movement to be completed by 12 o'clock to enable the Eleventh Corps to take its position.

The Eleventh Corps to be masked [sic] on the Plank Road, one mile in rear of the Twelfth, its movement to be completed at 2 o'clock.

1 division of the Second Corps to take position at Todd's Tavern and to throw out strong detachments on the approaches in the direction of the enemy. The other divisions of the corps to be massed out of the road near Chancellorsville.

The Third Corps to be massed on the United States Ford road about 1 mile from Chancellorsville, as fast as it should arrive, except for one brigade which would take position at Dowdall's Tavern (on the turnpike 2½ miles west of Chancellorsville).

General Pleasonton to hold his cavalry command at Chancellorsville.

The circular ended with the remark: "After the movement commences, headquarters will be at Tabernacle Church."

It is possible that Hooker had issued oral orders earlier than 11 A.M., the hour at which his circular was authenticated, for Meade's report states that the movement actually commenced about 11 A.M. Also, Hooker's circular does not mention the fact that Sykes' division of Meade's corps was to advance initially on the Turnpike, until after it had crossed Mott's Run. Thereafter Sykes was supposed to

_____

* Open country southwest of Banks' Ford. Editor.

move to the left, deploy, and open communication with Griffin on his left and Slocum on his right. None of this beautiful coordination was effected, however, as Sykes ran into the Confederates when he had advanced not more than a mile.

Hooker later testified before the Committee on the Conduct of the War that the above orders were in conformity with his intention of advancing for the purpose of uncovering Banks' Ford to shorten communications between the two wings of his army. It will, however, be noted that there was no intimation, in the phraseology of the orders or in Hooker's testimony, that he was going out to attack the enemy. If the English language means anything, all Hooker was telling his generals in this circular was that they were to place their troops in certain advanced positions. If Hooker had developed any sort of an operational plan in his own mind, there is no indication of it in the circular; no attack mission, no instructions to occupy a defensive line, no orders on what to do when the troops should reach the new positions. Even the closing sentence was ambiguous in stating that army headquarters would be at Tabernacle Church "after the movement commences." What movement was Hooker talking about—the shift of troops to the new position or a subsequent advance? The latter might possibly have been deduced by the corps commanders, since the designated command post was in front of the assigned position of the massed troops. But army commanders should not have to depend on crystal balls for the interpretation of their orders by subordinates. In point of fact, the Confederates were actually occupying the area around Tabernacle Church at the time Hooker issued the circular. It was a strange document for an army commander to issue under the circumstances, and the effect on the recipients can only be imagined. Conversely, they may have reasoned that half a loaf was better than no bread—at least some of them would be clear of the Wilderness!

Stonewall Jackson reached Tabernacle Church in advance of his 30,000 men at 8 A.M. May 1 to find 16,000 other troops under Anderson and McLaws, busily engaged in fortifying their position, a north-south line on a low ridge that ran for three miles from Duerson's Mill (see

MAJOR GENERAL LAFAYETTE McLAWS, C.S.A.

Map 12) on the right, to the unfinished railroad below the Plank Road on the left. This line cut across and effectively blocked Hooker's route from Chancellorsville to Fredericksburg by the three available roads.

Jackson's decision was reached almost immediately; to disregard the entrenching job and advance on Chancellorsville. His plan contemplated the withdrawal of Wilcox's Brigade from Banks' Ford and Perry's Brigade from opposite Falmouth, for Jackson's thought was to advance his whole force to the attack, and that included all the troops under his temporary command. Jackson had his occasional blind spots; the decision would have resulted in his playing right into Meade's hands if Hooker had just kept hands off. When Lee came up a few hours later, he noted the mistake and promptly corrected it by returning Wilcox's Brigade to Banks' Ford.

Aside from the fact that Jackson's instinct was offensive, he was thoroughly aware of the possibility that Sedgwick might break through Early's thin line at Fredericksburg, and was anything but intrigued with the idea of fighting in two directions at once. Two hours were required for his troops to form, and it was eleven o'clock before the advance got underway, Fitz Lee's cavalry brigade covering the left flank in the woods. Anderson's Division took the lead with one brigade on the Turnpike and two on the Plank Road, both preceded by a strong cavalry regiment and infantry skirmishers who were spread well out. McLaws' Division followed with Anderson's two remaining brigades, marching on the Turnpike, while the three divisions of Jackson's Corps, commanded respectively by Rodes, A. P. Hill, and Colston, followed by the main body of the artillery, took the Plank Road behind Anderson.

The two armies at this point were separated by a distance of not more than six miles. They could, therefore, be expected to meet head-on in a matter of two hours or less, either in column on the Turnpike or Plank Road, or in the fields and woods on either side, depending on how rapidly the leading elements would deploy in extended order. The situation had all the earmarks of an interesting meeting engagement fraught with a variety of possibilities. The advantage of numbers rested with the Union forces, but they were uninformed as to either the strength or disposition of the Confederate troops. Consequently they were obliged to advance blindly to a prescribed position without orders either to attack or defend if and when they should run into opposition.

The Confederates, on the other hand, moved out confidently to attack a known foe in a determined effort to repulse and drive him back to the Rapidan. Their commander, for the time being Stonewall Jackson, was marching with them in a position to make the best use of his men instantly and effectively as the battle developed. There would be no dilly-dallying on his part, while the Federal corps commanders, in the circumstances confronting them, would be obligated to send back to Hooker's headquarters at the Chancellor House for orders or they would have to do the best they could, in the absence of on-the-spot decisions, in a fight which inevitably would be as uncoordinated as could possibly be imagined.

The Chancellorsville Terrain

The Battle of Chancellorsville can be a very confusing study unless the reader is careful to orient himself thoroughly by fixing in mind the vitally important road net of which the Chancellorsville crossroads was the center. Equally important are the major reference points and the significant terrain features which played a vital part, such as Fairview, Hazel Grove, the Wilderness Run area, United States Mine and Banks' Fords, Salem Church, the unfinished railroad, and others. It is well also to note the eastern edge of the Wilderness, two to three miles east of Chancellorsville, and examine the character of the countryside between Fredericksburg and Chancellorsville (see Map 12).

The old mansion with its white columns, known as the Chancellor House, sat a few yards back from the Orange Turnpike, facing south in the center of a wide clearing several miles from the eastern edge of the Wilderness. From the crossroads the road that ran north reached a fork one mile from Chancellorsville, at which point two roads angled off; the one to the right curved for four miles to United States Mine Ford, main crossing point for the Federal reinforcements; the one to the left headed almost

CHANCELLORSVILLE IN 1884

This house was built on the site of the one burned during the battle. This photo, however, shows how the farm looked at the time of the battle. The Turnpike runs in front of the house, behind the white fence. The road running away from the reader, beyond the crossroads, goes north toward Bullock's.

straight to Ely's Ford on the Rapidan, less than five miles distant.

To the east the Orange Turnpike ran directly to Fredericksburg past Salem Church, while the Plank Road headed southeast in an arc which curved back to reunite with the Turnpike six miles to the east and a mile or so short of Salem Church. The road to the west was the Orange Turnpike, the key highway upon whose axis much of the bitter fighting occurred.

The other road which led from the crossroads was unimproved, and ran northeast to become the River Road that paralleled the course of the Rappahannock to Fredericksburg.

South of Scott's Dam, at a road fork, the tactically im-

MAP 12. THE ADVANCE TO CONTACT, MAY 1, 1863

This map portrays the situation about 11:30 A.M. Meade's V Corps has marched east on the River Road with two divisions, his third division moving on the Turnpike. Couch, commanding the II Corps, has directed French's division to move from its bivouac just north of Chancellorsville to Todd's Tavern. French got on the road, but the head of his column was halted by the passage of Slocum's XII Corps moving southeast on the Plank Road. Sickles' III Corps bivouacked the previous night at Hamet, two miles southeast of Hartwood Church. At 5 A.M. Sickles moved to U. S. Ford, crossed at 7:30 A.M., and marched to the vicinity of Chandler's (Bullock's). Howard's XI Corps has remained in about the same positions which it occupied late on April 30.

On the Confederate side, the three brigades of Anderson's Division climbed out of the trenches which they had been digging for over twenty-four hours in the Tabernacle Church-Zoan Church area, and started west, Mahone on the Turnpike and Posey and Wright on the Plank Road. Three of McLaws' brigades are following Mahone. The head of Jackson's Corps, moving up from the Hamilton's Crossing area, is just appearing on the Mine Road.

The opening gun of the battle has been fired, and in a few minutes Sykes will be in contact with Mahone.

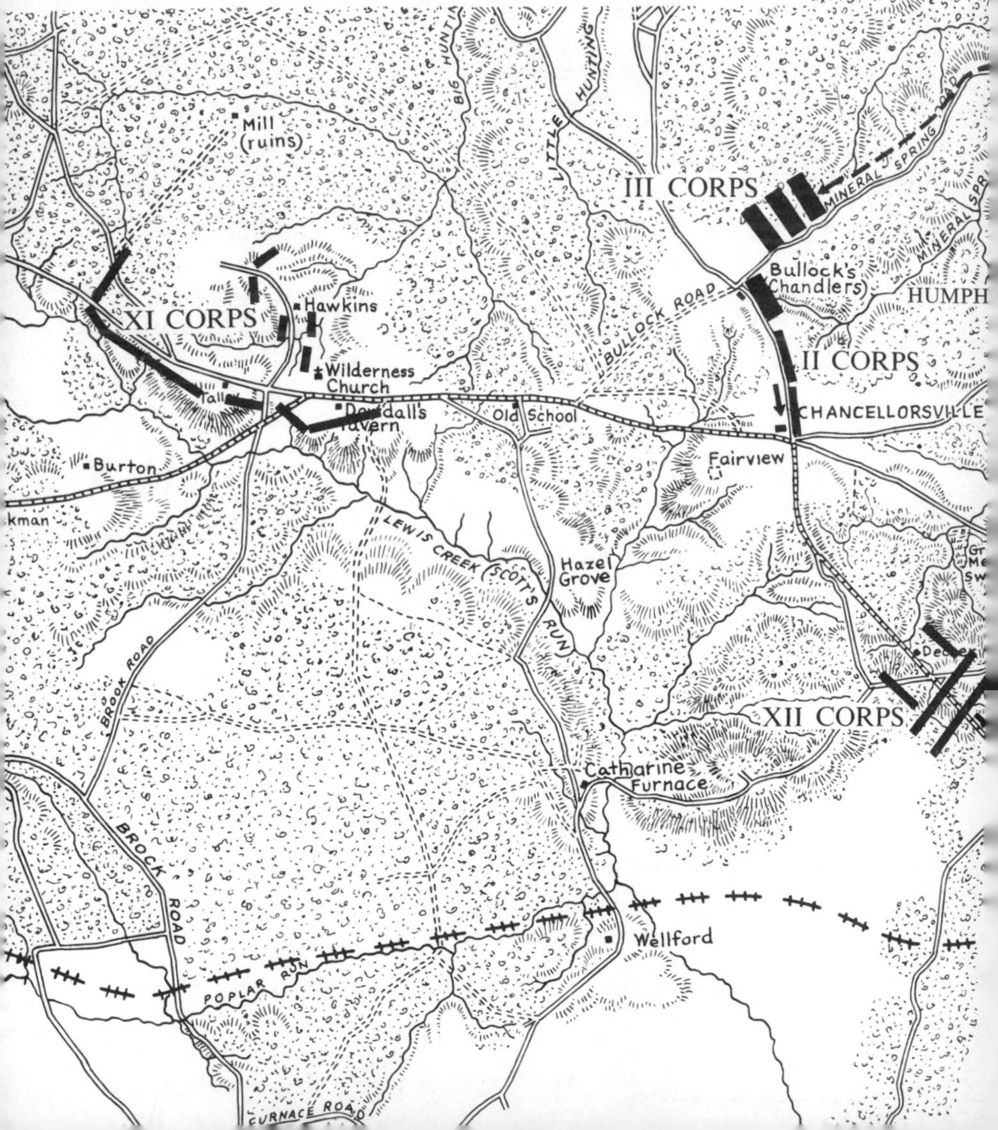

U.S. Mine Ford

PONTOONS

RAPPAHANNOCK

ROCKYPEN CREEK

Scott's Dam

Ballard's Dam

RIVER ROAD

RIVER

PONTOONS

GRIFFIN

Decker

Duerson's Mill

COLIN RUN

MOTT'S RUN

MINE ROAD

ORANGE

Mahone

McLAWS

Kershaw

Wofford

Semmes

ANDERSON

Zoan Church

Wilcox

Perry

PLANK ROAD

Posey

Wright

Tabernacle Church

MINE ROAD

CAVALRY

UNION

CONFEDERATE

N

JACKSON

3/4   1   2

SCALE-MILES

portant Old Mine Road led southeast across open country to Zoan Church* on the Turnpike. Four miles south of the Chancellor House an unfinished railroad, running east and west for some miles, was to play a part in the tactical dispositions of the Confederate forces. The major roles in the battle, other than the Turnpike, would fall to the Plank and Brock Roads winding through the Wilderness to the south; Fairview Plantation, less than a mile west of Chancellorsville; and Hazel Grove, the highest point on the battlefield, a tactical prize about a mile south of the Turnpike.

At the time of the Civil War, when hard-surfaced roads were few and far between, crossroads loomed importantly as strategic objectives because of their logistic and communication value, and as reference points that could be easily and quickly identified. This may have been one of the compelling reasons why the battles of Chancellorsville and Gettysburg were fought where they were.

Contact!

The Confederate column on the right had covered little more than a mile along the Turnpike when its advance cavalry ran into a small force of Federal horsemen, followed closely by a strong body of infantry from Sykes' division of the Fifth Corps. Both outfits deployed promptly, engaged in a sharp fight, and Sykes pressed the Confederates steadily back until he gained the position east of Mott's Run that he had been directed to seize. Jackson acted immediately to aid McLaws on the right, sending in a brigade from the Plank Road. Similar coordination, however, was lacking among the Federal corps commanders, with the result that Sykes, to avoid envelopment of both his flanks, reported his critical salient to Hooker and was told to withdraw in the direction of Chancellorsville.

---

* Also known as Zoar or Zion Church.

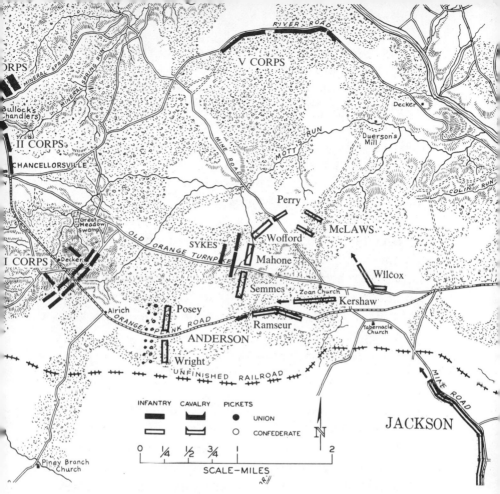

MAP 13. THE CONFEDERATE DEPLOYMENT

This portrays the situation at about 12:30 P.M., May 1, 1863. During the past hour Sykes has driven in the Confederate skirmishers on the Turnpike and is in contact with Mahone's Brigade. On the south flank, although Slocum's two divisions have not advanced, their skirmishers have forced back those of Posey on the Plank Road. Griffin and Humphreys have continued to move slowly northeast on the River Road. The II and III Corps remain in the Chancellorsville-Bullock's area.

On the Confederate side, Wofford and Semmes of McLaws' Division have deployed on either side of Mahone of Anderson's Division. Posey, also of Anderson's Division, has deployed on the south flank with Ramseur's (of Rodes' Division) and Kershaw's (of McLaws') Brigades coming up in support. Perry and Wilcox of Anderson's Division are going into position on the refused north flank, as a consequence of Humphreys' and Griffin's movement having been observed. Jackson himself is at Tabernacle Church, with the head of his corps continuing to advance via the Mine Road. He had sent Ramseur's Brigade of Rodes' Division on ahead to support Anderson.

[185]

The situation developed more slowly on the Plank Road, where Slocum's Twelfth Corps was proceeding with his two divisions abreast. The advance elements encountered Confederate skirmishers almost at once. The Federal divisions thereupon received orders to develop, that is, move from division column into columns of regiments or brigades, from which they could deploy quickly into line. This took almost two hours, so that it was nearly one o'clock when they resumed the advance. It is no wonder Sykes found his flanks in the air, with no supporting Federal troops in contact on either right or left. To meet Slocum's threat to his own left, Stonewall Jackson again reacted promptly to send in a brigade of infantry along the unfinished railroad, which endangered Slocum's right flank and forced his leading elements back on the main body.

While the meeting engagement along the Turnpike and Plank Roads was being fought, the two divisions of Meade's corps on the River Road were advancing with virtually no opposition until they came within two miles of Banks' Ford, the uncovering of which was a major objective of the entire movement. This development afforded a remarkable opportunity for Hooker to exploit what was obviously Lee's weak flank, had he energetically pushed either Couch's two-division corps or Sickles' three-division corps rapidly down the river road in support of Meade, with the mission of turning the enemy right. But Hooker's thoughts were defensive, and no effort was made to exploit Meade's easy progress.

It would appear that Corps Commander Meade was having too easy a time on the River Road, or his system of communications was inadequate. Certainly he did nothing to help Sykes, whose division was part of his own corps, when the former ran into difficulties on the Turnpike. Hooker had a right to expect Meade to maintain a working liaison with all of his divisions and to coordinate their efforts. For all of Meade, Sykes might just as well have been conducting an independent operation all by himself.

It was at 11:30 in the morning that Hooker had issued the following order to Sedgwick's left wing at Fredericksburg, through Chief of Staff Butterfield: "Direct Major General Sedgwick to threaten an attack at full force at 1 o'clock, and to continue in that attitude until further orders. Let the demonstration be as severe as can be, but not an attack."

Obviously Hooker was not yet aware of the fact that most of Lee's army had shifted during the night and was now moving against the advancing divisions of his right wing. Otherwise he would not have issued orders whose purpose could only have been to threaten the Confederates at Fredericksburg and to cause Lee to hold them there rather than to detach them to confront him at Chancellorsville.

Nor was Sedgwick at Fredericksburg any better informed as to the strength of the Confederates on his front. His lack of enterprise in failing to make at least a reconnaissance in force to determine what was before him, after having crossed the Rappahannock, can scarcely be excused on the basis of Hooker's orders, despite their indecisive character. It was certainly his responsibility to feel out the enemy sufficiently to find out whether Jackson's Corps was or was not still on his front. With a bit more aggressiveness, Sedgwick should have ascertained that only 10,000 men, not 40,000, were now occupying a thinly held seven-mile front on the heights west of Fredericksburg. Instead of this he sat tight.

At 12:30 P.M. Butterfield informed Hooker: "The enemy will meet you between Chancellorsville and Hamilton's Crossing. He can not, I judge from all reports, have detached over 10,000 or 15,000 men from Sedgwick's front since sun cleared fog." Yet at the very moment that

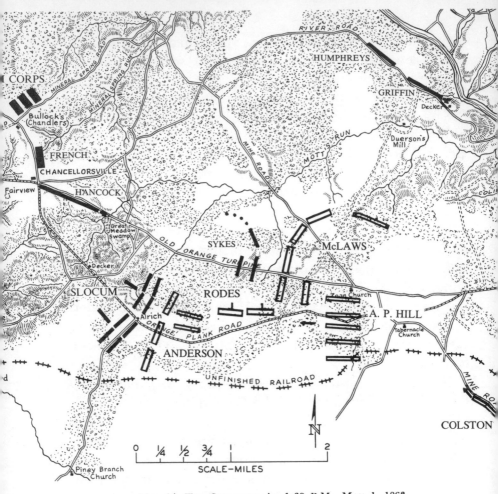

MAP 14. THE SITUATION AT 1:30 P.M., MAY 1, 1863

The Confederate deployment, especially on the south flank, has isolated Sykes and placed him in a precarious position. After Sykes reported this situation to Hooker, now at Chancellorsville, Sykes was ordered to withdraw. Hancock was directed to cover the movement. Slocum, who had advanced about half a mile, was also ordered to pull back to his position of the previous night. After some delay Meade likewise received a message to have Griffin and Humphreys return from their march along the River Road. It was after 5 P.M. before Griffin got the word. By that time he had reached Decker's, within a mile of Bank's Ford. His division and that of Humphreys retraced their steps at a killing pace.

Rodes, advancing west at the head of Jackson's column, has detached Ramseur's Brigade to assist Posey and Wright. He moved the remainder of his division by the right flank from the Plank Road and took up a position on the flank of Sykes, facing north. His division remained here until sunset. A. P. Hill came up in support, and Colston, at the rear of the column, was in reserve.

Butterfield was authenticating that message, Jackson's Corps had met and was pushing back the right wing a couple miles from Chancellorsville.

At 1:30 P.M. Hooker sent word to Slocum, concurrently with his retirement order to Sykes, to call off the advance and return to his former position at Chancellorsville. Howard's Eleventh Corps, ordered to follow Slocum, had scarcely gotten started from camp when it was ordered by Hooker to stand fast. Meade's Fifth Corps was ordered back about 1 P.M., when it seemed apparent to Hooker that his plans had gone awry, but the order failed to reach Meade. A second order followed the first. The latter was delivered to Meade at 3 P.M., when his column had arrived at a point not far from Banks' Ford, almost within reach of his objective. Humphrey's division responded immediately by returning to Chancellorsville at a rapid pace, but Griffin's division did not receive the order until after 5:00 P.M. Evidently realizing by that time that they had been isolated, the units of the division practically double-timed back to the Federal lines, still without being molested by the enemy, who appeared to be devoting all of his attention to the area of the Turnpike and Plank Roads.

General Couch, commanding the Second Corps, had been directed to go to the aid of the advance units, with particular attention to support of the sorely pressed but hard-fighting Sykes. Couch detailed Hancock's division for the job, and as usual Hancock performed handsomely and efficiently. Shortly after Hancock's men were in position, however, Couch received an order from Hooker "to withdraw both divisions to Chancellorsville." Couch has written that on receipt of the order he conferred with Hancock, Sykes, Warren, and others who were present; all agreed that the ground should be held because of its commanding position and the open country in front. Warren even went so far as to suggest to Couch that he should ignore the order, and took it upon himself to ride back to try and persuade Hooker to withdraw it. In the meantime, Slocum's corps had been ordered back, thus exposing Hancock's right, and Couch had no alternative but to carry out the order.

After Sykes' men had passed to the rear through Hancock's newly formed line, the latter complied with the orders to retire, a regiment at a time. By 4:30 P.M. all had withdrawn but two regiments, when Couch received a countermanding order from Hooker to hold his position until 5 P.M. Although no reason was given, Hooker's intention may have been to protect the withdrawal of Griffin's division on the left, but now it was too late. Couch, disgusted with Hooker's vacillations, understandably exploded, advising the courier to take this message back to the commanding general:

> Tell General Hooker he is too late. The enemy are on my right and rear. I am in full retreat.

The depressing effect on the Federal generals can best be described in Couch's own words:

> Proceeding to the Chancellor House, I narrated my operations in front to Hooker, which were seemingly satisfactory, as he said: "It is alright, Couch, I have gotten Lee just where I want him, he must fight me on my own ground." The retrograde movement had prepared me for something of the kind, but to hear from his own lips that the advantages gained by the successful marches of his lieutenants were to culminate in fighting a defensive battle in that nest of thickets, was too much, and I retired from his presence with the belief that my commanding general was a whipped man.

Lee's Instructions to Early

Lee was still on Lee's Hill opposite Fredericksburg on the morning of May 1, after inspecting Early's defensive preparations and before riding west to join Jackson, now in command of all the troops at Tabernacle Church. Lee had told Jackson the evening before that he was to take charge of McLaws' and Anderson's Divisions as well as his own and "make arrangements to repulse the enemy."

Before leaving Marye's Heights, Lee ordered up more artillery in order to give Early powerful gun support. It was vital that the latter's small force of 10,000 men should prevent Sedgwick from crashing through the line while Lee was dealing with Hooker's greatly superior force to the west. There was real danger that Lee's new line, halfway between Fredericksburg and Chancellorsville, might have to face strong attacks from both directions if Early should fail to hold Sedgwick in place. Early was told explicitly that, if forced to retreat, he was to move south; if however the enemy on his front turned out to be merely a diversionary holding force, then Early should send all the men he could spare to join Lee.

Having satisfied himself that everything was shipshape in Early's hands at Fredericksburg, Lee rode down the Plank Road early on the afternoon of May 1 to join Jackson and plan his next move.

Lee is Puzzled

The relative ease with which the Confederates were able to turn back the Federal divisions east of Chancellorsville caused Lee some concern. Could Hooker be baiting a trap that might snap shut if the Confederates should become too venturesome? Was it still possible that Hooker's major objective was Gordonsville after all, in spite of Stuart's positive identifications and the obvious objective, Chancellorsville, towards which his right wing had been headed the preceding day? Could it be that the meeting engagement of May 1 had been engineered by a portion of the right wing while the main body was being diverted on Gordonsville? It seemed improbable that Hooker would have come the long route by Kelly's Ford to Chancellorsville only to back away from Lee and head in the opposite direction, but it was possible.

The truth was that Lee did not know just what troops had crossed at United States Mine Ford, nor the extent to which Hooker had been reinforced. That he was now somewhat puzzled is evidenced by this message to General Stuart:

> Plank Road, 2 miles from
> Chancellorsville
> May 1, 1863, 4 o'clock.
>
> General:
> The captured prisoners agree in stating that this is Meade's corps with which we are now engaged, and that Howard's corps preceded them across the Rapidan, and has taken some other road. This is the only column that we can find in this direction. What has become of the other two?
> Meade appears to be falling back.
> I am, very respectfully yours,
> R. E. Lee,
> General.

It would appear from the above that Slocum's divisions had not become sufficiently engaged on the Plank Road to lose any prisoners, that Howard's corps had not even been spotted in rear of Slocum, and that Hancock's division of Couch's corps had succeeded in extricating Sykes without losing a man to the advancing Confederates. Furthermore, the fact that two of Meade's three divisions, which had almost reached Banks' Ford on the River Road before they were recalled, had entirely escaped Lee's notice, was of itself convincing proof that a golden opportunity was being missed by the Federals in that zone of the potential battlefield.

Jackson's Narrow Escape

As was his custom in the heat of battle, Jackson prowled around the front lines like a bird dog, looking for openings and observing the action of all elements of his command, to the extent possible for a single man on a horse. Meeting engagements were always a challenge to the austere instructor-turned-general, who was a strong believer in the advantages to be gained by personal reconnaissance, which he had so often utilized to ferret out the weak spot in his opponent's armor and then exploit it to the satisfaction of his own troops and the glory of Confederate arms.

About four in the afternoon, when the Federal divisions had withdrawn along the Turnpike and the Plank Road and disappeared from view in the woods, Jackson rode off to the left with an aide to examine the ground south of the Plank Road and to see for himself how his troops on the left were faring. About two miles south of Chancellorsville he met Jeb Stuart with a cavalry regiment in the vicinity of Catharine (Wellford's) Furnace. One of his infantry brigades was in the act of deploying and moving north to gain contact with the Federals. Jackson and Stuart rode ahead to a wooded crest to get a better view of the terrain to the west, but there was little to be seen because of the dense woods. About that time a nearby Confederate battery opened up and in reply received a shattering and well-aimed volley from close-in, concealed Federal batteries, indicating that the Confederates were not to have everything their own way. Canister and shell smothered the knoll upon which Jackson and Stuart were standing, as the terrified artillery horses a few yards off to the right screamed, reared, and fell in their traces. Jackson's aide was mortally hit, but the two generals miraculously escaped untouched. It was too hot a spot in which to linger. Jackson began to have second thoughts about his confident belief that Hooker would be found north of the Rappahannock come morning.

Meanwhile Lee had sent out reconnaissance detachments to ascertain, if possible, what the enemy might be up to at United States Mine Ford and whether the indications were that he intended to make a strong stand on the Chancellorsville line. Jackson's eyes were looking west, where Fitz Lee's cavalry was probing to map out the contours of the Federal line and to uncover any weak spots which might exist.

After Jackson and Stuart had terminated their little adventure to the south, Jackson and his staff joined A. P. Hill to take a look at the situation north of the Turnpike. What he saw there assured him that the Federal retrograde movement had come to an end, but he was still unconvinced that Hooker might not pull out under cover of darkness. Just before dark he galloped back to the Plank Road, followed it to its junction with the Furnace Road and there, at Decker's, met General Lee, who was anxious to talk and consider plans for the morrow.

By nightfall Jackson's troops, advancing steadily with little opposition from the Federals, occupied a line from the Mine Road on the right to Catharine Furnace, almost two miles southwest of Chancellorsville. McLaws' Division occupied the crest which topped the higher ground paralleling Mott Run; Anderson prolonged the line to the left across the Turnpike east of Great Meadow Swamp; while Jackson's Corps, disposed in depth along the Plank Road, bivouacked in the order, Rodes, A. P. Hill, and Colston, from front to rear.

The Meeting in the Woods

The sun had now set and the twilight shadows merged into the darkness of night, a blackness intensified by the density of the woods. The skirmishing was over for the day as Lee and Jackson moved off the crossroad, a particular target of a Federal sharpshooter who had apparently zeroed in during daylight, and was busily sniping from a convenient tree-perch from which the Confederates had had no success in dislodging him.

Moving into the pine thicket a few yards off the road, the two famous generals turned up discarded Federal hardtack boxes and went into a historic huddle from which great events were soon to stem. The flickering light from a campfire threw shadows in the dark woods to provide an eerie setting that drew the curious eyes of the handful of soldiers who can always be found on the outskirts of a conference. When such a meeting occurs in the vicinity of a crossroad close to the front and with such prominent central figures as Robert E. Lee and Stonewall Jackson playing the leading roles, it offers a special attraction.

Jackson reported to Lee that all the information he had been able to gather, coupled with his own observations, indicated that Hooker's left was firmly anchored on the Rappahannock, east of United States Mine Ford, and that the entrenchments along the center of his position were being energetically strengthened by earth parapets and abatis. He knew little about Hooker's right, however, and was waiting for the intelligence that Fitz Lee had been amassing during the afternoon. Jackson ventured to assert that all of Hooker's preparations were merely a cover-up to a planned further withdrawal during the night, but Lee had a different opinion. He just couldn't picture Hooker giving up quite so easily as all that.

As the moon slowly rose, within a few miles of where they sat some 70,000 Union soldiers and 50,000 boys in gray worked and loafed and fed themselves, while the conversation between Lee and Jackson canvassed the possibility of turning the Federal right flank, since the prospects for such a maneuver on the Federal left, so near the Rappahannock, appeared dim.

As they talked, Jeb Stuart rode up, dismounted, and was invited by Lee to join the conference and state what he had learned. Stuart, who had just come from Fitz Lee, with the collected reports of his cavalry scouts, was bursting with news. It seemed that his resourceful brigadier had been carefully feeling out the right of the Federal line, and discovered that it was definitely "in the air," did not extend to the Rapidan, or even rest on any substantial intermediate strong point. From the cavalry observations it was clearly apparent that the Federals expected danger chiefly from the south, for their right was but slightly refused north of the Turnpike and no Federal cavalry had been encountered in strength. The picture was almost too good to be true!

Lee and Jackson exchanged glances. It was good news that Stuart brought, and the case for a flank maneuver became a determination in the minds of the two leaders. After that the words tumbled fast. There had to be a road that would lead beyond the Federal right, it couldn't be too long, and it must be under cover. Secrecy was essential for the launching of a surprise attack. Without further ado, Stuart started out to learn if such a road existed.

Before midnight Lee's engineer officers returned from a moonlight reconnaissance to report that the Federal line was so strongly held under cover of the woods, and so generously supported by masses of artillery, that a frontal attack was in their opinion inadvisable, with little chance of success. The evidence for a flank attack was building up.

All that remained to convert Lee's strategy into orders was assurance that the mythical road that would meet the requirements for the flank march had been found. Jackson was still with Lee and now Lee made up his mind. Confident that Stuart would find a road, Lee turned to Jackson and informed him that the task was his. The tactical details would be left to Jackson, who was instructed to return before daylight to receive final instructions before putting his troops on the road. The response was brief and to the point: "My troops will move at 4 o'clock," said Jackson, as he saluted and went off by himself to snatch a few hours of sleep before calling his division commanders together to give them the word.

The night was chilly and the ground cold and hard. Unbuckling his sword Jackson leaned it against a tree and lay down with only his coat to cover him. Staff officers had occasion to remember later that Jackson that day had a heavy cold in the chest* and that he shivered when he arose stiffly to seek warmth from the dying embers of the fire kindled for him. They also recalled what in retrospect seemed to be a portent of personal disaster when, without being touched by human hand, his sword slipped sideways and fell to the ground with a loud clang!

Federal Dispositions, Night of May 1-2

At 4:20 P.M. on the afternoon of May 1, when practically all of his troops except Griffin's division had returned to their former positions, Hooker published an order that reads almost like an apology to his disgruntled army for having jerked it back on its haunches:

> The Major General commanding trusts that a suspension in the attack today will embolden the enemy to attack him.

"Fighting Joe" indeed! The order can hardly be described as a clarion call to battle, calculated to stir the blood of the fighting men who composed the Army of the Potomac. It was a far cry from the flamboyant language with which Hooker had regaled the army only the day before. Hooker was in truth a beaten man, as Couch said, and all his generals knew it and couldn't do a thing about it.

The position Hooker had selected for his troops to fortify and defend must be examined for a proper understanding of the events of May 2-3. Evidently the cross-

---

*Jackson survived the loss of his arm the next day, but died of pneumonia on May 10, eight days after he was wounded.

MAP 15. SITUATION UP TO MIDNIGHT, MAY 1, 1803

From dark until midnight the opposing armies occupied the positions shown; except Wilcox's Brigade, which was kept marching back and forth between Duerson's Mill and the Turnpike, owing to a succession of changed orders. The divisions of A. P. Hill, Rodes, and Colston have been kept reasonably well assembled, except for the detaching of Ramseur's Brigade of Rodes' Division. Anderson's and McLaws' Divisions are still somewhat intermingled.

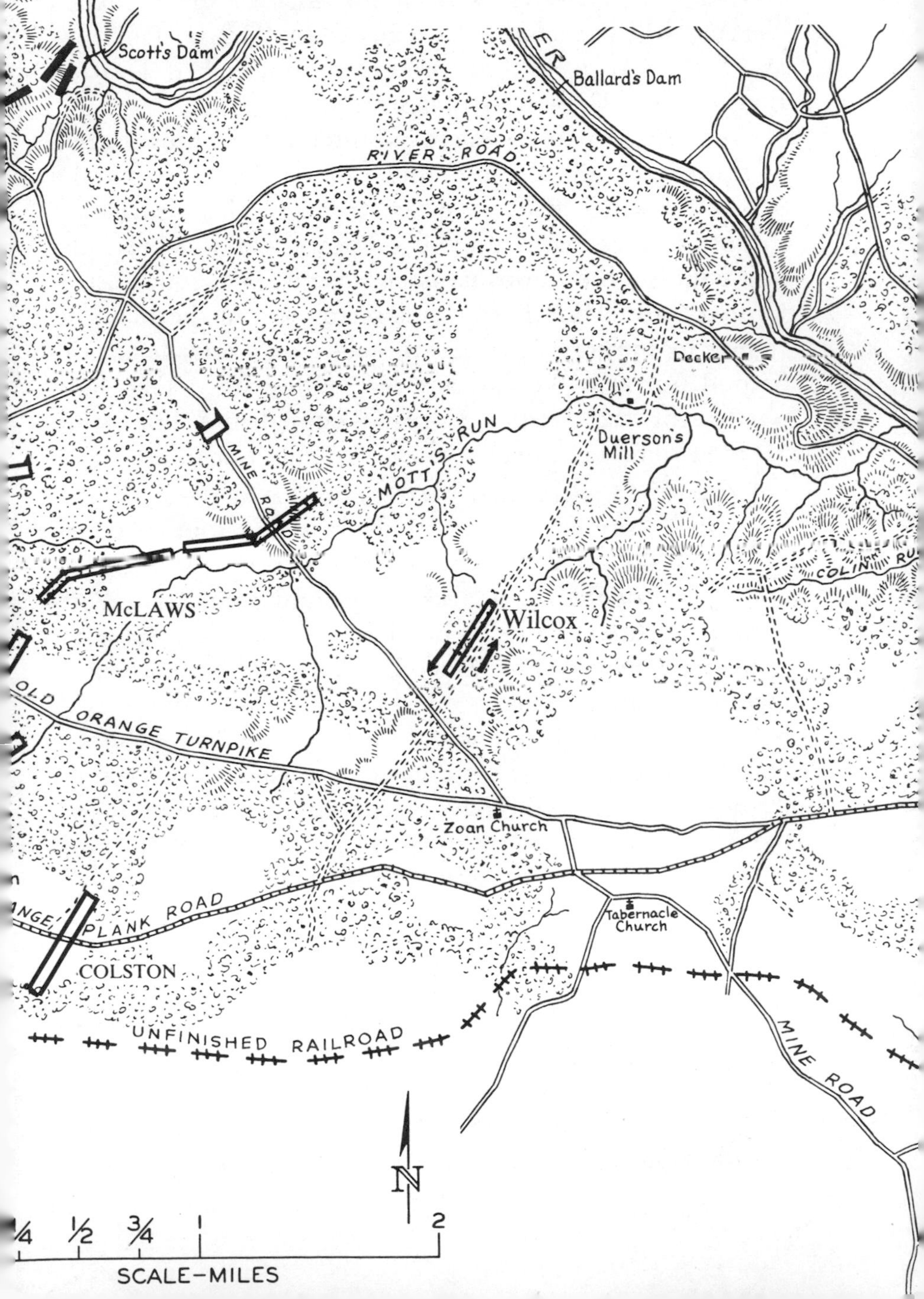

Scott's Dam

Ballard's Dam

RIVER ROAD

Decker

MOTT'S RUN

Duerson's Mill

MINE ROAD

COLIN RUN

McLAWS

Wilcox

OLD ORANGE TURNPIKE

Zoan Church

Tabernacle Church

ORANGE PLANK ROAD

COLSTON

UNFINISHED RAILROAD

MINE ROAD

N

1/4   1/2   3/4   1   2

SCALE—MILES

road at Chancellorsville loomed large in Hooker's planning, for he disposed his four corps, in front of and extended in two directions from the edge of the U-shaped clearing which enclosed the Chancellor House, Fairview, and Hazel Grove, all three on terrain of a higher elevation than the rest of the nearby landscape.

From the prominent enemy-pointed salient thus formed at the center, the defense line ran northeast to parallel Mineral Springs Run from in front of the clearing at Bullock's (crossing of the Ely's Ford and Bullock Roads) to a point on the Rappahannock several miles southeast of United States Mine Ford. This sector was in the main assigned to Meade's Fifth Corps, with one brigade of the Second Corps at the extreme left of the line. The main portion of the Second Corps occupied the line from Meade's right at Bullock's to the Orange Turnpike.

Slocum's Twelfth Corps rested both flanks on the Turnpike, in a curving bow which formed the southern face of the Chancellorsville salient to encompass Fairview and a part of the open neck of ground connecting Fairview and Hazel Grove. The perceptive student, looking at the map, may wonder, since Hooker had no objection to forming a salient jutting out from Chancellorsville, why he didn't establish a more effective one by including Hazel Grove in Slocum's defensive perimeter as well as Fairview. This would have given him possession of *all* the high ground in the area, with Scott's Run offering an obstacle to the enemy, and at the same time closed off the corridor of observation from Hazel Grove directly onto the very front porch of the Chancellor House.

A short distance north of Hazel Grove, Birney's division of the Third Corps connected Slocum's Twelfth Corps on the left with Howard's Eleventh on the right. The other two divisions of Sickles' corps bivouacked as army reserve in the woods north of the Chancellor House.

The ill-fated Eleventh Corps, slated to be the villain

of the Federal piece in the early evening of May 2, was drawn up along the southern edge of the Turnpike from Dowdall's Tavern, which Howard occupied as his headquarters, to a point more than a mile west of the Tavern. There the line bent north across the Turnpike for a pathetically short distance, while two and a half miles of

DOWDALL'S TAVERN

Wilderness, and a nice ridge at that, offered a tempting hole as big as a herd of elephants between the Turnpike and the Rapidan. All the Confederates had to do was to reconnoiter and then act, nor were they slow in doing both.

A line of Federal pickets was strung along the entire front, a mile or so out, to give timely warning of any hostile movement. This was of course a normal formation and served a purpose, but the line of observers would be of little use against a fast-moving, determined aggressor who could brush the screen to one side or overrun it almost before the word could be gotten back to the main position in the rear.

The Battle of Fredericksburg had introduced a new feature which, strangely enough, had never seemed to occur to either army during the earlier battles of 1862. That was the very sensible procedure of using earth and other protective materials to make it more difficult for the enemy to trample the defenders in an attack. Lee started it and both sides quickly learned its advantages; the individual soldier being quite ready to do a little digging when he found out how helpful a parapet or a depression in the ground could be in warding off bullets and shells. The Federals worked like beavers the night of May 1 to make their position as strong as possible; that is, most of them did so in the center and on the left, but on the right of Howard's corps there was apparently no real effort made to fortify the position. The oversight, or neglect, or whatever it was, couldn't have occurred at a worse spot, and the denouement would take a long time for the ill-starred Eleventh Corps to live down.

Hooker's last official act on the night of May 1-2 was to send orders to Butterfield at Falmouth, directing him to send Reynolds' First Corps at once to join him at Chancellorsville. The message was marked 1:55 A.M., but it didn't reach the Chief of Staff until 5 A.M. One division of the First Corps had already crossed the river below Fredericksburg and was operating under Sedgwick's command, where it was holding a small bridgehead. It was then necessary for Reynolds to assemble his divisions northeast of the river, and march by concealed routes (in ravines) to United States Mine Ford, where they would cross the Rappahannock again and continue the march to Chancellorsville.

JACKSON'S INITIAL OBJECTIVE—WILDERNESS CHURCH

Church is on left, Hawkins' farm on right. View is from in front of Dowdall's, on Turnpike.

CHAPTER 11

JACKSON'S HISTORIC FLANK MARCH

The bold Confederate plan to turn the Federal right flank has been variously attributed to both Lee and Jackson, but more likely it was a joint conception, arrived at independently. While the decision of course rested with the commanding general and his was the major risk, it was a triple play from Fitzhugh Lee (via Stuart) to Robert E. Lee to Stonewall Jackson that set the stage. For it was the cavalry brigadier whose thorough reconnoitering first discovered Hooker's exposed right flank; while Jackson's staff officers, Tucker Lacy and Jed Hotchkiss, made a vital contribution when they ran down the local resident who provided the intelligence as to the available road, without which the "concealed" march would have been impossible.

[203]

Nevertheless it was the army commander whose strategic sense and moral courage were the vital forces which sparked one of the great flank marches of military history. The specific blueprint and the execution were entrusted to Stonewall Jackson.

Faced with an opponent of vastly superior strength, Lee already had twice divided his force. Now he would subdivide the reduced segment for the third time. Not only that, he was about to march a number of divisions *across the front* of a strongly posted enemy, an undertaking considered by the professional tacticians to be the rankest kind of military heresy.

That however was the sort of thing that made Lee the great Captain that he was. Supreme master of the calculated risk, Lee had acquired the habit of daring greatly, with absolute confidence in his generals and troops. So far they had never failed him. True, his army had come close to disaster on more than one occasion, but each time his opponent had failed to exploit his opportunity, the Battle of Antietam having been the most recent example.

It cannot be doubted that in every one of the battles in which Lee took chances that would in all probability have boomeranged on a lesser chieftain, he had been careful to measure the deficiencies of the opposing Federal commander and accurately evaluate his probable reactions. Up to now the successive commanding generals of the Army of the Potomac had consistently accommodated him, and we may be sure the implications of Joe Hooker's surprising reversal were not lost on Lee.

The Reverend Beverly Tucker Lacy, Stonewall Jackson's favorite chaplain, had preached in and was familiar with the Fredericksburg-Chancellorsville area, where the name Lacy was an honored one. The chaplain's brother, Major Horace Lacy, was married to Betty Churchill Jones, who inherited historic Chatham, situated on Stafford Heights directly across the river from Fredericksburg and within shouting distance of Ferry Farm, where George Washington spent a dozen years of his boyhood. Chatham was known as the Lacy House when General Sumner used it as his headquarters during the Battle of Fredericksburg, but it was Ellwood Manor, owned by Betty Lacy's father, and situated a few hundred yards south of Wilderness Tavern, that would figure in a dramatic aftermath of the Battle of Chancellorsville.

Tucker Lacy of all people would know about the roads south of the Turnpike. Earlier that night he had given General Lee such information as he possessed, but the responsibility for marching the troops to the jumpoff position for the flank attack now rested with Stonewall Jackson. Lee and Jackson understood each other perfectly—Jackson must himself solve the problem.

As Jackson was warming his hands at the pre-dawn fire and sipping the coffee that a thoughful staff officer had wangled for him, Chaplain Lacy rose from among the recumbent forms of the staff and joined the general, who made room for him on the log upon which he was seated. Unmindful of the fact that he was conversing with his chaplain, Jackson talked about the military problem confronting the army. Almost casually he inquired if Lacy might know of a road by which the Confederates could get around Hooker's flank. Having already informed Lee, the chaplain told Jackson that such a road did in fact exist, and he traced it on the map that Jackson handed him. "Too close to the Federal line," was Jackson's comment, "wasn't there another road farther removed, by which they could march unobserved?"

Lacy didn't know, but remarked that the owner of Catharine Furnace, Colonel Wellford, would surely have the answer. Besides, he had a young son who could serve as a guide. Jackson lost no time in rousing Jed Hotchkiss, his dependable engineer officer and resourceful mapmaker. The two staff officers rode off posthaste on their mission.

By the time they returned, General Lee had joined Jackson. The generals eagerly received from Hotchkiss the news that a road had been found that met the specifications, that it was suitable for artillery, and was under cover all the way.

Producing the rough sketch that he had made, Hotchkiss explained that the Furnace Road ran south from where they stood, past Catharine Furnace, to join the larger Brock Road, which ran slightly east of south for three-quarters of a mile after crossing the unfinished railroad. The marching column would turn into the Brock Road there, and follow it for about a half mile to a point where a dirt road wound around to reconnect with the Brock Road below its junction with the Orange Plank Road. By following this route, a distance of something less than twelve miles, the column could debouch in rear of the Federal right flank. (Maps 16, 17, and 18.)

The missing piece of the puzzle had now been found. But it was approaching the hour of dawn. No more time could be lost—Jackson was already way behind the schedule that he had set when he told Lee he would march at 4 A.M.

"What do you propose to do?" was Lee's question.

"Go around here," replied Jackson, pointing to Hotchkiss' tracing.

"What do you propose to make the movement with?" was the next, and more important question.

"With my whole corps," said Jackson, not batting an eye.

"And what will you leave me?" inquired Lee, drily.

"The divisions of McLaws and Anderson," was the reply.

The dramatic exchange defies adequate description Here was a subordinate commander telling his commanding general that he proposed to risk the possibility that Hooker's powerful army of over 70,000 men and 182 guns would move a short distance to the front and annihilate the 12,900 men and 24 guns left with Lee, while Jackson with 31,700 men and 112 guns was winding his way a distance of twelve miles through the Wilderness to get on the Federal right and rear.

Lee must have been momentarily stunned at the bold conception, which went farther than even he had envisioned. But Lee possessed the capacity to think on a large-dimensional scale. Jackson's plan, if it should succeed, could achieve major results far beyond a diversionary effort that might merely serve to throw Hooker off balance temporarily. Jackson's plan *could* lead to a disaster for Federal arms. Lee was quick to recover and react.

"Well, go on," was all Lee said, calmly. But it was enough. Jackson moved rapidly to issue his orders and put the troops on the road: Fitzhugh Lee's cavalry in front and on the right to screen the column, to be followed by the divisions of Rodes, Colston, and A. P. Hill in that order. The ammunition wagons and artillery would follow immediately in rear of each division, but the supply and ambulance trains must take a longer and more round-about route to Todd's Tavern and west, so the troops would be between the enemy and the trains, while the latter would not delay the march of the combat elements.

Considerable time was taken in organizing the march and making certain that every man knew just what was expected of him. There was to be no noise, no straggling. Just to make sure of the latter, officers were instructed to use the bayonet on any laggards. The grim Jackson thought of everything—this was to be the march to end all marches —nothing would be left to chance. Stonewall Jackson was in his element, and his men rejoiced with him at the prospect.

It was shortly after 7:30 A.M., three and a half hours later than Jackson had planned, when the head of the column passed Decker's, near the junction of the Plank Road and the road running southwest to Catharine Furnace. The roads were still damp from a previous rain, which meant there would be no dust clouds to disclose

MAP 16. THE START OF JACKSON'S FLANK MARCH

At 8 A.M., a half hour after the head of Jackson's column passed the cross-road at Decker's, some of Birney's men at Hazel Grove could see a portion of the Confederate force moving over the high ground a mile to the south. Jackson may have been in the vicinity of Wellford at this time; the ground rises sharply at that point, and the road is running south, so that the Federals jumped to the conclusion that the Confederates were withdrawing from the area. This map also shows the Federal defensive position; Howard's corps on the right has its flank "in the air."

the movement. Lee stood at the crossroads to observe the start. As Jackson came by, mounted on "Little Sorrel," the two generals conferred briefly. Jackson rose in his stirrups, eyes gleaming, and pointed down the road. Salutes were exchanged and Jackson trotted forward. It was the last time Lee would see him alive.

The troops plodded steadily and cheerfully ahead. Soon they were spotted by the enemy as they crossed the high ground east of Scott's Run. Below Catharine Furnace the tree-covered road climbed a low hill and was also exposed above the tree tops to the view of the Federals a mile to the north. Federal artillery threw in a few bursts, whereupon officers were stationed on the near side of the open stretch of road, and the troops were directed to doubletime across the opening. A trail entered the road from the north at that point, and by Jackson's orders an infantry regiment was moved onto the trail and halted to provide security for the column against a sudden lunge by the Federals.

Lee Conceals His Weakness

There would be no halfway measures on the part of the small force of two divisions and supporting artillery which remained under Lee's control, in their efforts to divert Hooker's attention from Jackson's flank maneuver. No doubt remained in Lee's mind that Hooker wanted him to launch an attack. His tactics were therefore to encourage Hooker in that belief, and the best way would be to keep things stirred up all along the front. It would be fatal to Confederate hopes if Hooker were to discover what a weak force remained to oppose him; Lee would therefore keep him off balance and in a state of suspense until Jackson should achieve his expected success against the Federal right.

In accordance with that plan, several batteries opened on the Federals as Jackson's column took up the march, and the skirmishers of McLaws and Anderson introduced a hot musket fire from their positions on the Plank Road. All morning long, at intervals, the firing was aggressively kept up, with apparently satisfactory effect, since the Federals showed no disposition to assume an offensive posture.

At 8 A.M. Birney's division at Hazel Grove, some two miles southwest of Chancellorsville, had spotted Jackson's column crossing the exposed ridge, about a mile to the south. It was a long column and many wagons were observed sandwiched between the foot soldiers. The Federals were puzzled, however, by the fact that the Confederates were headed *away* from the front, for the road Jackson's troops were traversing ran south at that point and it looked to the Federals as though they were withdrawing. That was the way Hooker interpreted the reports, at any rate, no doubt highly pleased at this apparent confirmation of his prophecy that Lee must withdraw his army. It looked very much to Hooker as though Sedgwick's threat to Lee's direct communications with Richmond, by the railroad and Richmond Stage Road leading south from Fredericksburg, had forced Lee to retreat on Gordonsville.

The Aggressive Dan Sickles

Dan Sickles was a colorful character whose civilian and military traits revealed few if any inhibitions. He alone of Hooker's corps commanders was not a professional officer or a graduate of West Point, his prewar career having included active participation in politics, business, and a long series of amorous involvements, some at least of which were rather notorious. The most publicized of his extracurricular activities was probably his shooting to death of Philip Barton Key, not far from the Capitol in Washington, for having an affair with Sickles' wife. It was an interesting sidelight of that incident that Sickles' attorney was Edwin M. Stanton, who was soon to become Lincoln's Secretary of War.

Sickles, a proponent of offensive action, was not averse to expressing his own individual views whether or not they happened to conform to the overall tactics of his superior. He was on intimate terms with Hooker and did not hesitate to press his viewpoint on the army commander. When Generals Meade, Slocum, and Couch experienced the

MAJOR GENERAL DANIEL E. SICKLES

frustrating checkrein which Hooker applied to the right wing on the afternoon of May 1, Sickles' Third Corps was still en route from Fredericksburg to Chancellorsville, so his outlook on the strategic situation was presumably less restrained. The strength of his corps was almost 19,000 men, second in size to the largest corps in the army, Sedgwick's Sixth, and he was all for getting his divisions into action. Upon arrival at Chancellorsville his corps was posted as army reserve. This prospect did not appeal to Sickles' combative nature. In scouting around he discovered what looked to him like a weak link in the chain of defense between the Eleventh and Twelfth Corps, so with Hooker's approval he moved Birney's division into the line to strengthen the gap.

Again it was Sickles who took the initiative early on May 2 when he moved Birney forward to occupy the important clearing on the high ground at Hazel Grove, from which observation point the lateral movement of Jackson's Corps was first discovered by several of Birney's observers posted in tall trees. While it was a fact that the advance of Birney's division left a gap of one mile on Howard's left, the defect was not particularly serious in view of Hooker's great strength.

No matter what opinion may be held as to Sickles' military competence as a corps commander, he was an aggressive general who held to the view that the army was there to fight and not to sit on its haunches waiting for the enemy to make all the moves. During the morning, Birney reported on the Confederate column that was crossing his front in a never-ending procession of men, vehicles, and guns, all in full view. Sickles repeatedly importuned Hooker to allow him to move against the enemy with a view to cutting his column. But it was not until noon, four hours after the Confederates were first observed, that permission was finally and grudgingly granted. Sickles was told to "advance cautiously" to "harass the enemy," an insipid form of order that was scarcely couched in language to inspire the troops to heroic effort.

The persistent way in which Hooker was throwing away opportunity after opportunity for decisive action against the Confederates passes all understanding. After he had successfully placed his right wing on Lee's left rear, the fight appears to have gone entirely out of him. From that time on Lee took the initiative and pressed it, while everything that Hooker did or failed to do merely compounded his unaccountable failure to pursue his advantage on the afternoon of April 30.

Hooker's reasoning in allowing Jackson to move west, unopposed, for the entire morning of May 2 is obscure. An inviting and vulnerable target passed across the southern front, only a mile away, for four solid hours without interference. If indeed Lee was withdrawing on Gordonsville, as Hooker professed to believe, the logical reaction would seem to have been to attack and turn the retreat into a rout; to cut the column at several points; to send the cavalry at a rapid clip to block the march at the head of the column or at the very least to raise havoc along the flanks; and at the same time to send one or two corps in a driving attack against whatever Confederate force remained on Hooker's front, since it was obvious the latter couldn't be very powerful.

Jackson's Corps of 30,000 troops, confined to a narrow, tree-covered path through the Wilderness, and strung out over ten miles of road, was as vulnerable a target for an aggressive opponent as could be imagined. Weighted down by his division trains, unable to effectively deploy his troops if attacked, incapable of utilizing his artillery, Jackson was courting disaster every step of the way from early morning until late in the day when he came to the end of the trail and his greatest opportunity.

It was the good fortune of Lee and Jackson that the heavy risk they were taking did not end in the destruction of the Army of Northern Virginia. Nor does it detract one bit from the reputation of either to remark that it was Joe Hooker, alone and unaided, whose mental inflexibility and lack of moral courage created the climate which made possible, indeed almost inevitable, the successive actions that culminated in the wholly unnecessary and therefore disgraceful defeat and withdrawal of the Army of the Potomac north of the Rappahannock.

The more one thinks about it, the more amazing does Hooker's apathy appear. Spirited action, positive orders, prompt movements against the enemy—all breathing the spirit of the offensive, were clearly the need of the moment. But the spark was lacking. A smog of inaction, uncertainty, and timidity at the top imprisoned the Federal giant as

MAP 17. MOVEMENTS BETWEEN ABOUT 1:30 P. M. and 2 P. M., MAY 2, 18

This shows the march of Jackson's command around the right of Hoo
army. Birney (of Sickles' III Corps) has moved his division south from
Hazel Grove area to attack the tail of Jackson's artillery column, which
just cleared Catharine Furnace. Posey's Brigade of Anderson's Division
Thomas' and Archer's Brigade of A. P. Hill's Division are hurrying ther
aid Col. Best who with the 23rd Georgia Regiment is trying to stave off Birn
attack and protect the passage of the column. Gen Sickles is moving the
mainder of his III Corps to join in Birney's fight.

Jackson has just joined Fitzhugh Lee at Burton's farm, and is viewing
disposition of Howard's careless soldiery along the Turnpike near Dowc
Tavern. Jackson sends word to Rodes, who had started to turn northeas
Hickman, to continue north and halt with the head of his column at
Turnpike three-quarters of a mile west of Luckett's. Colston and A. P.
are following Rodes. The cavalry is moving between the main infantry col
and the Federals; and the trains are on an outside route passing thr
Piney Branch Church and Todd's Tavern.

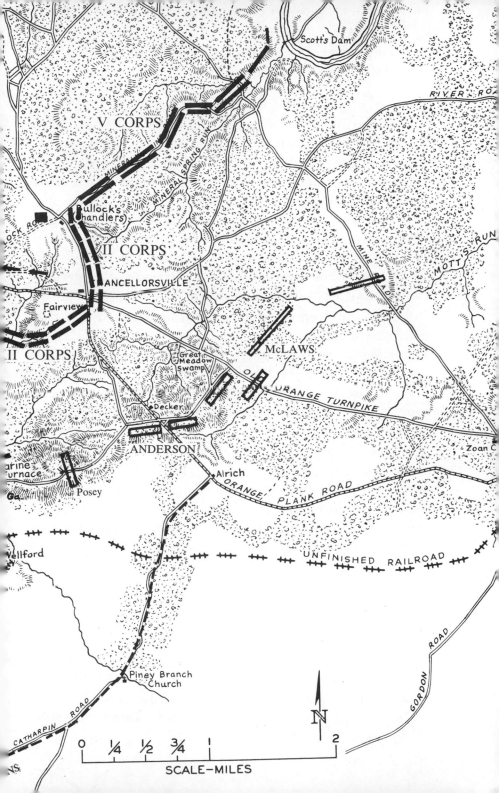

Scott's Dam

RIVER ROAD

V CORPS

MINERAL SPRING RUN

MINE RUN

MOTT'S RUN

Bullock's
(Chandlers)

II CORPS

CHANCELLORSVILLE

Fairview

II CORPS

McLAWS

Great
Meadow
Swamp

OLD ORANGE TURNPIKE

Decker

ANDERSON

Zoan C

arine
urnace

Alrich

ORANGE PLANK ROAD

Posey

Oa

UNFINISHED RAILROAD

ellford

GORDON ROAD

Piney Branch
Church

CATHARPIN ROAD

N

0   ¼   ½   ¾   1   2

SCALE—MILES

NS.

the Confederate David marched confidently forward with his slingshot at the ready.

Sickles Nips at Jackson's Heels

Preceded by several battalions of Berdan's famed sharp-shooters, Birney's advance brigade crossed Scott's Run (Lewis Creek), under orders from Sickles to pierce the Confederate column and seize the road upon which it was marching. Jackson's corps artillery was passing at the time, the main body of the infantry having already cleared. A lively scrap ensued with Colonel Best's 23d Georgia Regiment, which was covering Jackson's right in the vicinity of Catharine Furnace. Soon Posey's Brigade of Anderson's Confederate Division joined in the fray from the east.

Several captured Confederate prisoners stated that they had been marching to get on the Federal right and that things would start popping over there right soon. Sickles was skeptical, believed they were lying to mislead the Federals, a ruse the Confederates had learned to adopt with some success on other occasions. He felt sure Lee was retreating.

Hooker shared Sickles' opinion, but didn't feel the same urgency to go after Lee, at least not until he had thought it over some more. His compromise decision, after some time had elapsed, was to direct Howard to send his reserve brigade, of all outfits, to support Sickles' advance elements, while Pleasonton was told to take his cavalry down that way. No specific mission was mentioned other than to cooperate with Sickles, so Pleasonton conceived his own objective and decided that what he should do was to cut the Confederate column, establish communication with Sedgwick (a rather ambitious conception), and pursue the retreating enemy (which *did* make sense). But it would have made better sense if Hooker had placed his cavalry on the army right flank at the outset.

Jackson, informed that the rear of his column was under

attack and his trains endangered, directed the two rear-most brigades of Archer and Thomas to countermarch and dispose of the threat till the trains had cleared. While the contestants bickered in the thickets, the major portion of Jackson's column kept going. After a bit Archer and Thomas broke off the engagement and quietly went their way, leaving several score of prisoners, including most of the 23d Georgia, in Birney's hands as a consolation prize. There was no pursuit by the Federals, either with infantry or cavalry.

The events of the afternoon were sufficient to drive Hooker to at least one major decision. At 4:10 P.M. an order was dispatched to Sedgwick as follows:

> The major general commanding directs that General Sedgwick cross the river as soon as indications will permit; capture Fredericksburg with everything in it, and vigorously pursue the enemy. We know that the enemy is fleeing, trying to save his trains. Two of Sickles' divisions are among them.

This message to Sedgwick was slightly less negative than earlier "iffy" directions, but it was still discretionary, leaving it to the commander of the left wing to decide when "indications will permit." Professor Lowe's balloon and the signal stations had been sending a veritable stream of informative observations of enemy movements to Sedgwick and Butterfield. Those on May 2 particularly painted a picture of relative Confederate inactivity at Fredericksburg and the apparent departure of the bulk of the troops that earlier had crowded the hill positions west of the town. Furthermore, several of Hooker's messages during the morning stated positively that only Ewell's (Early's) Division had been left at Fredericksburg. Sedgwick had little excuse for not stirring himself more energetically.

Hooker's Achilles' heel was his right flank, as Jackson would soon demonstrate. But it needn't have been. For in disposing his right wing on the defensive line on the afternoon of May 1, after pulling his divisions back to Chancellorsville, Hooker had sent this order to Slocum and Howard at 4:45 P.M.:

> Let the right of your line fall back and rest at the sawmill ruin on Hunting Run, or in that direction, and have everything passed to the rear of it.

Hooker evidently forgot that Slocum was no longer the wing commander, with the chain of command down to Howard, otherwise the message would be unintelligible. Applied to Howard's corps on the extreme right it did make sense, although Howard claimed that the order never reached him. Both Howard and Slocum are reported to have protested against the instructions to refuse the right, on the premise that the Wilderness in that sector was impenetrable to troops except on the roads which they would have no trouble in holding. To fall back would in the opinion of the two corps commanders have the same demoralizing effect as a retreat.

The sawmill ruin was located about one and a quarter miles northeast of the extreme right of Howard's line along the Turnpike. A glance at the map will assure any Doubting Thomas that in planning a greater refusal of his line Hooker was right; Slocum and Howard decidedly shortsighted. Nevertheless Hooker allowed himself to be mollified, which probably was not too difficult in the light of his fixation that Lee must attack or withdraw. Hooker thus appears to have given at least passing thought to the possibility of a flank attack. His fatal mistake was in failing to insist on a strong extension of the right to insure strength on that flank, for he had ample troops to extend the line if he had decided to use them for that purpose rather than build up his powerful reserve north of Chancellorsville.

Had Reynolds' First Corps been transferred from Fredericksburg on May 1 instead of the following day, and placed on Howard's right to fill the gap to the Rapidan, Jackson's reception would have been quite a different one. There would still have been time if Hooker's order of 1:55 A.M. had reached Reynolds promptly, but its arrival was delayed until after daylight and the First Corps had a day's march ahead of it. As it turned out, Reynolds himself arrived at 6 P.M., but it was several hours later that his divisions got across the United States Mine Ford and forced their way along the crowded road to reach Chancellorsville. By then it was too late—the debacle had occurred. Furthermore, evidence is lacking that Hooker would have posted Reynolds on Howard's right even if he had arrived during the afternoon.

Having yielded to Slocum and Howard, and in spite of their conviction that the Confederates were physically incapable of penetrating the woods, Hooker was negligent in not checking carefully to make certain that adequate security measures had in fact been taken to prevent surprise, for it was generally conceded that the entrenchments and breastworks of Howard's corps were inferior to those thrown up by the Twelfth, Fifth, and Second Corps.

So far as can be determined, and in marked contrast to Lee's practice, Hooker made only one extended personal appearance among the troops of his army during the entire Chancellorsville campaign. That was a post-breakfast inspection ride which he took on May 2, accompanied by a number of staff officers, around the lines of the Chancellorsville position. What he saw seemed generally to satisfy him, for he was heard to remark at one point, "How strong, how strong!"—evidently referring to the character of the protective fortifications of earth and felled trees that his troops had zealously built overnight in accordance with his orders.

That Hooker had misgivings about the security of his right flank, however, was evidenced by a written message dispatched at 9:30 A.M. to the commander of the Eleventh

Corps, after he returned to his headquarters. The message called Howard's attention to the fact that his dispositions had been made to meet a frontal attack by the enemy, and directed that he examine the ground to the flank in order to be prepared to meet an attack from whatever direction it might come. The suggestion was added that Howard have "heavy reserves" well in hand to meet such a contingency.

Like all Hooker's communications to his lieutenants, this one lacked directness and decision. If Hooker as army commander felt that his right was insecure, he should have said so in no uncertain terms, indicated the corrective measures desired, and sent a staff officer to see to it that they were carried out to the letter, if he had any doubt as to the efficiency of the corps commander concerned.

O. O. Howard and the XI Corps

The still inadequately explained mystery of the Chancellorsville campaign was the yawning three-mile-wide Wilderness gap which Hooker allowed to exist on the right of his army between the Orange Turnpike and the Rapidan River to the north.

Hooker's strategic error May 1 in bringing to a grinding halt the gathering momentum of his offensive drive towards the rear of Lee's army at Fredericksburg did not prevent him from making a careful and comprehensive plan for defensive operations in the large, fortified semicircle around Chancellorsville. There in the dense wilderness it was his belief that the conditions of the Battle of Fredericksburg in December 1862 would be reversed and that the Confederate army would destroy itself in an attack against the impregnable line that his troops would construct during the night of May 1.

Hooker's conception must have contemplated solid anchors on either flank—the left on the Rappahannock below United States Mine Ford, the right on the Rapidan above the ford. His action in stripping Sedgwick's left wing of all troops except his own Sixth Corps and Gibbon's division indicated an apparent desire to be prepared at Chancellorsville with overwhelming defensive strength for the best Lee might offer. Nevertheless, since Hooker's inten-

MAJOR GENERAL OLIVER O. HOWARD

tion was clearly to have Sedgwick do all the offensive fighting for the army, and in the next few days two full corps at Chancellorsville were not even engaged, it is difficult to understand just what precise plan had really formed in Hooker's mind.

What manner of man was this one-armed major general, Oliver Otis Howard, who commanded the Eleventh Corps on the Federal right flank and became the scapegoat when Jackson's Corps surprised and routed him on the late afternoon of May 2?

An examination of his military record fails to yield much that helps to explain what happened at Chancellorsville. A graduate of the Military Academy in 1854, his first assignment of the Civil War was as Colonel of the

Third Maine Volunteers. He fought as a brigadier in the First Battle of Bull Run, in the Peninsular Campaign, and at Antietam in the fall of 1862. Then he was given a division, which he led at Fredericksburg. Twice wounded at the Battle of Fair Oaks, he left his arm on that field. When General Franz Sigel was relieved as commander of the Eleventh Corps, Howard was appointed to succeed him, on April 2, 1863, shortly before the Chancellorsville campaign.

Rightly or wrongly, the Eleventh Corps was held in low esteem by the rest of the Army of the Potomac. Composed partly of Germans and German-Americans, the corps was a newcomer to this army and the opinion was rather prevalent that its discipline was not of the best. In addition, the corps had a chip on its collective shoulders from the fact that its beloved former commander, Franz Sigel, had in the opinion of his men been given a raw deal by the high command. The result was that the new general, Howard, had two strikes against him when he took command just a few weeks before the army was scheduled to break camp for the spring campaign.

In retrospect, it is surprising that Hooker placed the Eleventh Corps on the important right flank at Chancellorsville, considering its reputation and the fact that the corps and its commander had only just gotten acquainted. But it is definitely to Hooker's discredit that, having placed it there, he failed to make certain that proper troop dispositions were made to secure so vulnerable a position.

A portent of things to come might have been noted in late April during the march of the right wing from Falmouth to Kelly's Ford. Hooker's orders to his corps were to travel as light as possible, keeping the number of ration wagons to the bare minimum for eight days' subsistence. But it developed that, while the other corps commanders conformed to the letter of the order, Howard's corps exceeded the authorized maximum by a large margin, to unduly clog the roads and impair the mobility of the entire wing.

Viewed objectively, it appears that both Hooker and Howard must be charged with gross negligence insofar as the security of the right flank of the army was concerned. It is no excuse to say that both generals were convinced that Jackson's observed flank march was to be interpreted as a withdrawal in the direction of Gordonsville. Insurance against surprise, whether expected or discounted, is one of the duties of a field commander. Neither Hooker nor Howard took out even a small policy against such a contingency.

Nor can it be said that Howard was not fully warned of the forthcoming threat, hours before Jackson struck. Howard felt so certain in his own mind that the Confederates could not crash the Wilderness, in the face of the heavy tangle of trees and interlacing underbrush, that he completely neglected to take the most fundamental precautions, apparently believing that an attack could come *only* from the south, the direction in which he faced the greater portion of his troops along the Turnpike. Only two small regiments, not over 900 men in all, were placed at right angles to the Pike, on the extreme flank, and even those on the Turnpike were unprepared when the attack occurred, for they were preparing for supper with their arms stacked at the edge of the road, no effort apparently having been made to keep even a fraction of each company or regiment under arms in a position of readiness for immediate action. Barlow's brigade, initially in corps reserve near Wilderness Church, was the only organized body that was not strung out in extended order. It was that brigade that Howard personally took forward to Hazel Grove, beyond reach of the right flank, when Hooker directed him to send a brigade to the support of the Third Corps in the course of Sickles' afternoon fight with the Confederate rear guard.

From the time of his arrival at Chancellorsville, Howard had established his headquarters at Dowdall's Tavern, which at the time of the battle was being occupied as a residence by Melzi Chancellor. It was located east of the junction of the Turnpike and the Plank Roads, about a mile from the extreme right of the Eleventh Corps. His main line extended generally along the southern edge of the Turnpike until near the Tavern, where it was several hundred yards south of the Turnpike; from there on it ran in a direction slightly south of east, crossing the Plank Road and hugging the north bank of the small creek that paralled Scott's Run, some 500 yards further south.

The three divisions of Devens, Schurz, and von Steinwehr were posted from right to left in that order, each division disposed in two lines of varying depth and strength. Schurz' Third Division held the center in the vicinity of Hawkins' Farm, with one brigade on the Turnpike and the other placed to the north in such position that it could face either south or west, although its attention was plainly directed on the Turnpike.

During the latter part of the morning, after Hooker had warned Howard to look to his right, Howard sent this message to headquarters:

Major Gen. Hooker, Comdg. Army.

General:

From Gen. Devens' headquarters (Taylor)* we can observe a column of infantry moving westward on a road parallel with this on a ridge about 1½ to 2 miles south of this. I am taking measures to resist an attack from the west.

Respectfully,
O. O. Howard,
Maj. Gen.

---

*Shown on the map as Talley, which is the correct name.

The last sentence of the message was pure eyewash, for not only did Howard take no measures worthy of the name to resist attack from the west; he repeatedly discounted the effort of at least a few of his subordinate officers to warn him of the impending danger.

Confederate cavalry during the early afternoon had been feeling out his line on the west, and his own pickets brought in two prisoners who stated they had lost their way from a column that was moving around the Federal right. Infantry patrols sent out from Howard's corps to the front discovered enemy skirmishers about a mile and a half from the Turnpike, and enemy infantry patrols had reconnoitered Howard's front shortly before noon. All signs pointed unerringly to the fact that the enemy was on the move and getting closer all the time.

At two o'clock Howard's division commander on the right, General Devens, was told by his outposts that the enemy was moving around his right. The officer of the day made a similar report, but was advised, curtly, not to start a panic. A short time later, in repeating the warning he was told in no uncertain terms not to be a coward— the enemy was retreating!

Devens was a Regular, newly assigned to the Eleventh Corps and regarded askance by the men of the division for the reason that their former commander, Brigadier General Nathaniel C. McLean, had been downgraded in order to make room for Devens to take command of the division. Whether Devens or McLean was the better man is beside the point. A slot apparently had to be created and McLean stood in the way. But the appointment was not a popular one and Devens must have been aware of the fact that he was not welcome.

McLean was given command of the Second Brigade of Devens' division. His regiments were posted at the extreme right of that portion of the Eleventh Corps line that was strung along the Turnpike, with Von Gilsa's brigade occupying the refused angle north of the Turnpike. And it was McLean's officers and men who repeatedly brought the warning reports that Devens chose to treat in so cavalier a fashion, almost as though he had made up his mind that nothing constructive could be expected from the personnel of the Eleventh Corps. Devens would have cause to regret his attitude in a very short time.

At 2:45 P.M. a major from the outpost on the right sent the division commander an urgent message which should have startled him:

> A large body of the enemy is massing in my front. For God's sake make disposition to receive him.

Devens was sufficiently impressed to forward that intelligence to General Howard, but the latter's mental bloc was so pronounced that he simply brushed the information off. A similar message at 3:00 P. M. received the same treatment.

Is it any wonder that historians have placed the blame for the debacle of the Eleventh Corps equally on Hooker and Howard? Even with their low opinion of the morale and discipline of the Germans, it cannot be said that their attitude was calculated to effect any improvement or to encourage a courageous fighting spirit either among the junior officers or in the ranks.

Confirmatory evidence of Hooker's complacency, and confidence that Lee was retreating, is found in a circular which he sent around to his corps commanders at 2:30 P.M. The order directed them to replenish their supplies and make ready for an early start the next morning, presumably in pursuit of the "retreating" enemy. And it was as late as 4:10 P.M. that Hooker informed Sedgwick by telegram that the enemy was "fleeing."

Just how wrong can a general be?

At 4:30, with Sickles still engaged and the remainder of the army idly sitting it out, Slocum was ordered forward to support Sickles. All he did in compliance was to send forward Geary's division to link up with Sickles' left and close the gap that existed between the two corps as a result of Birney's forward move earlier in the day.

Lee Maintains the Pressure

Lee anxiously awaited the noise of Jackson's guns far to the left. As the afternoon dragged slowly on, he kept up the pressure of McLaws' and Anderson's Divisions against the center of Hooker's line at Chancellorsville. The pronounced salient in the Federal position, greatly enlarged by Sickles' advance from Hazel Grove, would under normal circumstances have been seized upon by the watchful Lee, had his strength permitted, to launch a powerful arrow against the base of the salient, with an excellent chance of severing the Federal troops at Hazel Grove and below from the main body. As will be seen later, just such an effort was made by an energetic Confederate unit shortly before midnight that night, and although it was unsupported and failed to panic Sickles, it did temporarily sever his communications. The important effect of the isolated attack, however, was that Hooker became thoroughly alarmed and, according to Couch, "at once made preparations to withdraw the whole front, leaving General Sickles to his fate."

The skirmishing along the lines was especially severe on the front occupied by Hancock's division of Couch's Second Corps, which held a position between Slocum's left and Meade's right, at the apex of the Federal bulge at Chancellorsville. At no time, however, did it assume the aspect of a decisive attack and consequently, after a number of local exchanges, the Federal troops appraised the Confederate exercises for what they were, mere distractions.

Developments at Fredericksburg

As the calm before the storm continued throughout the

afternoon on the Chancellorsville front, a similar situation prevailed at Fredericksburg, where Sedgwick, as the direct result of Hooker's spasmodic, conditional messages, was in the unenviable position of wondering which end was really up.

It appeared initially that his main job had been to hold Lee at Fredericksburg by demonstrations and then to attack if conditions should justify. He had every reason to believe that Hooker planned a two-pronged attack to squeeze Lee to death if he remained. But the real expectation was that Sedgwick would shortly be called on to pursue the fleeing Confederates towards Richmond. Then Hooker sat down at his end of the line and began sapping Sedgwick's three-corps strength until only his own Sixth, plus half of Gibbon's division, remained. Finally, about an hour before Jackson's thunderbolt struck, Hooker wired his left wing commander to capture Fredericksburg and vigorously pursue the enemy, without letting him in on the secret as to which direction Hooker expected the enemy to take or what Hooker's huge troop concentration was going to do about the matter.

Hooker was becoming more and more incoherent as time went on. He became thoroughly enmeshed in the net of his own cerebrations, if such a term is justified in this case, which may be doubted. Although Sedgwick gained no laurels for brilliant planning and execution in this campaign, he was more sinned against than sinning, and it is not too surprising that the uncoordinated performance of his left wing was somewhat short of satisfactory.

From the tenor of Hooker's order, Sedgwick could fairly assume that a Federal victory had been achieved at Chancellorsville, or the message surely would not have spoken so positively of Lee's retreat. The mere fact that Sickles' corps was "among the enemy trains" spoke volumes. It would thus seem that Sedgwick's mission was comparatively simple

—pursuit of a fleeing enemy, so he set about the task of fulfilling the mission early on the evening of May 2.

While Sedgwick was in the process of preparing to move, the situation at Chancellorsville had exploded. Another order came in from Hooker about 11 P.M. This one directed Sedgwick to "cross the Rappahannock at Fredericksburg immediately upon receipt of the order" and move in the direction of Chancellorsville until he connected with Hooker. He was told to attack and destroy any force on the road, and be in Hooker's vicinity at daylight.

Confusion still reigned in the area of army communications. Surely Hooker knew that Sedgwick was *already* across the Rappahannock. But the professional soldier is trained and conditioned to follow orders explicitly, and this order said to cross *at* Fredericksburg. Sedgwick's reaction was something akin to that of the newspaper man with whom it is second nature to "follow the copy out of the window (if necessary)." The order was a puzzler, sure enough. Should Sedgwick recross the river and follow the north bank of the river to Chancellorsville? That wouldn't make sense, because there were no Confederates there to attack. Well then, should he recross and re-recross a second time, in order to "follow copy" and avoid embarrassment to the major general commanding? Inconceivable as it may sound, that possibility was actually considered, but common sense came to the rescue. Sedgwick decided simply to move northward from the plain on which his entire corps was spread, seize Fredericksburg, and then take off for Chancellorsville by the shortest route.

CONFEDERATES STORMING HOWARD'S BREASTWORKS

CHAPTER 12

THE STORM BREAKS

WHILE Lee's thoughts on the afternoon of May 2 were centered on Jackson's dramatic sweep through the Wilderness, upon which the fate of the Army of Northern Virginia depended, unremitting Confederate pressure was kept up against the Federal position before Chancellorsville. Whether the local action at that point was chiefly to divert Hooker's attention from what was transpiring in the depths of the forest to the west, or Lee anticipated a collateral gain from the effect of pushing Hancock's troops closer to the Chancellor House, in order to extract the maximum advantage from the expected rolling up of Hooker's right at Dowdall's Tavern, the Confederates did exert unusual efforts against the center of Hooker's position.

Lee's generalship at this critical juncture is pleasant to contemplate. Not for a minute would he yield the initiative that he had seized May 1 from Hooker, who was now so far off balance that light, constant taps were apparently all Lee need administer to maintain the status quo until Jackson should burst from cover in his crashing attack.

The god of war was smiling on Thomas Jonathan Jackson in his last great adventure on earth, for the march of his powerful column was not interrupted by the Fed-

LIEUTENANT GENERAL THOMAS J. JACKSON, C.S.A.

erals, thanks mainly to Hooker's obsession, which seems to have filtered down through the ranks to the point of paralyzing inaction in the zone where the greatest danger threatened.

Yet, despite Jackson's strict orders against straggling, and the intense eagerness with which he personally repeated his demand that his men "press on, press on," the famous march was conducted at a relatively slow pace for divisions that had by their repeated successes in earlier forced marches become known as Jackson's "foot cavalry."

The conditions were favorable for a rapid gait, for there was no possibility of losing the way, and nothing to slow the column. Yet by 1 P.M. the cavalry advance guard had advanced only eight or nine miles after a lapse of six hours, a rate of march not in excess of 1½ miles an hour. True enough, the column had been subjected to sporadic shelling as it crossed the clearing at Wellford's Farm, but the effect should have been to accelerate the march rather than retard it. To some extent the great length of the column itself contributed to the slow pace, for there is always a certain amount of telescoping between units, except where perfect march discipline is maintained. And it is unlikely that Jackson's own sense of urgency was reflected in the toiling ranks of the enlisted men, especially on such a warm spring day.

As the leading element of the advance cavalry reached the crossroad 1½ miles south of the Turnpike, it turned right on the Orange Plank Road, which led directly to Dowdall's Tavern, Howard's corps headquarters at the junction of the Plank Road and Turnpike, the very heart of the Federal position along the latter. This was the route Jed Hotchkiss had marked in the expectation that it would bring the Confederate column to a jumpoff position beyond Hooker's right flank. (See Map 17).

The Confederate cavalry, with the Second Virginia in the lead, continued the march for half a mile to Hickman's, where the Germanna Plank Road from the northwest joins the Orange Plank Road. There the regiment halted and dismounted to give their horses a breather, while one squadron moved down the road a bit further as security for the rest of the outfit. Running into a small body of Federal cavalry on the road, the Virginians drove them back and then returned to Hickman's. But they had galloped far enough in their pursuit to look across the open fields of Talley's Farm to the Turnpike where Federal infantry in considerable strength was posted. The squadron commander returned posthaste to report that he had "gotten a view of the right of the Federal line."

Half a mile east of Hickman's was Burton's Farm, set on high ground in a clearing to the north of the Plank Road* and not over 1,000 yards from the center of Howard's position. The squadron commander's report was quickly relayed to Fitzhugh Lee, at the junction of Brock Road and the Plank Road. At the same moment Jackson himself rode up at the head of his infantry. With suppressed excitement Lee invited Jackson to ride with him to the clearing—he had something interesting to show him. After halting the infantry, the two officers rode on to Burton's to take a good look.

An Expensive Delay

Jackson had no need of his field glasses to disclose what must have been a disappointing sight—Federal infantry all along the Turnpike, as far as he could see, and well to the left (west) of the road upon which he had counted to bring him quickly on to the Federal flank and rear. It was now two o'clock and, unfortunately, a lot more marching had to be done before he could place his divisions for the attack. A few minutes of further silent observation was sufficient. Summoning a courier to his side, Jackson sent a message back to General Rodes, commander of the leading division of the Second Army Corps, instructing him to continue on the Brock Road across the Orange Plank Road and halt when he reached the Turnpike. There Jackson would join him and issue further orders.

The additional three or four mile approach march was to prove a serious if not fatal deterrent to the full exploitation of Jackson's forthcoming destruction of the Federal Eleventh Corps. For it would be well after five o'clock in the afternoon before the attack commenced, and night came early in the dark forest at this time of year, even though it was springtime.

Lee's cavalry, supported by a brigade of infantry, was

---

*This clearing does not exist in 1958.

[233]

placed in observation on the Plank Road, to mask the final phase of the march of the main column, and as insurance against possible aggression by the Federals. By 2:30 P.M. Rodes' leading division had reached the Turnpike a short distance from Wilderness Tavern and moved east for almost a mile towards Chancellorsville to Luckett's, still without running into enemy troops. Seemingly the Federals were entirely oblivious to the threatening storm about to break.

Jackson had sometime before sent off his last message to General Lee, shortly after observing the Federal position from Burton's Farm:

> Near 3 P.M. May 2, 1863.
>
> General,—The enemy has made a stand at Chancellor's which is about two miles from Chancellorsville. I hope as soon as practicable to attack. I trust that an ever-kind Providence will bless us with great success.
>
> Respectfully,
>
> T. J. Jackson, Lieutenant General.
>
> The leading division is up, and the next two appear to be well closed.
>
> T. J. J.

It was high time the corps move off the road and develop an attack formation, if complete success was to be attained before darkness should force a halt. The deployment was effected smoothly and, despite a certain amount of noise, without the Federals becoming aware of the vast troop movement taking place within a mile of them. Preparations for the evening meal occupied the attention of Howard's unsuspecting soldiers, whose arms were stacked and who sat or lolled around in as unprepared a posture as though they were comfortably secure in their camps at Falmouth.

Moving silently off the Turnpike to right and left as they advanced, Jackson's brigades formed in extended order facing east, overlapping the Federal flanks to the north and south in such strength that their attack, when launched, should be irresistible. It was no easy task for some 25,000 men to form battle lines in the tangled forest, but Jackson was determined that the job be done right, despite the passing of the precious minutes, The lines were carefully dressed as the deployment continued and finally, sometime after five o'clock, the preparations were complete.

The character of the landscape was as though made to order for the Confederate dispositions, and they took full advantage of it to assure complete surprise. Dowdall's Tavern was set on the eastern fringe of a large clearing, with Talley's Hill some hundreds of yards to the west, while Hawkin's Farm extended the cleared area to the north. There was open ground as well in the triangle formed by the Turnpike and the Plank Road as far as Burton's Farm, but beyond that the forbidding Wilderness again closed in, to conceal the preparatory maneuvers of the wily Jackson and his corps. It was under cover of the heavily forested area that the thunderbolt was fashioned, ready to be launched in the open terrain the minute Jackson should give the word.

For an overall length of almost two miles the gray lines, three of them, extended on either side of the Pike leading to Chancellorsville. First a line of skirmishers, four hundred yards in front of Rodes' division, which was formed in a single line with brigades abreast. Several hundred yards in rear of Rodes came Colston's Division, similarly deployed. Last of the three lines was composed of A. P. Hill's men, disposed partly in line and partly in column.

Jackson's plan for the actual attack had been carefully explained to his three division commanders and additional time allowed for them to give detailed instructions to their brigades and regiments, so there would be no hitch. There would be depth as well as breadth to the attack and the supporting divisions were told to drive resolutely ahead through the forest, capture the successive objectives which Jackson indicated, and allow nothing to halt the forward

MAP 18. THE SITUATION AT 5 P. M., MAY 2, 1863

Archer and Thomas reached Catharine Furnace at 3:30 P. M. to assist Col. Best. An hour later they resumed the march. Meantime Anderson's and McLaws' Divisions kept up a lively demonstration to divert the Federals' attention from Jackson.

Sickles was engaging in a private war of his own near the furnace. He saw a chance to cut off part of the Confederate column, but needed help. Barlow's brigade of the XI Corps (of all units!) was sent to him. Slocum

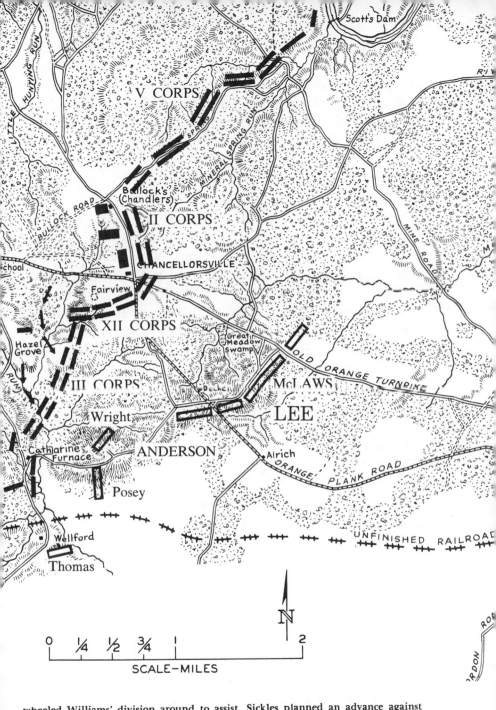

wheeled Williams' division around to assist. Sickles planned an advance against the flank and rear of Anderson. Before this could be executed, Jackson struck.

Jackson reached the Turnpike at 2:30 P. M., turned east at Luckett's, and deployed astride the Pike with Rodes in the assault, Colston in support, and A. P. Hill in reserve. The last three brigades of A. P. Hill's Division had not yet come up. The deployment, except for these three brigades, was completed by about 5 P. M. Shortly thereafter Jackson gave Rodes the word to move out to the attack.

push. Flank protection was provided for, and the artillery was prepared to gallop to the front to crack any islands of resistance which the Federals might be able to form.

Zero hour had arrived. Jackson sat his horse, shoulders hunched, watch in hand, the dial showing 5:15 P.M.

"Are you ready, General Rodes?" he asked.

"Yes, sir."

"You can go forward, sir," said Jackson.

That was all. Suddenly a bugle sounded and eager trumpeters, all along the line, sounded the charge. The skirmishers moved out with a rush, as the long lines dashed forward like an uncoiled spring, thousands of excited throats making the dark forest ring with the nerve-shattering Rebel yell.

The surprised Federals heard the shouts and cheering at the same moment the startled denizens of the forest fled in all directions. "Like a cloud of dust driven before a coming shower," wrote General Howard, "the first lively effects of the steady Confederate advance appeared in the startled rabbits, squirrels, quail, and other game flying wildly hither and thither in evident terror, and escaping, where possible, into adjacent clearings."

Howard's two inadequate, small regiments facing west on the north side of the Turnpike had just time enough to seize their weapons and offer token resistance because of the suddenness of the attack, for the Confederate lines so far overlapped the Federal right and left, and the assault struck with such power and depth that the defense crumbled in a few moments, the men falling back in disorder.

At the very moment when the massive attack started, General Howard was returning to his headquarters at Dowdall's after visiting Sickles at Hazel Grove. His absence from the vital right flank at this critical moment was serious, but it is to be doubted that he could have taken any constructive steps to reduce the impact of the Confederate assault even if he had been on the spot. At such a time,

the presence of the commander in person is imperative chiefly for its influence on morale, but there would have been no time for Howard to issue effective orders and even less time for them to be transmitted and executed. It was General Couch's opinion, expressed later, that "no corps in the army, surprised as the Eleventh was at this time, could have held its ground under similar circumstances."

There was no stopping the cheering, exultant men of Jackson's big divisions. Wild with enthusiasm, the irresistible Confederates rolled over brigade after brigade of the successive lines of Howard's corps, as the retrograde movement of the overwhelmed regiments quickly turned into a confused rout which gained momentum as the Confederate avalanche ground steadily forward towards Chancellorsville.

The sight that greeted Howard as he galloped up to Talley's Hill was one to cause the heart of the bravest general to turn over. Men in blue were fleeing for their lives in every direction, throwing away their rifles as they

[239]

ran. Equipment was strewn everywhere, terrified artillery horses were rearing and plunging, men were falling rapidly, and fleeing cattle clogged the road. All efforts to rally and reform the fugitives were unavailing. The panic in that first wild melee was complete.

There were plenty of brave men and courageous officers in the Eleventh Corps, and under a different set of circumstances the corps might have made a worthier stand. But its low morale, as previously explained, and the lack of confidence which the higher commanders displayed in so many of its regiments, were enough to make the corps a sitting duck for the Confederate hunters almost without the assist gratuitously made by the generals of the corps as a result of their wholly inadequate security measures.

Somewhat further to the east, in the direction of Chancellorsville, Major General Carl Schurz's Third Division of the Eleventh Corps, with a strength of about 5,000 men, had sufficient warning, from the noise of the conflict and the rush of men to the rear, to form a hasty line of defense that extended from the wood opposite Hawkin's Farm, past Wilderness Church, to Dowdall's Tavern on the Turnpike. But the time available was too short to make the position strong or to prepare the men psychologically for the impending shock and the wild flight of their fellow-soldiers. The fast driving Confederate bolt soon hit that line with solid force and it too quickly melted.

By six o'clock, less than an hour after Jackson first struck the unprepared Federal right, the Confederates had firm possession of Talley's Hill. One last despairing Federal effort to salvage something from the wreckage was made east of Wilderness Church, but the panic had by now infected the entire corps and this final line was quickly broken and streamed to the rear in company with the others.

John L. Collins, an officer of the 8th Pennsylvania Cavalry with Pleasonton's brigade, who had become separated from his command in the fighting near Hazel Grove and was trying to find his way back to his troops, has testified to the heroic efforts of General Howard to stem the rout of his corps.*

In the very height of the flight we came upon General Howard, who seemed to be the only man in his own command that was not running at that moment. He was in the middle of the road and mounted, his

HOWARD TRYING TO STOP THE ROUT OF HIS TROOPS

*Battles and Leaders of the Civil War, Vol. III page 184.

Map 19. The Situation At 7:15 P. M., May 2, 1863

Soon after Jackson launched his attack, the broken XI Corps was fleeing east in great disorder. Sickles by 7:15 P. M. had broken off his movement to the south and southeast and had faced Birney, Whipple, and Williams back toward the Turnpike to stem the Confederate advance. But the first unit sent north to assist Howard was the 8th Pennsylvania Cavalry, then near Hazel Grove. This regiment promptly marched north, ran into the Confederates moving along the Turnpike, made its heroic but costly charge, after which the surviving members made their way back to the Chancellor House where they were re-formed.

Federal artillery at Hazel Grove and Fairview is firing effectively. Sykes has moved northwest along the Ely's Ford Road. Reynolds, who had received orders at 7 A. M. that day to march to Chancellorsville, has reached U. S. Ford with two of his three divisions; his third division is some six miles to the rear.

Barlow's brigade of Howard's corps has not yet received orders to break off its advance south.

The Confederate attack has lost its initial momentum, the units at the front having become disoriented and intermingled in the darkness and the woods. Jackson has ordered Hill to pass through Rodes and resume the assault.

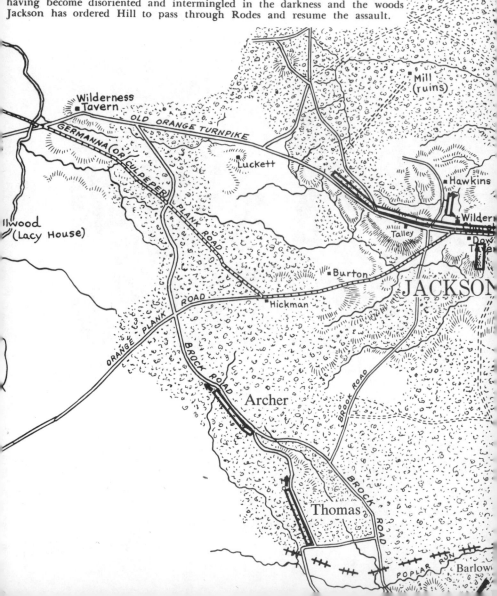

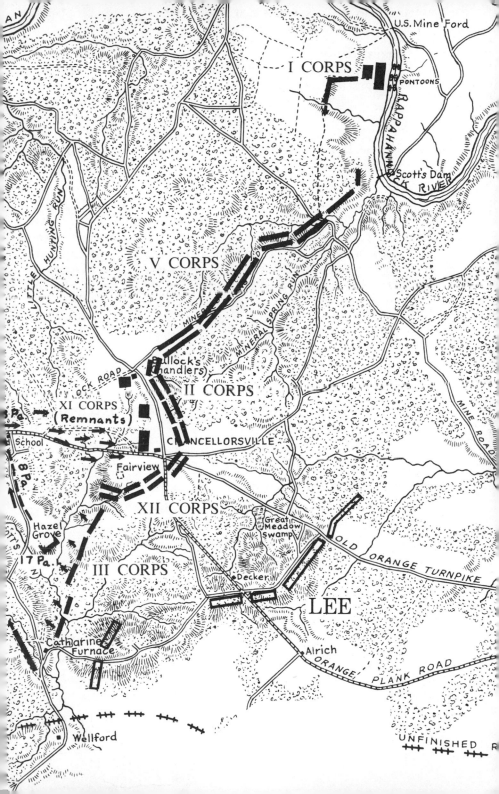

maimed arm embracing a stand of colors that some regiment had deserted, while with his sound arm he was gesticulating to the men to make a stand by their flag. With bared head he was pleading with his soldiers, literally weeping as he entreated the unheeding hordes. . . . Pharaoh and his chariots could have held back the walls of the Red Sea as easily as those officers (Howard and several members of his staff) could resist this retreat.

My course was right oblique from the road, and I had not gone far before I saw lines that I knew were not retreating. Their flags were flying, and my heart took a bound as I beheld battery after battery galloping into position, and regiment after regiment wheeling into line behind them. A line of battle showed itself at last; the Third Corps had come up to stop the successful charge, and Jackson's men would find a difference between attacking the Third Corps in front and the Eleventh in rear.

The Federals Make a Stand

It was 6:30 P.M. before General Hooker received the news of the disaster to his right. That seems strange until one remembers that this was the year 1863, radio communication was unknown, artillery fire almost nonexistent in the Wilderness except on the roads and from prearranged positions in the clearings, and the sound of musket firing was localized by the very denseness of the forest. Still, it would seem that at least one mounted staff officer might have had the presence of mind to take an extended gallop to warn the army commander of what had occurred. On the other hand, the reception given by Howard's division commanders and Howard himself, earlier in the afternoon, to those who had anticipated trouble, had not been of a kind to encourage further initiative on the part of either the line or staff. Poetic justice seemingly had prevailed.

Hooker was seated peacefully on the porch of the Chancellor House when suddenly the first wave of fleeing men, horses, cattle, and vehicles was seen coming at a run down the Turnpike. The sight struck Hooker like a thunderclap, but it must be said to his credit that he reacted immediately and decisively—a pleasant change from his recent complacency. Quickly mounting his horse, the general galloped out to meet the retreating mass, sized up the situation as the old fighting division commander would have done, and at once snappy orders began to crackle.

Guns were ordered to Fairview, down the road a short distance toward Dowdall's to block the Confederate advance. One of Couch's brigades was posted across the road running north from the Chancellorsville crossroads to halt the rout and the Confederates alike. Hiram Berry's division of Sickles' corps was moved forward to the Fairview area to offer organized resistance. A division of Meade's Fifth Corps was shifted to the crossroads, near Bullock's, and a message dispatched to Pleasonton to send a cavalry regiment immediately to Howard. Order of a sort was being restored.

Meantime Sickles, having become acutely aware of the excitement on both sides of the Turnpike to the north of him, took things into his own hands, broke off the fighting below Hazel Grove, which had about petered out anyway, and headed north where things were getting hot. Nor had Pleasonton waited for Hooker's order to exercise his own initiative. Taking two of his cavalry regiments and as many guns as he could quickly get his fingers on, Pleasonton moved energetically to operate against the head and right flank of the Confederates advancing east along the Turnpike.

Reynold's First Corps, coming up from Fredericksburg, was crossing United States Mine Ford at this inauspicious moment, just in time for his column to help clog the already crowded road from the ford to Chancellorsville. Although Hooker had neglected to inform Reynolds where he intended to employ the First Corps, there is reason to believe that it would have been posted on Howard's right, to close the then existing gap and to anchor the right of the Federal semicircular defense line on the Rapidan River. It was now too late for that, and Reynolds was directed "to occupy the ground vacated by the Eleventh

MAJOR GENERAL JOHN F. REYNOLDS

Corps." This in itself was a rather weird, hopeless mission which no doubt gave the solid Reynolds some food for thought, particularly after he had learned the extent of the debacle on the army right.

The shades of night were now beginning to fall, to the considerable advantage of the Federal forces, for Stonewall Jackson's divisions were under the strictest injunction to let nothing stop them in their impetuous and so far thrillingly successful drive to inflict a crushing defeat on their old foe. Jackson could well have used a few more hours of daylight to put the finishing touches to his outstanding performance. Despite the superlative achievement of his Second Corps, entirely too much time had been taken in covering the dozen miles from Decker's. Yet the fault was not Jackson's. His blazing spirit seemingly could not multiply itself to accomplish the march and development in less time. But it is not unreasonable to conclude that his corps could have cut through to seize United States Mine Ford if he had started at 4 A.M. as planned. What slowed him down during the early hours of twilight, after the virtual destruction of Howard's Eleventh Corps, was a combination of Confederate troop confusion in the darkness of the forest, weariness, disorganization, and the resulting loss of momentum in the ranks of his attacking divisions, and a stiffening of resistance by the Federal corps other than the Eleventh. The sharp edge of Jackson's penetration had finally been blunted and the Confederate waves were now breaking ineffectually against hard rock in place of yielding sand.

Worth His Weight in Gold

His ear acutely cocked to sounds from the west, Lee acted promptly to order into action the divisions of Anderson and McLaws as soon as the noise of the conflict on the Turnpike reached him. The two Confederate generals threw their divisions, or as many of the troops as were in contact, into a vicious attack on Hooker's center at Chancellorsville. This nicely coordinated drive was calculated to overrun the important crossroads, smother the units protecting the Chancellor House, and either cut the Federal line or keep the enemy so fully occupied that no troops could be detached to interfere with Jackson's efforts on the flank.

There was to be no rest for the fleeing fugitives from Howard's corps, who had escaped from the pursuing Confederates at Dowdall's only to run smack into a flurry of fighting on the Chancellorsville front. The frightful confusion can only be imagined. Ambulances, baggage wagons, caissons, loose animals, camp followers, and frenzied soldiers flowed rapidly east in a tide of human flotsam that might have brought to an inglorious end the resolute Army of the Potomac, had it not been made of sterner stuff.

This was not the first time the Confederates had in-flicted a near disaster on a Union army. But the Army of the Potomac as a whole did not panic easily, and once again its sturdy regiments rose magnificently to the occasion in spite of the crumpling of their right flank and the write-off, for all practical purposes, of an entire corps of three divisions.

Hancock's division of the Second Corps was posted at the center across the Turnpike and thus received the heaviest weight of the collateral Confederate blow, deliver-ed with artillery and infantry by Lee's two divisions. The strongly fortified front line on Hancock's sector was under the command of an unusually keen young officer named Nelson A. Miles, whose skillful and determined handling of the battle at that point, in refreshing contrast to much that happened elsewhere that afternoon of May 2, would win for him a retroactive Congressional Medal of Honor. Repeatedly and violently the Confederates concentrated their attack on Miles' regiment, but each time were vigor-ously repulsed. It was a shining example that the young officer set for the rest of the army and the action was conspicuous in the midst of the infighting which raged over much of the Wilderness.

Division Commander Hancock, watching that part of the front in company with Corps Commander Couch during one of the Confederate attacks, was so impressed by Miles' conduct of the defense that he impulsively turned to a member of his staff with the remark: "Ride down and tell Colonel Miles he is worth his weight in gold." To which comment Couch added the prophetic remark: "I shall not be greatly surprised to find myself some day serving under that young man." Thirty-four years later, in 1897, Nelson A. Miles became Chief of Staff of the U.S. Army.

The months of disciplinary training in the Federal camps above Falmouth were now paying off. The steadiness in the ranks of the Second, Third, Fifth, and Twelfth Corps, and their refusal to panic as Howard's refugees streamed through them to the rear and even beyond Chancellorsville into the arms of the Confederates, gave assurance that the Confederates had begun to sail into rough waters. These Federal veterans were undisturbed by the tumult and shouting and shooting—it was all in the day's work, and had Hooker only known it, his army was in shape and in sufficient strength to recapture the initiative, launch a counterattack against Jackson's weary troops, and more than cancel the debt.

Perhaps that was too much to expect from the Hooker of April 30-May 2, whose defensive psychology had become a fixed attitude that nothing could shake. The Army of the Potomac would save him from himself, but its personnel were powerless to do any more in spite of their capabilities and the willingness to make the most of them, given competent leadership at the top.

The Federal Cavalry Has an Adventure

Cooperating with Sickles at Hazel Grove and the Furnace, Pleasonton's cavalry was given the mission of going to the aid of Howard's hard-pressed corps on the Turnpike. Sickles' two divisions, under Birney and Whipple, in company with the 6th New York Cavalry, which covered Sickles' flanks, were pretty well isolated from the rest of the army at Hazel Grove and hence in danger of being cut off. By the same token, however, they were a thorn in Lee's side in holding what may fairly be termed the key position on the battlefield. Sickles for one was keenly conscious of its strategic importance and confident that his corps, properly supported, could hold the position.

Pleasonton had the 8th and 17th Pennsylvania Cavalry Regiments with him at the western and northern edges of Hazel Grove, within several hundred yards of the southernmost element of Howard's Eleventh Corps. Both regiments were relaxing at ease but ready for any contingency, although restricted to the extent that they had been sent there to cooperate with Sickles and thus were not free to go off on independent adventures of their own.

When Pleasonton was informed of the stampede of the Eleventh Corps he has said that he sent the 8th Pennsylvania to find and help Howard, and moved the 17th Pennsylvania off into the woods to the left to hold the enemy in check until he could get artillery into firing position. By dint of great exertion and considerable good fortune he managed to assemble 22 guns in a formidable line and, facing west rather than east, was ready for Jackson's men when they came up about dusk, after forcing their way through the tangled forest.

The 8th Pennsylvania Cavalry, Major Pennock Huey commanding, moved north on the road running to the Turnpike,* in a column of twos, with the three squadrons also in column. Huey's account of this and the following action declared that he was told only to assist Howard, nothing having been said of the disaster that had already engulfed the Eleventh Corps. His troopers, laboring under the inspired delusion that Lee's army was retreating, were in high spirits in spite of the gathering darkness and uncertainty of the situation. They were completely unaware that a large force of Confederates was advancing at right angles to their direction of march, and just a short distance away.

The head of the regiment had almost reached the Plank Road, sabers still in the scabbards and pistols holstered, when they were startled to discover the road filled with Confederates, whose skirmishers lapped over on both flanks of the Federal cavalry. Huey's lively account of what followed is given in his own words:

It was here that I gave the command to "draw sabres and charge," which order was repeated by

---

*The Plank Road and the Turnpike coincide between Wilderness Church and Chancellorsville.

Major Keenan (comd'g the first battalion) and other officers. On reaching the Plank road it appeared to be packed about as closely with the enemy as it could be.

We turned to the left, facing the Confederate column, the regiment crowding on, both men and horses in a perfect frenzy of excitement, which nothing but death could stop. We cut our way through, trampling down all who could not escape us, and using our sabers on all within reach, for a distance of about 100 yards, when we received a volley from the enemy, which killed Major Keenan, Captain Arrowsmith, and Adjutant Haddock, three of the noblest and most gallant officers of the war, besides a large number of men.

This was one of the unplanned, accidental lethal encounters that constantly occur on battlefields, make their unrecorded impact for good or ill on the plans of the generals, and are forgotten by history unless some participant preserves the episode in writing for the edification of posterity. The charge of the 8th Pennsylvania Cavalry was a great surprise both to the enemy and itself. It had no choice but to charge or surrender, and no one can say whether or not it proved anything, or how long it took for the elements of the regiment who survived to regain the cohesiveness of an organized unit. After receiving the destructive volley the survivors made their way east to Chancellorsville, where they were formed again in line, to intercept stragglers.

Nevertheless, it is not beyond the realm of possibility that the unexpected boldness of a single regiment of Federal cavalry, appearing suddenly in the very midst of the infantry fighting, made a marked impression on the minds of the Confederate foot soldiers. The result could very well have been to cause the latter to be extraordinarily alert to the possibility that other Federal cavalry was prowling about in the forest, and that it was that form of trigger-happiness that led directly to the wounding and subsequent death of Stonewall Jackson.

Federal Artillery at Hazel Grove

The diversion caused by the 8th Pennsylvania Cavalry was of a temporary character. On the Confederates came, through the woods, solid masses of men in skirmish line and column, carrying a Union flag taken from the Eleventh Corps, or possibly picked up off the ground. It was growing darker by the moment as the Confederates burst from the woods into the clearing at Hazel Grove and let loose a volley of musketry from thousands of muskets as they rushed into the open.

The Federal command to fire rang out and 22 guns answered almost with a single roar. At pointblank range the carnage among the Confederates was indescribable. Quickly reloading, the guns fired a second time, and then for twenty minutes poured canister into the torn gray ranks and, as Pleasonton remarked, "the affair was over."

It was Rodes' Division that tried to take Hazel Grove and failed. Pleasonton was later to record that the Confederates would have succeeded if their infantry fire had been more accurate and aimed lower to take advantage of ricochets. As it happened, most of the musket balls passed harmlessly over the heads of the Federal cannoneers, who for their part aimed low and made their bursts fully effective.

General Henry Hunt, Chief of Artillery of the Army of the Potomac, would have been proud of his artillery that day had he been present. But one of Hooker's many errors of judgment at Chancellorsville had been to relieve the architect of his superb artillery corps of field command, leaving him with only administrative responsibilities, until almost the eleventh hour, when he was again given full charge of all the artillery, both administrative and tactical. The way in which the Federal artillery functioned was a lasting tribute to the years of dedicated, intelligent preparation and training which Hunt had devoted to the guns and those who served them. Hunt would have approved of the way those 22 guns stopped cold the attempt of Rodes' Division to overrun Hazel Grove, and he was entitled to share with them the credit for preventing two divisions of Sickles' corps, at the same time, from being irretrievably cut off from the main body of the army.

Hunt would likewise have been thoroughly pleased had he been in position to observe the heroic work of another artillery outfit, Dilger's Battery of Howard's Corps, during the first mad dash of the Eleventh Corps to the rear. Hubert Dilger had learned what makes a good artilleryman tick during service with the horse artillery in his native Germany, which he left to join the Union Army. They gave him command of an Ohio battery and before

DILGER'S BATTERY STAYING JACKSON'S ADVANCE

long, under his skilful and loving care, it became Dilger's Battery, Eleventh Corps. There was none better.

The story of Dilger's Battery on the Plank Road, facing almost alone the onrushing mass of Confederates, and fighting an incredible rear guard action without benefit of infantry for a good half-hour, is excitingly told by Fairfax Downey in *Sound of the Guns.** Single-handedly the indomitable captain, manipulating his gun crews with tactical skill and courage, denied the use of one of the only two roads open to Jackson and inflicted heavy damage on the advancing Confederates until they managed to swarm in on his embattled guns from the woods on either side of the road and force a withdrawal barely in time to avoid capture. To what extent Dilger's lone battery was able to buy time for Hooker's divisions in rear to readjust their lines to meet Jackson's advance can only be conjectured, but there can be little doubt that his bold conduct accomplished greater results than all the rest of the Eleventh Corps put together.

All during the early hours of the night the Federal artillery, emplaced at Fairview, Hazel Grove, Chancellorsville, and other points to the north, poured shell and canister into the temporarily jumbled brigades of Jackson's Corps, giving them no peace and, in the darkness, making it difficult to reconstitute them as efficient units. In spite of which, Jackson's zeal to "press on" had not abated, and he was prompt to urge A. P. Hill, whose division was in better shape than the other two by reason of having been the tail-ender in the attack column, to rush a brigade to cut Hooker off from United States Mine Ford. Before the attempt could be made, both Jackson and Hill were wounded, and the day's fighting came to an end.

---

*The Story of the American Artillery, David McKay Co., N. Y., 1955, p. 145 et seq.

JACKSON IS WOUNDED

CHAPTER 13

JACKSON'S LAST BATTLE

FIGHTING continued sporadically far into the night of May 2, which was an almost unheard-of occurrence during the first half of the Civil War. But the aftermath of Jackson's flank march, the fighting on the right of Hooker's army, and the disastrous foot race of the Union Eleventh Corps, which could have led to the complete defeat of the Army of the Potomac, had keyed up both armies to such an extent that precedent was shattered.

The fierce drive which animated the spirit of Stonewall Jackson, in his famous maneuver and the devastating surprise attack into which it led, had not diminished in the least when darkness closed in over the battlefield. His divisions had taken the initial objectives he had designated; it was the enemy that was "ingloriously flying." The thought uppermost in Jackson's mind at this stage was how best to exploit the victory already so handsomely won on a part of the field.

The none too easy ten-hour march had been followed immediately by a difficult deployment in the Wilderness on a two-mile front, then a raging attack through thickets that the Federal generals regarded as impassable. Who can doubt that the driving force of General Jackson, despite the foregoing, would have pressed the attack through the night, so that he might reap the fruits of victory? It was his hope that by continuing the attack he could squeeze Hooker between Lee and himself, block the Union army off from United States Mine Ford, cut Hooker to pieces in the process, or at the very least link up with Lee's wing before Chancellorsville to drive the Federal army into the Rappahannock.

The mere fact that his own divisions were tired out, could have used some food to advantage, and were badly in need of reshuffling after the wholesale intermingling of organizations during the early hours of the attack, would not deter the impatient Jackson; neither would the increasing resistance of the remaining corps of the Union army which succeeded the confusion attending the roll-up of its right flank. Jackson was the kind of general who would figure that the time to press the attack is when the enemy is demoralized, and he suspected that to be the case with Hooker's divisions, if the example of the Eleventh Corps could be taken as the criterion. Even though his troops were confronted with the tough assignment of further fighting in the darkness, their morale was high and the enemy would be facing equal difficulties. He, Jackson, had gained the ascendancy and was determined to hold the initiative as long as his men were able to remain on their feet.

Rodes' Division, in the van of the attack, had by this time lost all semblance of a cohesive unit, as was to be expected. That level-headed commander decided that the cause would be better served were he to take time out to pull his units together for more effective work, so he called a halt to the advance and requested that A. P. Hill's Division, in the third line, be brought forward to take the lead and continue the attack. That made sense to Jackson, who was up front and in close touch with the forward elements, as he always was in the heat of battle. He at once gave the order to a staff officer, who put spurs to his horse and in a few moments Hill reported to receive the corps commander's instructions.

"Press them, Hill. Cut them off from the United States Ford. Press them!" ordered the taciturn Jackson, the direct actionist who was a believer in short, concise oral orders. Jackson knew what he wanted done, quickly, and the fiery Hill, his smoldering feud with his corps commander forgotten for the moment, was not one to ask questions. Galloping off, and no doubt enthused by the opportunity for the Light Division to take the place of honor at the front of the corps, Hill sped to his troops to put them in position on either side of the Turnpike, ready to leapfrog the advance brigades.

A bright moon had arisen to throw an eerie light on the Turnpike and the occasional clearings, intensifying the shadows and giving to the terrain and natural objects that unnatural appearance with which every soldier is familiar who has marched or maneuvered at night. Because they were unfamiliar with the Chancellorsville terrain, neither Jackson nor any of his generals knew exactly where they were or the precise trace of their front-line position. The moon helped, of course, and there must be a road or roads that would lead to United States Mine

Ford in rear of Chancellorsville. It wouldn't do to push much further ahead without that knowledge, so Jackson, still the direct actionist, decided to find out for himself.

Accompanied by several members of his staff and one of Stuart's couriers, who had brought a message from the cavalry commander and was retained by Jackson as a guide familiar with the countryside, the small cavalcade of mounted men started out on the personal reconnaissance that was to mark Stonewall Jackson's last ride. Moving at a walk along the Turnpike, which coincided with the Orange Plank Road from Dowdall's Tavern to the Chancellorsville crossroads, Jackson halted at an old schoolhouse, one of the more familiar landmarks of the region. Across the road could be seen two roads branching off to the northeast, the nearer of which Stuart's courier identified as the Mountain Road, a spur paralleling the Turnpike for only a short distance and leading nowhere; the other was a road leading to Bullock's Farm, about a mile north of Chancellorsville.

That was important intelligence, but Jackson had to know more. How close was the enemy? What were they doing? Down the Mountain Road went the little group of horsemen, the staff growing increasingly nervous as they found themselves in a no-man's land ahead of their own lines and an unknown distance, perhaps half a mile, possibly only a few yards, from the enemy. It was no place for a lieutenant general to play scout, and one of the staff officers questioned the advisability of going any further. Jackson assured him that all was well, the enemy was on the run, they would continue.

After a bit the general halted, motioned for silence, and cocked his ear. Noises to the east and not too far off! An officer giving a command to some men; the sound of axes! That was what he had come out here for. The Federals were close by and fortifying their position.

Turning their horses, the little group started to retrace

WHERE JACKSON WAS SHOT

Grave of unknown Union soldier within a few feet of monument marking the spot where Jackson was wounded.

their steps to their own lines. Taking up the trot, as though symbolic of Jackson's urgent anxiety to renew the attack, fortifications or no fortifications, and to galvanize A. P. Hill into action, the Confederate horsemen rapidly approached the line of their own outguards. Trigger-happy and understandably nervous, the Confederate skirmishers out in front along the Turnpike heard the clatter of hoofs, saw the shadowy figures coming towards them at a rapid gait, and mistook them for a detachment of Federal cavalry looking for trouble. A single shot rang out, then another, followed by a volley as Hill's men opened up to repel the imagined threat, killing a captain and a sergeant in Jackson's small party.

"Cease firing. You are firing on your own men!" shouted one of Jackson's staff officers as he leaped from his horse and ran excitedly toward the Confederate lines. But it was too late. Jackson's frightened horse bolted, galloping wildly in the direction of the enemy.

With difficulty the general managed to get the animal under control sufficiently to turn its head towards his own lines, when another volley from a North Carolina regiment on the north side of the Turnpike found its mark, three bullets striking Jackson as he fought to rein in his now almost unmanageable horse. One bullet lodged in his right hand; another passed through the left wrist and came out through the palm of that hand; the third passed completely through his left arm between the elbow and the shoulder, badly shattering the large bone and cutting the main artery, rendering the arm useless. Little Sorrel plunged into the thicket, knocking the general's hat off and badly scraping his face. Fortunately he had by that time reached the line of pickets, where ready hands caught at the reins of the trembling animal and carefully assisted the disabled corps commander to dismount. Already weak from loss of blood and shock, Jackson was placed on the ground in a grove just north of the Turnpike and first aid of a sort administered.

Bad news travels fast, and in a short time A. P. "Powell" Hill, who had also been reconnoitering along the front in close proximity to Jackson, hurried up, to be joined almost at once by other staff officers, including Captain James Power Smith, one of Jackson's aides. Smith had been acting as a communication center between the artillery reserve at the rear and Jackson's moving command post in the saddle, during the attack and pursuit of the early evening.

Young Smith, who was later to enter the ministry, has

left an authentic first-hand report of Jackson's removal from the battlefield. Remaining with the wounded general from then on throughout the night, his story, among many, has the ring of truth*:

The writer reached his side a minute after, to find General Hill holding the head and shoulders of the wounded chief. Cutting open the coat-sleeve from wrist to shoulder, I found the wound in the upper arm, and with my handkerchief I bound the arm above the wound to stem the flow of blood. Couriers were sent for Dr. Hunter McGuire, the surgeon of the corps and the general's trusted friend, and for an ambulance. Being outside of our lines, it was urgent that he should be moved at once. With difficulty litter-bearers were brought from the line near by, and the general was placed upon the litter and carefully raised to the shoulder, I myself bearing one corner. A moment after, artillery from the Federal side was opened upon us; great broadsides thundered over the woods; hissing shells searched the dark thickets through, and shrapnels swept the road along which we moved. Two or three steps farther, and the litter-bearer at my side was struck and fell, but, as the litter turned, Major Watkins Leigh, of Hill's staff, happily caught it. But the fright of the men was so great that we were obliged to lay the litter and its burden down upon the road. As the litter-bearers ran to the cover of the trees, I threw myself by the general's side and held him firmly to the ground as he attempted to rise. Over us swept the rapid fire of shot and shell—grape-shot striking fire upon the flinty rock of the road all around us, and sweeping from their feet horses and men of the artillery just moved to the front. Soon the firing veered to the other side of the road, and I sprang to my feet, assisted the general to rise, passed my arm around him, and with the wounded man's weight thrown heavily upon me, we forsook the road. Entering the woods, he sank to the ground from exhaustion, but the litter was soon

*Battles and Leaders, page 211.

brought, and again rallying a few men, we essayed to carry him farther, when a second bearer fell at my side. This time, with none to assist, the litter careened, and the general fell to the ground, with a groan of deep pain. Greatly alarmed, I sprang to his head, and, lifting his head as a stray beam of moonlight came through clouds and leaves, he opened his eyes and wearily said: "Never mind me, Captain, never mind me." Raising him again to his feet, he was accosted by Brigadier-General Pender: "Oh, General, I hope you are not seriously wounded. I will have to retire my troops to re-form them, they are so much broken by this fire." But Jackson, rallying his strength, with firm voice said: "You must hold your ground, General Pender; you must hold your ground, sir!" and so uttered his last command on the field.

Again we resorted to the litter, and with difficulty bore it through the bush, and then under a hot fire along the road. Soon an ambulance was reached, and stopping to seek some stimulant at Chancellor's (Dowdall's Tavern), we were found by Dr. McGuire, who at once took charge of the wounded man. Passing back over the battle-field of the afternoon, we reached the Wilderness store, and then, in a field on the north, the field-hospital of our corps under Dr. Harvey Black. Here we found a tent prepared, and after midnight the left arm was amputated near the shoulder, and a ball taken from the right hand.

It was during the heavy Federal bombardment described by Jackson's aide, while the disabled corps commander was being transported to the rear, that A. P. Hill received his wound in company with many another Confederate. Hill's wound, while slight, proved sufficiently disabling to require his removal for treatment. Several shell fragments had struck him in both legs, resulting in painful but not serious injury.

Hill managed to move under his own power a short distance to the rear, where he conferred with his nearby brigadiers. Although Rodes was the senior division commander after Hill, he was not a major general, and all agreed that Hill should send word to Jeb Stuart that he was their choice to succeed Jackson as acting corps commander.

Pandemonium in the Moonlight

Conscious of the isolation of his two divisions at Hazel Grove, Birney's and Whipple's, but at the same time aggressively aware of the fact that his position, between Lee's right wing facing Hooker at Chancellorsville and Jackson's Corps driving in from the west, served as a Federal wedge to prevent a junction of the two Confederate wings, Sickles had been urging Hooker to permit him to launch an attack. His purpose ostensibly was to recover several guns which had been abandoned during the early part of the evening, when Rodes' troops were stopped in their tracks by the artillery Pleasonton had commandered at the Grove to meet the Confederate assault. But Sickles was full of fight and temperamentally allergic to passive resistance at any time, and besides, his tenuous line of communication with Chancellorsville could stand strengthening, having already been temporarily cut by an enterprising body of Confederates. All in all, a vigorous attack would in Sickles' opinion be a salutary move that should not be delayed till morning lest it then be too late to derive the collateral benefits.

At ten o'clock the desired permission was received from Hooker and preparations for the attack in the moonlit forest got under way. Staff officers were sent to division commanders Williams, of Slocum's Twelfth Corps, and Berry of Sickles' own, to inform them of the plan and assure their cooperation. Williams' division, which was the nearest, found that his line was at right angles to Sickles' at Hazel Grove. Fearful of confusion in the darkness, Williams requested that the attack be deferred until Slocum, then at army headquarters, could approve, but the

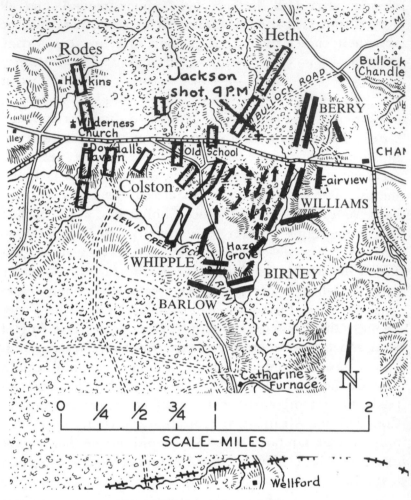

MAP 20. SICKLES' NIGHT ATTACK

This portrays the situation about midnight, May 2, 1863. Sickles has just made his night attack and the troops—those who could be rounded up—have returned to the positions from which they jumped off. Barlow's brigade returned from its fruitless expedition south of the unfinished railroad just in time to witness the mob scene in the moonlight. The men are supperless, having left their knapsacks at Dowdall's, but doubtless happy not to have participated in the action of the XI and III Corps.

courier either garbled the reply on his return to Sickles, or the latter disregarded the request, for the attack proceeded as planned.

With bayonets fixed, Birney's division moved out shortly before midnight, in column of brigades, regiments abreast and formed in line of companies, each company in column of fours. The center regiment of each brigade marched astride the road leading north to the old schoolhouse on the Turnpike, almost a mile distant, which at this time was occupied by the advance elements of Jackson's Corps, although Sickles wasn't aware of that and Birney's regiments only knew that they were likely to encounter the enemy at any moment.

It was not long before pandemonium broke loose in the darkness. Birney's regiments on the right ran into William's Federal troops while those on the left overran Lane's Confederates. The regiments on the road reached the Turnpike but failed to hold it. Musketry firing became general all over the lot, friendly and enemy troops shooting promiscuously at one another; at the same time Slocum's artillery opened up on his order, since no one had informed him of the projected Third Corps attack, and he was taking no chances.

As a coordinated attack the effort proved somewhat abortive. If Sickles expected Williams and Berry to make a concerted effort to drive back the Confederates on the Turnpike, he failed to make it clear just what form their cooperation should take. The attack turned out to be a unilateral one on Birney's part, but it did serve a useful purpose. For Sickles was able to improve his position, somewhat further advanced in the direction of the Turnpike, and to secure ground to the right that enabled his pickets to connect with those of the Twelfth Corps. Furthermore, the heavy fire which was directed into the mass of Confederate troops on the left had the effect of cooling their ardor for any further adventures that night.

The confusion in the ranks of Jackson's Corps as a result of the intermingling of units collateral to their impetuous advance, the difficulties inherent in fighting in the darkness on unfamiliar terrain, particularly that of the Wilderness, and the depressing moral effect of the loss of Jackson and Hill within a few minutes, combined to set the Confederates up as likely candidates for a severe reverse at Federal hands. Had Sickles and Slocum taken time to put their heads together to plan a coordinated counterattack with the two corps working together as a team, instead of getting in each other's way and killing each other's men, there would have been a good possibility that the panic of the Federal Eleventh Corps might have been duplicated, with the Confederates on the receiving end. But that was not to be, and the Federals were forced to content themselves with the thought that valuable time at least had been bought and they were still in the fight.

General Rodes, temporarily in command of Jackson's Corps after A. P. Hill was wounded, now called a halt in the attack, countermanding Jackson's earlier order to Hill's Division (presently commanded by Harry Heth) to push on to United States Mine Ford, and the two armies settled down to a few hours of doubtful rest before morning and certain resumption of the fighting.

The interesting speculation presents itself as to what might have happened during the night if Jackson had not been wounded. It is almost certain that the attack by A. P. Hill's Division up the road through Bullock's would have been continued with the object of cutting in behind Hooker's position at Chancellorsville. But then what? Meade's unused Fifth Corps was ready for action and Reynold's First Corps was now on the field, tired after its forced march but capable of giving a good account of itself. Without knowing the topography, without any preparation beyond the command to "press forward and cut them off from the United States Ford," without coordination between the three divisions of his corps, and unable to use his artillery in the dense forest, Jackson's chances for an effective nighttime exploitation of his daylight success cannot be said to have been of the best.

A Lost Opportunity

Hooker's ineptly conceived and ineffectual employment of his cavalry during the Chancellorsville campaign has been mentioned, but little has been said about the activities of the cavalry division of 3,400 sabers, commanded by Brigadier General W. W. Averell, following his duel with Fitzhugh Lee and Averell's failure to destroy the latter in the March affair at Kelly's Ford.

It will be recalled that in late April Stoneman's cavalry corps was split into two columns for the raid on Lee's communications with Richmond and each column given a separate mission, Averell's being to take on the enemy cavalry at Culpeper and presumably keep it off the backs of Hooker's right wing as the latter advanced on Chancellorsville.

Averell's division ran into advance elements of Rooney Lee's Brigade at Brandy Station, drove them back on Lee's main body at Culpeper, and then continued on to Rapidan Station, pushing the Confederates ahead of them. A packet of mail captured at Brandy Station disclosed a letter which said that the Federal cavalry was being followed by Hooker's whole army and that Jackson's corps of 25,000 men was at Gordonsville preparing to resist Hooker. This "intelligence" Averell had forwarded to Hooker with the comment that it was "believed to be reliable and important."

During these movements Averell received several dispatches from Stoneman which were somewhat ambiguous and in at least one instance at variance with Hooker's original instructions to the cavalry corps. Purporting to guide Averell's actions, they were badly phrased. Stoneman's intentions, as explained in his official report, were not discernible in the wording of the messages. Averell interpreted the instructions to mean that he was to keep the enemy cavalry in the vicinity occupied, while Stoneman avers that the intent of the orders was for Averell to block off his immediate opposition and then promptly rejoin the main army.

The net result of the badly mishandled situation was that Averell remained inactive for two nights and a day at Rapidan Station, with Rooney Lee facing him across the river and apparently quite content with being able to pin down such a large force of enemy cavalry with but a fraction of their strength. Rapidan Station was only twenty miles west of Chancellorsville, less than half a day's march for cavalry. Somehow Hooker got wind of what was going on and sent word to Averell directing him to bring his whole outfit to Chancellorsville (where his regiments could be used to advantage). Nothing happened. A repeat message on the afternoon of May 2 finally brought action, and in due course the cavalry division found its way to Ely's Ford, only five miles distant from the battlefield, where again it came to a halt on the north side of the river and simply marked time. Up to now Averell's score had been only one man killed, and two officers and two men wounded, which explains his ineffectual operations more eloquently than a dozen reports.

Here was a case of another lost opportunity for the Army of the Potomac, which if understood and grasped could have changed the course of the battle. The word "could" is used advisedly, for there can be no assurance that Hooker would have employed Averell's cavalry any more effectively than he did Pleasonton's, which *was* at hand in brigade strength and could have secured the army right flank if Hooker had so directed. The upshot of the matter was that Hooker relieved Averell of command of his division, but stopped short of preferring charges, merely stating that "in detaching him from this army my object has been to prevent an active and powerful column from being paralyzed in its future operations by his presence."

Stuart Takes Command

With the launching of Jackson's flank attack against Hooker's right, Jeb Stuart, whose cavalry had covered the march of the Second Corps, found time hanging heavy on his hands. His horsemen were now idle, their mission completed for the present. It therefore appeared to Stuart that he could operate more constructively if he should move up to Ely's Ford, where reports had it some Federal wagon trains had been parked. Receiving Jackson's permission, about 6 P. M. Stuart led a force of 1,000 men composed of infantry, cavalry, and a battery of artillery and soon arrived at the Ford where he found Averell's Federal cavalry division occupying the north shore. That was an interesting development, which Stuart decided to exploit by way of a preventive, diversionary attack.

But there was far more important work in store for General Stuart than a night encounter with Blue cavalry. As he was making his dispositions for the attack, a staff officer reported from A. P. Hill with a message that both Jackson and himself had been wounded, that Stuart was now the senior officer in the Second Corps, and that he was to return at once to assume command. Sending word to Fitzhugh Lee to secure and hold the road from Ely's Ford to Chancellorsville, to restrain a possible ambitious move by Averell (about which he apparently need not have worried), Stuart galloped off through the darkness to take over.

Ambrose Powell Hill

A. P. Hill, considered by Lee to be the best division commander in the Army of Northern Virginia, was a stormy petrel whose propensity for doing battle was by no means confined to the enemies of the Confederacy. A Virginian whose roots were deeply imbedded in the Old Dominion, Hill had been sent by his financially embarrassed family to West Point as an economic measure. He took kindly to the military profession and by the time of his death at the hands of a Union private before Petersburg in 1865, at the age of 39, he had established a combat reputation among Lee's lieutenants that compared favorably to that of Longstreet and Jackson.

Originally a classmate of Jackson and McClellan, and roommate of the latter at the Military Academy, Hill was forced by illness during his cadetship to drop back a year, graduating in 1847. During the decade before the Civil War he is perhaps remembered best as a rival suitor of McClellan's for the hand of beautiful Ellen Marcy. That was one battle that Hill lost, chiefly because McClellan was then a civilian vice president of the Illinois Central Railroad. The young lady's father, an army man himself, took a dim view of his daughter marrying into the army, for in those days it was difficult for officers to make financial ends meet. Colonel Marcy wanted Ellen to aim higher, opposed Hill's request for her hand, and gave his blessing to her union with George B. McClellan. No doubt both former roommates recalled the competition for Ellen's favor, although with different emotions, when Hill became the willing instrument by which Lee was able to forestall a resounding victory for McClellan at the Battle of Antietam in September 1862.

To his handsome features and slender figure, surmounted by red hair and a red beard, Hill added color by habitually going into battle wearing a flaming red shirt and carrying an ever-ready sword, with which he was wont to smite a skulking soldier or even a recalcitrant officer whose aggressiveness appeared to the general to be in question. A skilled horsemen, absolutely fearless and always impatient to rush headlong into danger, Hill was frequently imprudent, even reckless, and his troops as a rule suffered heavier casualties than most of the other divisions of the army. But the Light Division, which Hill personally led in all the major battles from May 27, 1862, when he was promoted to major general, until he was given command of the newly formed Third Corps after Chancellorsville, always seemed to be selected for the vital battle assignments. Mistakes were made, of course, but the dependence which

MAJOR GENERAL AMBROSE P. HILL, C.S.A.

was increasingly placed on the Light Division, and the manner in which it invariably performed, achieved for its commander and itself a reputation for excellence that was second to none in the Army of Northern Virginia.

Hill's fiery spirit not unnaturally was accompanied by a temper that led him to take offense easily. In a lesser character, or in one whose solid virtues were less evident and unproven on many battlefields, the quick temper might easily have led to personal disaster. Hill's loyalty to his subordinates was an outstanding characteristic, but the quality of his subordination to his superiors was something else.

The merits of his controversy with Longstreet after the

Peninsular Campaign in 1862, and his long feud with Jackson, which ended only when the latter was mortally wounded by Hill's men at Chancellorsville, will have to be fully weighed elsewhere.

Analyzing the hostility between Jackson and Hill, which started before the battle of Antietam, it might appear to those of military mind that Hill's justification was greater than that of Jackson, who frequently, if not habitually, neglected to take his generals into his confidence or give them any advance information about his battle plans or intentions. He was also prone to bear down heavily on them for what seemed to him to be infractions, without investigating the basic cause. And to cap Jackson's seemingly cavalier attitude, there were several historic occasions when he committed the unforgivable military sin of issuing direct orders to Hill's subordinate officers without taking the trouble to notify the division commander. That sort of treatment naturally infuriated Hill, as it would any officer of spirit. The net result, however, was that both of Lee's distinguished corps commanders were goaded at different times into placing General Hill under arrest. As late as a week before the Battle of Chancellorsville relations between Jackson and Hill had become so strained that Jackson wrote Lee asking that Hill be relieved of command in the Second Corps. It required all the patient diplomacy of which R. E. Lee was possessed to reestablish harmonious (on the surface) relations between the warring factions.

The historic fact appears to be that Lee could not afford to spare any one of the three, regardless of the friction between them. It would have taken far more than a seeming personal affront to one at the hands of any one of the others for Lee to allow his most valuable generals the luxury of a personal victory over a fellow-Confederate, no matter what his rank or position. As it turned out, Longstreet and Hill ultimately composed their differences, while the Jackson-Hill feud ended with Hill solicitously supporting the wounded Jackson on the battlefield within a stone's throw of the enemy. Significantly, both Lee and Jackson, with their last breaths, were subconsciously thinking of the impetuous A. P. Hill, for they both called on him by name to bring up his troops as they passed into the Great Beyond.

Two Arms are Lost

Several hours after the ambulance arrived that conveyed Jackson to the corps hospital tent, set up several hundred yards east of Wilderness Run in a field along the Turnpike, chloroform was administered by Doctor McGuire and the left arm amputated just below the shoulder. Tucker Lacy and Captain Smith remained with Jackson throughout the night. In the morning the chaplain removed the severed member to the Lacy farm, which was about a mile distant from the hospital, buried it in a spot near the house, and erected a marker for the dubious benefit of posterity.

After Jackson had regained consciousness, Major Sandy Pendleton came to report that Hill had been wounded, Stuart had reached the field to take command, and he had been sent to learn whether Jackson had any instructions. The drugged general brightened, made an effort to concentrate, and seemed about to respond with his customary incisiveness; then his features fell and he answered feebly: "I don't know—I can't tell; say to General Stuart he must do what he thinks best."

Stuart was in a very difficult position at this juncture. He hadn't the remotest idea what Jackson's followup attack plan might have been, nor was he informed until he arrived on the field as to what shape the corps was in or just where the positions of its several elements might be. General Hill and Captain Boswell, Jackson's Engineer Officer, were the only two who knew that Jackson had directed Hill to advance the Light Division through the darkness to the White House (Bullock's), north of Chancellorsville, to cut Hooker's line to United States Mine Ford; but Boswell had been killed and Hill wounded. Although Stuart must at the first opportunity have consulted Hill on his stretcher and learned of Jackson's plan, common sense dictated a pause for reorganization, with a view to renewing the attack at daybreak. That would give Stuart a few hours to gather up the reins of his unfamiliar steed and to proceed more confidently, instead of jabbing blindly at the Federals with but a foggy conception of the tactical situation.

A note dictated by Jackson was handed to Lee at the Chancellor House after the successful Confederate assault of May 3* had forced Hooker to take up a new line further removed from Chancellorsville. Greatly moved, Lee replied, expressing his deep regret at Jackson's loss in a message that revealed the character of the great leader: "Could I have directed events, I should have chosen for the good of the country to be disabled in your stead. I congratulate you upon the victory, which is due to your skill and energy."

Lee's habitual thoughtfulness for others led him, while the battle was still raging, to direct that Jackson be removed to a safer spot lest through some mischance he be taken prisoner. By a roundabout road, therefore, the wounded general was transported by ambulance to the home of his friend, Mr. Chandler, at Guiney's Station, where he was placed in comfortable quarters which would, it was hoped, afford an opportunity to convalesce in quiet surroundings and with his wife present. For several days his condition showed encouraging improvement, but pneumonia developed and he began to grow weaker. Chaplain Lacy reported to Lee Jackson's turn for the worse and the fear of the doctors that the disease might prove fatal. Lee, who would not accept that dire forecast, sent Lacy with a mes-

*See Chapter 14.

sage to Jackson: "Give him my affectionate regards and tell him to make haste and get well, and come back to me as soon as he can. He has lost his left arm, but I have lost my right."

On Sunday, May 10, Jackson was told that the end was near. Soon he became delirious, and began to issue battle orders. "Order A. P. Hill to prepare for action. Pass the infantry to the front!" Then, calmly, as though in benediction: "No, no, let us pass over the river, and rest under the shade of the trees." With which words the spirit of Stonewall Jackson passed quietly into Immortality.

HOUSE IN WHICH JACKSON DIED

SECOND LINE OF FEDERAL POSITION
Near the V at Bullock's.

CHAPTER 14

THE SITUATION AT 5 A.M., MAY 3

THE Confederates at Chancellorsville were ready for a rest when the fighting ended late on the night of May 2-3. It had been a tough day for all of their divisions. The entire force had been engaged, with Jackson's Corps having borne the heavier burden of marching and fighting. But the right wing—McLaws and Anderson—had also done their share. Hooker's flank had been neatly turned, at a heavy price, to be sure, in the loss of Jackson and Hill, but the morale of the Confederates was heightened by their satisfaction at having inflicted a crushing blow on the enemy. The initiative remained in Lee's hands, and to a man the Southerners were prepared to press their advantage early Sunday morning in a renewal of their driving attack on the Federal positions.

On the opposite side, despite the disaster which had put the Eleventh Corps hors de combat, the Army of the Potomac had quickly recovered its equilibrium and was full of fight—everywhere but at the top. Out of a total of five Federal corps on the battlefield, only two, the Eleventh and Third, had been fully engaged and, of the latter, Birney's division had seen limited action for but a short time. The Second Corps (except for one brigade), the entire Fifth Corps, and one division of the Twelfth Corps, can hardly be said to have been in action at all. In effect, then, more than half of Hooker's 70,000-man main striking force had merely stood to arms, manning their fortifications. If that was Hooker's idea of how to fight a battle, Lee's mental graph of his opponent's ability must have shown a sharply descending curve.

Reynold's First Corps, having spent the better part of May 2 on the road from Fredericksburg en route to join Hooker, had started to cross United States Ford during the evening. This was just in time to aid in slowing down the mad rush of the terrified fugitives of the Eleventh Corps, who seemed determined to escape by way of the pontoon bridge over which Reynolds' divisions were coming on the field. Marching by way of Hartwood Church, it had occured to Reynolds to cross at Banks' Ford and take the River Road on the south side of the Rappahannock. But he thought better of it, doubtless because the pontoon bridge that was on hand at that point had not yet been thrown. Had he decided to cross there, it could have led to interesting possibilities, the most intriguing of which was the chance of coming in on Lee's rear from the east, while the latter was preoccupied with a holding attack against the center of Hooker's line at Chancellorsville. Equally rewarding, by occupying Banks' Ford on the southern side, Hooker's operational flexibility would have been vastly increased, cooperation with Sedgwick assured, and almost anything might have happened. A mentally alert

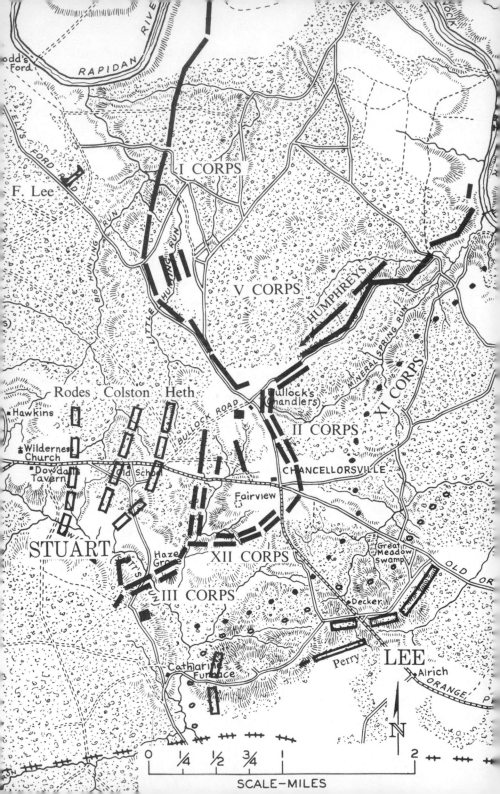

army commander in Hooker's place would certainly have made better use of such a huge, available reenforcement.

The sudden, shocking revelation that Lee's army, instead of retreating on Gordonsville as Hooker had been insisting, was attacking vigorously after a well-planned and executed march that effectively outflanked the outflanker, had the odd effect of increasing Hooker's defensive-mindedness, if that were possible. His smug assurance that Lee, if he should attack, would shatter his army against an impregnable Federal position, had been replaced by fear for the safety of his own army. Hooker had lost confidence in himself, that was certain, but the tragedy of his psychosis was that it implied as well a wholly unjustified lack of faith in the Army of the Potomac, which was ready, willing, able, and even desperately hopeful that some miracle would happen to jolt their bemused, timid commander out of his strange lethargy.

It would seem that Hooker's wing of 70,000 (net after casualties) should have been more than enough to fight a defensive battle against Lee's 45,000 who confronted the Federals at Chancellorsville, without overcrowding the position with Reynolds' added strength of more than 16,-000. Hooker had not reckoned with Lee's superb ability to maneuver offensively, but the frame of mind of the Federal commander was such that even 86,000 men would not be sufficient, in the face of his woeful lack of effective combat leadership, to gain the ascendancy over the alert and confidently aggressive Confederates.

Upon Reynolds' arrival in advance of his corps, Hooker issued instructions that the First Corps should take position on the army right "his (Reynolds') right to rest on the

---

MAP 21. THE SITUATION AT 5 A. M., MAY 3, 1863

This shows the troops' dispositions just before Stuart launched his attack to clear Chancellorsville and effect contact with Lee's right wing. Sickles has just received orders to move to the right, reinforcing the lines facing west from Fairview. Humphreys is moving toward Bullock's.

Rapidan, on the east bank of Hunting Run, and extending to the crossing of the Chancellorsville and Ely's Ford Roads, and thence along that road in the direction of Chancellorsville." Reynolds' left was to connect with the right of Sykes' division of the Fifth Corps. This order superseded an earlier order for Reynolds "to seize the position vacated by the Eleventh Corps," which had indeed been wishful thinking of a high order.

Hooker Pulls in His Horns

The best that Hooker could come up with at the tail end of Saturday, May 2, was the creation of an inner or second defense line, a V-shaped affair with the point at Bullock's Farm, the base the curving line of the Rappahannock, and the sides occupied by three of the six corps present. Reynolds' First Corps occupied the army right, or west side of the new line, along Hunting Run; Meade's Fifth Corps was shifted to the center, generally along the Ely's Ford-Chancellorsville Road; the remains of Howard's shattered Eleventh Corps occupied the army left or east side of the line along the Bullock Road, somewhat farther to the west than the original position of the Fifth Corps. One brigade of Couch's Second Corps was held in reserve on Howard's left rear, just in case. The contracted line was a strong one for defense, both ends anchored on the river, but the concept of fighting with one's back to a river is not regarded by the military experts as a particularly healthy exercise; especially when the defender has lost the initiative and reminds one of a spiritless boxer shielding his head with both arms against the rights and lefts of his lighter but more aggressive opponent, while waiting hopefully for the bell to mark the end of the round.

To the south of the V were the other three corps of the army, the Second, Twelfth and Third, forming an awkward salient which jutted out in a semicircle from the apex of the second line of defense, and interposed between the two wings of Lee's army. Slocum's Twelfth and Couch's Second Corps formed the U around Chancellorsville and Fairview, with Sickles' Third Corps way out on the tip of the salient at Hazel Grove. Salients are traditionally vulnerable pieces of real estate, but this one would not have the opportunity of either proving or disproving the doctrine, because Hooker docilely yielded Hazel Grove without a fight on Sunday morning. Probably it was just as well that he did, considering his mental state, because the Third Corps could not have held the position against strong pressure from two sides unless ordered support from other corps should aid in levelling out the salient by means of a forward movement on one or both flanks.

Hazel Grove was a position worth a fight to retain and the risk of the salient was justified as a temporary expedient. But it was an unsafe position unless the army commander was determined to make a positive effort to reduce its vulnerability by exploiting its inherent and acquired advantages.

Shortly before daylight on Sunday morning, May 3, Hooker rode out to see Sickles at Hazel Grove. That high ground, in conjunction with Fairview, if productively utilized was the key to dominance of the battlefield. Guns posted at the Grove could make Fairview untenable; if in Confederate hands they would be able to enfilade both the western and southern exposure of Slocum's Twelfth Corps, which presently held a lease on Fairview.

Not since the arrival of his right wing on April 30 had Hooker made any serious offensive gestures in the direction of the enemy. All he had done was to pull in additional corps from Fredericksburg, one after the other, until he had six of his seven corps at Chancellorsville, with an initial strength of about 90,000 men. Surely with such preponderance the army had a right to expect at least a modicum of initiative from its commander after more than two days in the Chancellorsville area.

Jackson's Corps under Jeb Stuart's command passed the night of May 2 in the area initially occupied by Howard's Federal Eleventh Corps, in a position of readiness from which it could attack in any one of three directions: to the northeast towards United States Mine Ford and Hooker's communications; directly east, down the Turnpike to Chancellorsville; or in a southeasterly direction against Hazel Grove to connect with the divisions of McLaws and Anderson, which under Lee's immediate command were disposed from the unfinished railroad and Catharine Furnace, across the Plank Road and the Turnpike, to a point on Mott Run about a mile east of the Chancellorsville crossroad.

Lee was snatching a few hours of sleep in a pine grove along the Furnace Road when he was awakened shortly before 2:30 A.M. by the arrival of a member of Jackson's staff, come to report to the Commanding General on affairs on Jackson's front. It was the first eyewitness account of the stirring events of the preceding evening, and Lee was eager for the details. He was told of the wounds suffered by Jackson and A. P. Hill and Stuart's succession to command and, in a general way, the present dispositions in the area of Dowdall's Tavern.

Lee was at once alert, particularly when the officer told him that Jackson's intent had been to cut Hooker off from United States Mine Ford. In Lee's view, however, the important thing was first to effect a junction of the two separated wings. A message to that effect was soon on its way to Stuart:

> It is necessary that the glorious victory thus far achieved be prosecuted with the utmost vigor, and the enemy given no time to rally. As soon, therefore, as it is possible, they must be pressed, so that we may unite the two wings of the army.

Endeavor, therefore, to dispossess them of Chancellorsville, which will permit the union of the whole army.

I shall proceed myself to join you as soon as I can make arrangements on this side, but let nothing delay the completion of the plan of drawing the enemy from his rear and from his positions. I shall give orders that every effort be made on this side at daybreak to aid in the junction.

Relative Capabilities

This was the situation as the two armies rested briefly before resuming the battle on the morning of May 3. Hooker had been reenforced by 16,000 men of Reynolds' First Corps, which more than made good the loss of a large part of the Eleventh Corps. His effective force at Chancellorsville now exceeded 86,000, with 244 guns, against Lee's separated wings aggregating approximately 45,000 men and 132 pieces of artillery. The Confederates had won a partial victory but had failed to shake the confidence of the main body of Hooker's army, which was still full of fight.

For all practical purposes, the majority of the troops comprising the Federal Second, Fifth, and Twelfth Corps had borne no part in the fighting May 2, and now the fresh First Corps had joined the ranks. The disaster to the Eleventh Corps was not really felt by the rest of the army. because there existed no feeling of comradeship with "the foreigners"--unfair as the attitude may have been. Except for the uneasy feeling created by Hooker's strange attitude, his army was confident and self-assured and would enthusiastically have fallen on the foe with every reason to expect success, relative strength considered.

But the buck had been passed by Hooker to Sedgwick, who was under orders to attack Lee's rear at Chancellorsville, first brushing aside the opposition immediately confronting him. Hooker with 86,000 men would wait supinely while Sedgwick with 23,000 was expected to carry the burden of a 10-mile march and then a battle.

In reality the only defeatist in the Federal ranks was Hooker himself, but since he was calling the shots there was little likelihood that the Army of the Potomac would be asked to do more than cower in its fortifications and beat off such further attacks as Lee might choose to unleash.

Early's Confederate Division continued to maintain its defensive position on the heights of Fredericksburg, after having made a false move during the day as the result of a misunderstanding. Lee's chief-of-staff, Colonel Chilton, had been instructed to deliver verbal orders to Early to send Lee any troops he might feel able to spare, if the Federals showed signs of withdrawing. Instead he told Early at 11 A.M. May 2, to leave one brigade at Fredericksburg, with artillery, and proceed with the rest of his force to join Lee at Chancellorsville. Under protest, Early obeyed, but as soon as Lee learned of the mistake, he immediately corrected it, and Early lost no time returning to his position, fortunately without interference from the Federals.

The fact that Sedgwick failed to capitalize on the fleeting opportunity thus presented to him reflects no credit on the alertness of that general, and suggests that the contact which he should have been maintaining with his much smaller opponent was decidedly inefficient. It would almost seem that Hooker's lack of initiative at Chancellorsville had infected his left wing commander at Fredericksburg.

Viewed in retrospect, the numerically inferior Army of Northern Virginia at this stage held only a moral and psychological advantage over the Army of the Potomac. Hooker at Chancellorsville now had nearly a two to one strength advantage over Lee, while Sedgwick's corps at Fredericksburg contained three men for every one of Early's Confederates. Literally Hooker's divisions had hardly begun to fight, but the chief drawback was that their general persisted in keeping them in a combat straitjacket. He seemed to be completely barren of ideas for either maneuver or fighting that would afford his capable subordinates the opportunity to show their mettle by uncovering any one of a number of tactical plans that will readily occur to the reader of military competence who takes the trouble to study the relative capabilities of the separate wings of the two armies at Chancellorsville and Fredericksburg.

Therein lies the fascination of the Chancellorsville campaign. As a huge game of chess it would be difficult to find a battle in which a greater variety of strategic and tactical opportunities were offered to both commanders. Chancellorsville is considered by most historians to have been the greatest battle Lee ever fought, and the reasons for that opinion are readily apparent. The unique character of the battlefield, situated in the depths of a dense forest, with open country within reach, furnished a provocative stage to begin with. On the face of it, Hooker's impressive superiority in men and guns gave him a great advantage, which was materially increased by his initial strategic success in placing three corps on Lee's rear by a surprise march. His nutcracker technique looked like a sure thing, until he lost his nerve, but from then on Lee was in the saddle and riding hard.

By midnight, May 2-3, however, it could still have been anybody's battle. Lee had the edge and held the initiative, but only because Hooker lacked the intestinal fortitude, in his own person, to wrest it from his calm, collected opponent. Hooker still held the key positions on the field, but didn't know what to do with them. All he could think of was of a passive nature, how best to keep from being hurt. A more disgusted bunch of generals than Meade and Couch and Reynolds and Slocum and Sickles would be hard to find; and as for Sedgwick, solid citizen that he was, that unfortunate left wing commander had been placed in such a confused state of mind by Hooker's successive messages that one can only sympathize with him in his predicament.

On balance, then, the advantage still lay with Hooker. The Battle of Chancellorsville was far from over. But the outcome was almost a foregone conclusion. Because Lee was imbued with the will to victory and Hooker was already a defeated man, had been in fact for almost forty-eight hours.

HOOKER'S HEADQUARTERS ON MAY 2

GEARY'S DIVISION, NEAR CHANCELLOR HOUSE

CHAPTER 15

SAVAGE FIGHTING AT CLOSE QUARTERS

HOOKER'S pre-dawn visit to Sickles' position at Hazel Grove conceivably was seized upon by the Third Corps Commander as an opportunity to present the case for a buildup of strength in that area, to justify an offensive move by the Federals. That would be in the Sickles' character; his two divisions had staked out a claim to that valuable position and had successfully contested an effort by Rodes' Confederates to dispossess them the preceding evening. Sickles could see no valid reason for cravenly pulling out, feeling confident that he could hold the Grove if given effective support, a commendable attitude that should have made sense to a superior with a semblance of fighting spirit.

Whatever passed between the two generals is not known, but it is obvious that Hooker had but one thought, to concentrate his divisions behind the fortified lines that he had decreed as the new and shortened defensive position to the north. Lee was prepared to take losses in order to capture the important key to the battlefield, a major obstacle to a junction of his two wings, but Hooker generously and gratuitously volunteered to save him the trouble. Sickles was forthwith directed to withdraw from Hazel Grove at daylight and take position at Fairview, perpendicular to and astride the Turnpike, to reenforce the line held by the Twelfth Corps and Berry's division of his own Third Corps.

Sickles promptly complied and in short order had marched his troops out of the salient, barely ahead of Jeb Stuart, who had already mounted a dawn attack in that direction. Stuart's purpose was to adjust his line, but the order was misunderstood, and the engagement became general. The Confederate blow found its target on the move and managed to mess up Sickles' rear elements sufficiently to capture several guns, but that was all. Stuart lost no time in putting Archer's Brigade on the vacated position, at the same time running up thirty guns whose gunners found themselves in the happy position of being able to enfilade the Federal position at Fairview, together with one of Slocum's divisions intrenched to the southeast of Fairview.

In conformity with his conviction that Sickles' corps at Hazel Grove should not be left out on a limb, but before actually directing its withdrawal, Hooker had ordered Pleasonton's cavalry on the night of May 2 to pull out and go into camp on the north side of the Rappahannock. Pleasonton initiated the retrograde movement at four o'clock on Sunday morning, but in the course of the march the morning battle of May 3 erupted. The cavalry was temporarily sidetracked by an unusual assignment which required it to form a buffer line across Fairview, under orders to stop and turn back escapees from the front line. If the curious mission emanated from Hooker, as it prob-

ably did, the order was in keeping with the current attitude of mind of the commanding general. In any event, no further combat seems to have been required of Pleasonton's force, which could and should have been used as dismounted cavalry where it would have done the most good. Furthermore, Averell's cavalry division had now moved up to United States Mine Ford, with nothing to do. In combination, then, Hooker had over 5,000 able-bodied cavalrymen to utilize as reserve in addition to the 30,000 men of the First and Fifth Infantry Corps, but there was no spirit left in the army commander.

The collateral advantage handed to the Confederates without a struggle was the removal of the Hazel Grove roadblock to an easy junction of the forces under Stuart and Lee. The early morning withdrawal by Sickles consequently got the Confederates off to a favorable start and they lost no time in exploiting their improved fortunes with murderous artillery fire effect.

Stuart's eagerness to launch his attack as early as possible after sunrise, and his relative unfamiliarity with the capabilities of his newly-acquired infantry, taken together resulted in a somewhat uncoordinated initial effort by the Confederates of the left wing. The first advance by the several brigades of the leading attack echelon was consequently disjointed and ineffectual. The Federal position at Fairview had been strongly fortified by log emplacements as much as three feet in height in some places. On the front manned by the divisions of Berry and Williams, facing west, the woods had been cleared to a considerable width to provide an effective field of fire that materially strengthened the defense.

From the artillery standpoint, possession of Hazel Grove gave Stuart a decided advantage over the Federal guns at Fairview. If nothing but an artillery duel should develop, the contestants would exchange compliments on fairly even terms, so far as position was concerned. But for punishment to the infantry, the Federals, closely massed, would be likely to suffer more than the Confederates, who were disposed for the attack in three successive waves, with a distance of some three hundred yards between lines.

Stuart had improved his time by moving to the front during the night all the guns he possibly could. The result was that after the Confederates occupied Hazel Grove they had 50 guns in position there and on the Turnpike near Melzi Chancellor's (Dowdall's), capable of directing a powerful converging fire on the Federals at Fairview, their only remaining bulwark in front of Chancellorsville, and on Hooker's headquarters, the Chancellor House, as well.

The Hooker-imposed absence of Artillery General Hunt at Banks' Ford was now to be keenly felt. From time to time Hooker had been shifting guns *away* from the front line into his secondary defense in rear of Bullock's, and even as far back as United States Mine Ford, until 40 guns remained at Fairview, giving the Confederates a 5-4 advantage. The disparity was further emphasized by the fact that the Federal artillery at Fairview could not place its shells

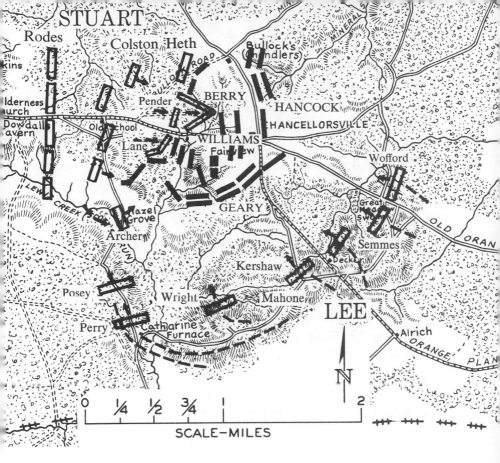

MAP 22. THE FIGHT FOR CHANCELLORSVILLE

This shows the situation about 7:30 A.M., May 3, 1863, in the Chancellorsville area. Heth's (formerly A. P. Hill's) Division has advanced against the Federals on the Fairview heights and against Berry's division north of the Turnpike. On the right flank of Heth's Division, Archer has wheeled against the withdrawing column of Sickles' divisions and is repulsed. Lane and Pender have crashed against the center between Berry and Williams, and a seesaw battle ensues for an hour and a half. On the south, Anderson's and McLaws' Divisions are executing a wheeling movement to come up abreast of the right of Heth, thus making the contact which Lee had directed.

directly in front of its own infantry, but only on the enemy at a distance, which imposed on the foot soldiers almost the full responsibility of repelling attacks, without benefit of artillery support.

The heavily wooded character of the terrain and the aggressive attitude of the Confederates led to piecemeal attacks, lacking central direction and with varying success. Liaison between organizations was poor and units repeatedly advanced without support on either flank, frequently without even the knowledge that the troops to their right or left were in motion or even present.

The Fighting Becomes General

By 7 A.M. the fighting along the Turnpike had become general and everybody in the vicinity began to get in the act. Two Confederate brigades, concentrating on the Federal center near the pike, hit a regiment composed almost wholly of recruits, on the extreme right of Slocum's line, and broke through with a whoop and a rush, driving the bewildered and inexperienced outfit to the rear. This first break in the line caused a gap that exposed the flank of Berry's division. One brigade of that division quickly lost an entire regiment, which retreated beyond Chancellorsville, and when stopped could only muster 100 men. The pressure on Berry became so heavy that he dispatched a staff officer to Hooker's headquarters to inquire whether he should try to hold. Berry then crossed the Turnpike to confer with his brigade commander in that sector. Recrossing to his division command post, he was killed on the road by a Confederate sharpshooter posted in a nearby tree, the first division commander of either army to lose his life in this battle.

During the early morning hours the infighting waxed fast and furious on the mile or so of front covered by the advanced portion of the Federal line. The determined Confederates under Stuart's urging attacked repeatedly, with varying success. Much of the fighting was at close quarters. Berry's troops, taking the brunt of it, after a time began to yield ground.

As the Confederate pressure directed on Berry's division mounted in fury, portions of the line commenced to crumble. The disintegration was hastened by the somewhat less than courageous action of Brig. General Joseph W. Revere, a descendant of the Revolutionary hero, who commanded the Second Brigade of Berry's division. When Berry was killed, Revere mistakenly assumed that he was the senior brigadier and therefore in command of his sector. Taking advantage of what he considered his prerogative, and concluding that it was too hot a spot for the comfort of his brigade of all New York regiments, Revere led the entire outfit to the rear with disastrous effect on the brigades which remained. This embarrassed the fighting men of the Excelsior Brigade, formerly commanded by Sickles, who were justly proud of their reputation, and wholly unaccustomed to what they rightly regarded as action approaching cowardice on the part of their brigade commander. Sickles was on another part of the field when this occurred, but when he learned of it, he flew into a towering rage at the subordinate who had acted contrary to his own orders, summarily removed Revere from command, and relegated him to the limbo of temporarily inactive generals.

If Hooker's mind had not been so preoccupied with defensive considerations, he might have given thought to the actual situation that existed at daylight, May 3. The fact was that Stuart's wing was in an extremely ticklish position. His front and right flank were in danger of attack from 25,000 men of Sickles' and Slocum's corps but his left flank was potentially even more vulnerable. The 30,000 men comprising the two corps of Meade and Reynolds, in effect a reserve line but available for an attack, could easily have been moved a short distance to the right and thrown powerfully against Stuart's left flank while he was engaged with Sickles and Slocum's troops at Hazel Grove and Fairview.

This was only one of the repeated occasions when Hooker would have been wise to recall and invoke Lincoln's prophetic words to himself and Couch on the occasion of the Presidential visit to the army in April: "Gentlemen, in your next battle put in all of your men!" It cannot be doubted that Stuart could have been overrun and possibly decimated in a two-pronged attack, unleashed by the simple expedient of an encouraging and eagerly awaited order to the disappointed Federal corps commanders: "Gentlemen, you may attack." Instead of which, the veteran troops of the First and Fifth Corps, all hardy fighters, remained virtually idle in a position of readiness, while Sickles and Slocum and Hancock's division of Couch's corps were allowed to fight the battle with the immediate odds in favor of the Confederates, who profited by the virtual guarantee of noninterference from Hooker's strong and unused reserve.

While the battle raged on the Federal right, Anderson's Confederate Division was assaulting the Federal center and McLaws its left, where Hancock's division of the Second Corps and part of Slocum's Twelfth were covering the two parallel roads leading east towards Fredericksburg.

Soon Stuart's continuous hammering and the defection of several Federal regiments on the right of Berry's division, which peeled off, one after the other, as their respective flanks were turned, endangered the entire Federal right. Fortunately French's division of the Second Corps was thrown in at the psychological moment to save Hooker's right from caving in. French drove the Confederates back, only to be in turn outflanked on his right. Further support from other troops, however, redressed the balance and the danger to the all-important Bullock's Farm strongpoint was temporarily averted.

The Chancellor House had already taken considerable

punishment from the tireless Confederate artillery, the continual roar of guns and rattle of musketry making it impossible to carry out any kind of staff operations at army headquarters. Hooker himself doesn't seem to have made the slightest effort to direct the actions of his various corps or even to coordinate their actions. There is no evidence that he issued any combat orders beyond answering inquires with the inadequate reply that the units in question were to "retire when out of ammunition." There was no attempt to replenish ammunition, at least so far as Hooker personally was concerned, and seemingly no real interest in the subject. Nor is there any evidence that the army commander made any move to visit any part of the convulsive battlefield during the desperate fighting on the right flank. Had General Hunt been on hand, it is safe to say that the resupply of the guns would have been given intelligent direction, but as it was, the corps of both Sickles and Slocum soon exhausted their ammunition and had no choice but to displace to the rear behind the support line, giving up Fairview in the process.

At nine o'clock Hooker stood on the porch of the Chancellor House, with worried face, leaning against a pillar and with ears cocked in the hope of hearing Sedgwick's guns from the direction of Fredericksburg. He had ordered Sedgwick the evening before to come in on Lee's rear at Chancellorsville, the instructions being to arrive at daylight. There was of course no sign of Sedgwick, and it was now more than three hours past the deadline, which in itself should have been enough to convince Hooker that Sedgwick was confronted with something more than an easy march, and that all of Lee's troops consequently were not facing Hooker. That should have been the signal for Hooker to snap out of his lethargy, go over to the offensive, and turn the tables on Lee.

While in this brown study, wondering what to do, a solid shot from a Confederate battery on the Plank Road struck the pillar against which Hooker was leaning, throwing him heavily to the ground. For a few moments he was stunned and unable to move; then he recovered, rose to his feet, and mounted his horse. By that time Sickles' divisions and a part of Slocum's corps had been forced to withdraw, all requests for support having been refused, leaving only Geary's division of the Twelfth Corps, Hancock's reduced division of the Second Corps, and a battery of guns between the semidisabled Hooker and Lee's army. Geary's division was slowly being turned and disaster loomed.

When Hooker was knocked senseless for a few moments, his second-in-command, General Couch, whose Second Corps was nearby, was told that Hooker had been killed, which if true would automatically place him in command of the army. Dismounting quickly, Couch rushed to the Chancellor House, saw the shattered pillar, but couldn't find Hooker. Speculating on what steps he would take to restore the morale of the army and the fortunes of the battle, he suddenly came upon Hooker and members of his staff, all mounted and apparently in good shape.

But that was the last Couch saw of the commanding general anywhere near the front. Although Hooker moved to the rear to relax in a more secure climate, he neglected to communicate with Couch or offer any advice on the further movements or actions of the divisions still under fire and in contact with the enemy. Couch was left to his own devices to salvage what he could at this critical stage, just as Sickles was abandoned to his fate at Hazel Grove the evening before.

Like Sickles, Couch was a fighting general. He addressed himself courageously to the task of preventing a complete disaster to the Federal forces. Even at that eleventh hour, he felt that the day could be saved. Several dozen guns, rushed into position to the right of the Chancellor House, now burning furiously from the fire caused by Confederate shells, could in his opinion drive from their lodgment

CHANCELLORSVILLE IN 1922

Today even this fragment of the old building has fallen, leaving nothing but the foundations.

the Confederates pressing Geary's flank and then neutralize the thirty deadly guns that were pounding the Federal line from Fairview, not 600 yards away. Couch had already had one horse killed under him as he moved from point to point in his strenuous efforts to keep intact the hard-pressed troops of Geary and Hancock and to bring additional guns and men to their support. It was love's labor lost, however, because Hooker had made up his mind to abandon the field, according to Couch, or he would not willingly have permitted Sickles' corps and most of Slocum's to withdraw from contact.

While engaged in this task, a staff officer summoned Couch to army headquarters. Hancock was left in command of the field, as Couch followed the messenger, to find Hooker half a mile in rear of Chancellorsville, lying on a cot in a tent at the far side of an open field. Other officers were present, including General Meade, who was still hoping that his corps would be allowed to take part in the battle. As Couch entered the tent, Hooker raised on his side with the remark: "Couch, I turn the command of the army over to you. You will withdraw it and place it in the position designated on this map," pointing to a field sketch.

There was nothing for Couch to do but follow instructions, no matter how strongly he felt about Hooker's lack of courage, for the latter was still the senior. His relinquishment of command was conditional and oral, and could have been countermanded just as easily if Couch had shown the nerve to take matters into his own hands. Hooker was still acting somewhat dazed from the severe bruising he had received, but he appeared to be in full possession of his mental faculties, which was most unfortunate for the army. It would be interesting although futile to speculate on how the Battle of Chancellorsville might have turned out if Couch, Meade, Reynolds, Slocum, Sickles, and some of the division commanders had at this point put their heads together, called in a senior surgeon with guts, and declared Hooker physically incapable of retaining control of the army. That's the way it would probably have turned out in a dramatized version, but as it was, Couch hastened to obey the order, which was to further contract the V-shaped inner line and remain strictly on the defensive. It is, nevertheless, a striking commentary as to the effect of Hooker's intransigence on the strong mind of a superior type of general officer, that after Chancellorsville had passed into history Couch refused to serve further "under such an officer."

In the opinion of Major General James H. Wilson, reviewing in a newspaper article Major Bigelow's *The Campaign of Chancellorsville,* neither over-indulgence in liquor nor complete abstinence from his customary drinking habits was responsible for Hooker's mental vacuum during the battle. Neither were the "paroxysms of pain" which he suffered at intervals following his injury at the hands of a Confederate shell, although it is said that in later life he became partly paralyzed on the injured side. In Wilson's words, "His loss of power to command with his normal intelligence was due mostly to constitutional defects brought out by the overwhelming disaster 'the best army on the planet' had met with under his overconfident leadership from an army 'that God Almighty couldn't save'."

Hancock and Geary

There was little opportunity during the Chancellorsville campaign for Union generals to distinguish themselves by acts of heroism or tactical feats, chiefly because the battle was a Hooker-imposed static one for the Army of the Potomac after gaining contact with Lee's army— that is, all except for Sedgwick's corps. And in that case it is not surprising that Sedgwick failed to achieve success in the face of Hooker's confusing orders and less than bold attitude in withholding from one-fifth of his army even a semblance of cooperation from the remaining four-fifths.

Hooker had in his army any number of capable generals both as corps and division commanders—Couch, Meade, Slocum, Reynolds, Berry, Hancock, Sykes, Geary, Williams, and others. Virtually all were forced by the army commander's lack of enterprise to do little else than ward off Confederate attacks in a defensive posture after they had reached the end of the line in the wilderness at Chancellorsville.

Winfield Scott Hancock was an outstanding example of a promising combat leader who was allowed no scope to demonstrate his capabilities. Yet at Gettysburg, two months later, he was to prove the man of the hour in bringing order out of chaos on Cemetery Ridge on the afternoon of the first day; as one of the major factors at the high water mark when Pickett's charge was turned back; and in urging Meade to counterattack as he (Hancock) was carried off the field on a stretcher after receiving a disabling bullet wound in the thigh.

Grant in his *Memoirs* referred to Hancock as "the most conspicuous of all the general officers who did not exercise a separate command; who commanded a corps larger than any other one, and whose name was never mentioned as having committed in battle a blunder for which he was responsible. His personal courage and his presence with his command in the thickest of the fight won for him the confidence of troops serving under him."

Hancock was every inch a soldier—it was in his blood and he loved everything about soldiering, even paperwork. He had an aggressive, enthusiastic, martial temperament; the danger and excitement of battle stirred every fiber of his being. Hancock represented the highest standards of the professional soldier and exemplified the type of general who, if given half a chance by the vainglorious Hooker, could in company with other capable generals have provided for the Army of the Potomac the opportunity that was denied it of fulfilling its destiny on the field of Chancellorsville.

Less than two divisions, commanded by Hancock and Geary, now remained in position to face the concentrated fury of Lee's entire force, which had been united automatically by the successive withdrawals of the Federal corps from Hazel Grove and Fairview. Two of Hancock's brigades had previously been detached, Caldwell's to United States Mine Ford and Meagher's Irish Brigade from the time the army first crossed the Rappahannock. Geary's flank had already been turned, but he still fought tenaciously against heavy odds, although the inevitable result could be foreseen.

Hancock's depleted division fought manfully along Mott's Run, but his fate too was a foregone conclusion. The only uncertainty was how long it would take to finish him off. With the increasingly rapid pace of the Federal disintegration process, Hancock soon found his division virtually the only cohesive Federal unit still fighting. His position quickly became critical. A full Confederate division was centering its attention on Hancock, whose line was under the direct charge of the same Colonel Miles who had earned the admiring comments of his superiors in the fighting of May 2. Assailed from two directions, and to protect the flank of Geary's line which faced south and crossed the Plank Road, Hancock was forced to face the eleven regiments of his division both east and west, with the result that his troops were now fighting back to back, only a few hundred yards separating the two parallel lines.

The conditions were far from healthy. Hancock's horse went down with a bullet in its brain. Couch was slightly wounded, but stayed on the field. Miles was seriously wounded. The Chancellor plain became a veritable inferno of screaming shells and zipping bullets. Geary's division was overrun and forced to retire as best it could to Bullock's. But Hancock's depleted division hung on, buying time at a heavy cost and fighting alone where a few hours earlier three army corps, seven divisions, had fought. Finally the word came down that the First Division could withdraw, and it was none too soon, if there was to remain any semblance of an organization to be withdrawn.

By ten o'clock the field surrounding the Chancellor House had been vacated by the Federals, all of whom had retired in fairly good order to the north and in rear of the newly constructed intrenchments centering on Bullock's. The dazed and bone-weary but exultant Confederates moved in and took possession, but they were so nearly exhausted by their efforts of the past few days that little or no attempt was made to effect the capture of enemy guns or men.

Perhaps the victors suspected a trap, for the Federal units had retired in what appeared to be a well-disciplined movement on the whole, even if it was in successive fragments; or else the Confederates were too tired to care.

MAP 23. THE CONFEDERATES CAPTURE CHANCELLORSVILLE

The situation about 10 A.M., May 3, 1863, as Lee's two wings unite for the
final drive to clear Chancellorsville. Hooker has ceased to function, and his
divisions—still full of fight—reluctantly pull out to the north.

But when General Lee, some time after ten, rode up to the ruined and still fiercely burning house that had been Hooker's headquarters, his weary, powder-blackened men suddenly awoke to a realization of the magnitude of their triumph and began to cheer their commanding general with unrestrained enthusiasm. "It was the supreme moment of his life as a soldier," wrote Douglas Southall Freeman*. "The sun of his destiny was at its zenith. All that he earned by a life of self-control, all that he had received in inheritance from pioneer forebears, all that he had merited by study, by diligence, and by daring, was crowded into that moment."

Gradually the firing died down and a weird sort of spontaneous armed truce took the place of the bitter fighting that had marked the early hours of what under more peaceful conditions would have been a beautiful May Sunday morning. The human body can take a lot of punishment, but there comes a time when nervous energy has been sapped and a period of recuperation is necessary. That stage had been reached and passed by both armies, save for the 30,000 men of the fresh First and Fifth Federal Corps, whose hands were tied by a nonfunctioning army commander who simply let nature take its course without lifting a finger to help shape the course, and without delegating his responsibility to others who were both competent and willing.

Cessation of the actual fighting was followed by an uneasy and, of course, unacknowledged truce, during which both armies turned their attention to straightening out their lines, reassembling units within their own divisions, attending to such wounded as could be reached, and generally restoring internal order of a sort.

Roaring flames were now threatening large numbers of men who had become lost in the forest or wounded in the fierce ebb and flow of the action below Chancellorsville.

*R. E. Lee, Vol. II, Charles Scribner's Sons, New York, 1934.

The heavy shelling of the morning had set fire to many wooded areas where the dry leaves, abatis, and dead wood of the forest provided ideal fuel for the licking flames. Many of the wounded, who would otherwise have been saved either by friendly troops or as prisoners, could not be reached and were left to be consumed alive by the flames. By common consent of those who went over the battlefield after the carnage was ended, the charred bodies —many of which were found clinging close to what they evidently hoped would be sheltering trees, others with supplicating hands outstretched until a merciful death came to their relief—bore mute witness to the frightful fate which overtook literally hundreds of the wounded.

The Scene Shifts to Fredericksburg

It will be recalled that Hooker's Saturday evening order to Sedgwick, in command of his own Sixth Corps and Gibbon's division of the Second Corps at Fredericksburg, caused Sedgwick to believe that Lee was retreating on Gordonsville, with Sickles harrying his trains, and that all Sedgwick had to do was to march the intervening 10 miles to Chancellorsville, brushing Early aside in passing.

[304]

Lowe's balloons had reported withdrawals by the Confederates manning the heights west of Fredericksburg. The prospective mission appeared to be a relatively easy one, at least in its initial stages. What would happen when Sedgwick had completed his march was left up in the air. Without being too specific, Hooker had given Sedgwick the impression that at daybreak, May 3, he was expected to attack Lee's rear while Hooker assaulted him in front.

The Sixth Corps, already across the river before receipt of Hooker's order, moved north at midnight towards Fredericksburg, while Gibbon's division awaited the laying of his bridge before crossing at Falmouth. Early's skirmishers held up the advance with fire, and it was daylight before Sedgwick could occupy Fredericksburg and prepare to attack Marye's Heights, where Early's reenforced division was strongly intrenched, although spread thinly along the row of hills to the Howison House, where his right was anchored.

Once again Hooker's plan had miscarried, due mostly to his own shortsightedness, lack of imagination and tactical ingenuity, and almost complete absence of logistical foresight. It was nothing short of stupid to predicate the action of his main army on such a thin reed of probability as Sedgwick's arrival at Chancellorsville by daylight, and it was almost criminal for Hooker to hold 86,000 men idle in a defensive posture while expecting 23,000 to carry the major burden of the attack.

Events on the Chancellorsville front on Sunday morning apparently had no effect in causing Hooker to make the slightest revision in his estimate of the situation, or his appraisal of the relative combat capabilities of the two forces at either end of the corridor. His sole thought, if indeed he did any thinking after being stunned by the concussion, seemed to be to pull into an even smaller shell and wait supinely for help to come to him from down Fredericksburg way.

THE SUNKEN ROAD, AFTER SEDGWICK'S SUCCESSFUL ATTACK

CHAPTER 16

THE SIXTH CORPS AT FREDERICKSBURG

MAJOR GENERAL JOHN SEDGWICK, "Uncle John" to the men of the Sixth Corps, Army of the Potomac, with which his name is indelibly linked, was a favorite in the army. Idolized by his own command, despite the rigid discipline which he enforced, he had a jovial smile and was looked upon as a father always zealous in the interest of his children. He was not a brilliant leader, being somewhat slow on the uptake, but his common sense was proverbial, and, although modest and unobtrusive, he possessed an iron will and soldierly courage; when committed to battle he always seemed to grow in stature and mental capacity.

Born in Connecticut in 1813, Sedgwick's forebears were fighters, including Major General Robert Sedgwick, sent by Oliver Cromwell as Commissioner to Jamaica, and his grandfather, also named John Sedgwick, a major in Washington's Army at Valley Forge. Graduating from West

Point in 1837, in the same class with Joseph Hooker and Jubal Early, Sedgwick served as an artillery officer during the Florida war, against the Indians, and in every engagement of the War with Mexico, following which he was appointed a major of one of the new regiments of cavalry, with which branch he again served against the Indians and in garrison duty until the outbreak of the Civil War.

After being wounded in the Peninsular Campaign and receiving his promotion to major general, he commanded a division at the Battle of Antietam, where he was twice wounded, once through the body. Recovering after a period of convalescence, he was given command of the Sixth Corps, following the First Battle of Fredericksburg, and led it through the campaigns of Chancellorsville, Gettysburg, the Wilderness, and Spotsylvania Court House, at which place he was instantly killed by a Confederate sharpshooter.

The Sixth Corps was the largest in the army by several thousand men, numbering 23,667 "present for duty equipped," of which 5 percent were officers, according to the official strength returns for April 30, 1863. Hooker had 404 guns in the Chancellorsville campaign, 54 of them assigned to Sedgwick. According to Livermore, 93 percent of the men reported as present were, for the army as a whole, considered as battle effectives, which would give the Sixth Corps in round figures 22,000 men. Including Gibbon's division of approximately 4,500, Sedgwick commanded a force of over 26,000 men to which were opposed the 10,000 of classmate Early's reenforced division on the heights west of Fredericksburg.

Although the topography of the area in the immediate vicinity of Fredericksburg was new to Sedgwick, it was familiar ground to the three divisions of the Sixth Corps, still under the command of Brigadier Generals W. T. H. Brooks, Albion P. Howe, and Major General John Newton, and to Colonel Hiram Burnham, now commanding the Light Division, which had recently been detached from its partly-divisional status and given an independent role as a separate division of the corps.

At the first Battle of Fredericksburg, December 13, 1862, the Sixth Corps, under the command of Major General William F. Smith as part of Franklin's Left Grand Divi-

MAJOR GENERAL JOHN SEDGWICK

sion, crossed the Rappahannock below Fredericksburg and deployed on the plain in company with Franklin's other corps. But Burnside's incompetence and Franklin's inability to use his own discretion resulted in almost complete inactivity by the Sixth Corps, disposed along the Richmond road, while Reynold's First Corps did all the fighting on that portion of the battlefield.

When the Chancellorsville Campaign opened in late April, the Sixth, First, and Third Corps, under Sedgwick (as both corps and wing commander), Reynolds, and Sickles respectively, were secretly moved from their camps above Falmouth to crossing positions in rear of Stafford Heights, below the town of Fredericksburg. Sickles, held in reserve, was soon ordered to Chancellorsville, where Hooker was massing the main body of the army after the successful flank march of the Fifth, Eleventh, and Twelfth Corps.

Shortly before daylight on Tuesday, April 28, Brooks' division at Deep Run and Wadsworth's (of Reynolds' corps) a mile below at Pollock's Mill, crossed the Rappahannock in boats and established bridgeheads, while the remaining divisions of the two corps were held in readiness to cross to the other side the following day. Some skirmishing occurred during the morning as five bridges were laid, three at Franklin's Crossing and two below, but the better part of the time of the Confederates was devoted to entrenching, with an occasional burst of artillery fire thrown in Reynolds' direction at the southern end of the plain.

Barksdale's Brigade of McLaws' Division, later supported by Hay's Brigade with the rest of Early's Division in reserve, held the Confederate line from the Rappahannock, across from Falmouth, to the Howison House, a distance of about 2 miles, on the morning of Saturday, May 2. By that time Lee's army, less Early and Barksdale, had left for Chancellorsville, the intervening days being spent by Sedgwick in making demonstrations and crossing the rest of his two corps, reduced to one corps when Hooker pulled Reynolds out during the night of May 1-2.

Butterfield's Role

The understanding sympathy of those who have served as chiefs of staff goes out to Major General Dan Butterfield, Hooker's chief, who was forced to spend almost his entire time during the campaign at Falmouth in charge of what in later wars would be called the rear echelon of the army command post. Hooker's judgment may be open to question in relegating the general who occupied the exalted position of army chief of staff to a spot where his chief task was to coordinate the operations of the widely separated wings of the army. Not that the function was not a vital one, but in this case Hooker was holding all the strings of planning and execution tightly in his own hands. For such a restricted role, without discretionary authority, an intelligent, experienced staff officer of lesser rank could have done all that Butterfield was permitted to do. The chief of staff could have rendered more effective service, even though limited to coordination, at Chancellorsville, where in effect after May 1, when the battle was joined, Hooker's army functioned virtually without a real head.

One has only to read in the *Official Records* the contents of the vast number of telegraphic messages sent every few minutes by Butterfield to Hooker throughout Sunday, May 3, to be convinced that the chief of staff was making every effort to keep the commanding general informed. His reports were so complete and clearly expressed that developments that day on the Fredericksburg-Salem Church front are portrayed like an unrolled, continuous panorama. Butterfield painted the picture in so businesslike a manner that Hooker's failure to carry out his announced purpose of attacking Lee from Chancellorsville in support of Sedgwick's advance cannot be attributed to lack of intelligence; on the contrary, it only serves to compound the failure in the eyes of history.

More perceptive than his commander in his awareness that President Lincoln would be anxiously awaiting word of what was transpiring along the Rappahannock, Butterfield took it upon himself to send Lincoln a telegram on Sunday morning, couched in diplomatic language that must have started the President burning with impatient curiosity. It was the first word Lincoln had received. The message read:

Headquarters Army of the Potomac,
May 3, 1863—8:50 A.M.

ABRAHAM LINCOLN,
President of the United States:

Though not directed or specially authorized to do so by General Hooker, I think it not improper that I should advise you that a battle is in progress.

DANIEL BUTTERFIELD,
Chief of Staff

In striking contrast, a telegram from Hooker's headquarters to Butterfield four hours later, at 12:45 P.M., told of Hooker's reluctance to even intimate the dire straits of the army to the President:

General Butterfield:

I think we have had the most terrible battle ever witnessed on earth. I think our victory will be certain, but the General told me he would say nothing just yet to Washington, except that he is doing well. In an hour or two the matter will be a fixed fact. I believe the enemy is in flight now, but we are not sure.

RUFUS INGALLS,
Chief Quartermaster.

A fair comment on that message, considering what had happened Saturday night and Sunday morning at Chancellorsville—Jackson's flank attack, the Federal withdrawal from Hazel Grove and Fairview, the disabling of Hooker, the contraction of the army's defense line, and the occupation of the Chancellor clearing by Lee's forces—would be —who is kidding whom? The only element of consistency in the message was Hooker's patent attempt to keep alive in Sedgwick's mind the fiction that he was going to attack simultaneously with Sedgwick, to pin Lee between them. To give any other impression to Sedgwick might be to cool his enthusiasm for the prescribed offensive.

Butterfield's anxiety to see some of the action away from his desk was revealed in the telegram he sent Hooker at 1:15 P.M. Sunday, expressing regret that the general was "even slightly wounded" and inquiring somewhat pathetically if he could not be permitted to join Sedgwick, since it was now impossible for him to join Hooker even had the authority been granted. The message closed with the almost despairing cry: "while I do not know who would replace me here, I am heartsick at not being permitted to be on the actual field, to share the fate and fortunes of this army and my general."

Still thinking of Lincoln and determined that he would do his best to make up for Hooker's taciturnity, Butterfield again wired the President at 1:30 P.M.:

> From all reports yet collected, the battle has been most fierce and terrible. Loss heavy on both sides. General Hooker slightly, but not severely, wounded. He has preferred thus far that nothing should be reported, and does not know of this, but I cannot refrain from saying this much to you. You may expect his dispatch in a few hours, which will give the result.

In the meantime, Hooker apparently reached the belated conclusion that it might be advisable to let the President in on the progress of the battle, so he drafted a telegram and sent it at 1:15 by orderly to United States Mine Ford, where it was put on the wire and reached Lincoln at 4 P.M.

Headquarters Army of the Potomac,
May 3, 1863—3:30 PM

> We have had a desperate fight yesterday and today, which has resulted in no success to us, having lost a position of two lines which had been selected for our defense. We may have another turn at it this P.M. I do not despair of success. If Sedgwick could have gotten up, there could have been but one result.

As it is impossible for me to know the exact position of Sedgwick as regards his ability to advance and take part in the engagement, I cannot tell when it will end. We will endeavor to do our best. My troops are in good spirits. We have fought desperately today. No general ever commanded a more devoted army.

Joseph Hooker,
Major General.

His Excellency A. Lincoln
President of the United States

Inferentially at least it was all Sedgwick's fault, and the remark does Hooker no credit. Indeed it suggests the small boy out walking with his parents who runs ahead a half-block in play, stumbles, falls, and calls back to mother and father in a shrill, reproachful voice: "Now see what you made me do!"

By 4:30 Lincoln's impatience for further news overcame his desire not to burden field headquarters in the midst of the battle as he telegraphed Butterfield:

"Where is General Hooker? Where is Sedgwick? Where is Stoneman?"

Confusing Orders from Hooker

Hooker's mental gyrations and strategic ineffectiveness, from the time Lee seized the initiative and commenced to outmaneuver and outfight him, are clearly portrayed in his series of telegraphic orders to Sedgwick from morning to night on Saturday, May 2. The instructions to his corps on the field at Chancellorsville were in many cases oral and fragmentary, and therefore lacking substance for a study in continuity, but those to Sedgwick, ten miles away, were perforce reduced to writing.

Because Lee had been so aggressive and had pressed his attacks on Hooker from three sides with such marked success, the latter felt sure that practically the entire Confederate army was in contact with him. Therefore, he assumed Sedgwick must be faced at Fredericksburg with merely nominal opposition, which seemed to present him with a favorable opportunity to deliver a strong blow against Lee's rear and thus achieve one of the original objectives of the pincers movement, even though belated.

Acting upon that strategic conception, Hooker had dispatched the first of his series of messages to Sedgwick, through Chief of Staff Butterfield, at 9:30 A.M., Saturday, May 2. The gist of the order was for the Sixth Corps "to attack the enemy on his front if an opportunity presents itself with a reasonable expectation of success." At that time, of course, Jackson was engaged in marching around Hooker's flank and the wishful thinking Federal commander cherished the illusion that Lee was retreating.

Hooker probably received a message shortly thereafter which advised that the enemy remained strong on Sedgwick's front, for at 9:45 A.M. he sent word to Sedgwick:

"You are all right. You have but Ewell's (Early's) Division in your front; balance all up here (Chancellorsville)."

By afternoon the bemused Hooker had fully convinced himself that his earlier estimate as to Lee's withdrawal was correct, so he sent off a priceless message to Sedgwick (just one hour before Jackson charged into his own right flank):

> 4:10 P.M. May 2: You will cross the river as soon as indications will permit; capture Fredericksburg with everything in it, and vigorously pursue the enemy. We know that the enemy is fleeing, trying to save his trains. Two of Sickles' divisions are among them.

Shortly after that message sped over the wires to Sedgwick the sky fell in on Hooker, who for several hours had no time to think about his left wing. At 7:05 P.M., however, Sedgwick was puzzled to receive the next message:

> The Major General commanding directs you to pursue the enemy on the Bowling Green road.

What Hooker was thinking about when he dictated that order is anybody's guess. Presumably he pictured Sedgwick as having already completed his 4:10 mission, but Hooker was certainly shooting arrows into the air and developing fantasies of his own, because Sedgwick would naturally have to pursue his enemy in the direction the Confederates would choose to withdraw, if any, and it didn't have to be in a southerly direction by the Bowling Green Road.

However, Sedgwick tried to follow instructions, as the following message which he sent to Hooker via Butterfield at 8 P.M. indicated:

> General Brooks has taken the Bowling Green road, in front of him; is still skirmishing, and will advance as long as he can see, and will then take position for the night. Newton is moving in the direction of Hamilton's Crossing, and at daylight the entire corps will be in motion.

Sedgwick was still trying to make sense of Hooker's wishes insofar as they could be interpreted from his disjointed and peremptory combat orders when the crowning message, dispatched at 9 P.M. from Hooker's headquarters reached him at 11 P.M. below Fredericksburg:

> The major-general commanding directs that General Sedgwick cross the Rappahannock at Fredericksburg on receipt of this order, and at once take up his line of march on the Chancellorsville road until you (sic) connect with us, and he will attack and destroy any force he may fall in with on the road. He will leave all his trains behind, except the pack-train of small ammunition, and march to be in our vicinity at daylight. He will probably fall on the rear of the forces commanded by General Lee, and between us we will use him up. Send word to General Gibbon to take possession of Fredericksburg. Be sure not to fail.

Sedgwick was of course already across the Rappahannock with his whole corps and engaged in developing the Confederate position, when the last message was received. But it was now clear that, traveling light, Hooker wanted him to take Fredericksburg, brush aside any Confederates in his path, and proceed with all dispatch to Chancellorsville by the most direct route, which was certainly not the Bowling Green Road leading to Richmond. "Uncle John" therefore made plans accordingly, which of course took some time in the darkness, involving as it did the issuance of new orders to his three division commanders and the commanding officer of the Light Division.

The Second Battle of Fredericksburg

Taking his cue from Hooker, Butterfield kept needling Sedgwick to lose not a minute's time in getting the show on the road, the final attempt being made exactly at midnight in a message delivered to Sedgwick in person by one of Hooker's aides who had come down to Fredericksburg from United States Mine Ford to give Butterfield a more complete fill-in on the Chancellorsville situation than was possible by telegraph.

> From the statement brought by General Hooker's aide, it seems to be of vital importance that you should fall upon Lee's rear with crushing force. He will explain all to you. Give your advance to one who will do all that the urgency of the case requires.

Both Hooker and Butterfield were under the misapprehension that Early's Confederate Division had been greatly reduced, a presumption that was undoubtedly built up by the frequent messages, from the signal stations and Professor Lowe's balloons opposite Fredericksburg and at Banks' Ford, reporting the observed movements of Confederate units and trains in rear of their position on the heights west of Fredericksburg. Present day veterans of recent wars will recall similar fallacies put out as facts by higher headquarters whose personnel, going by the book or in pursuance of a purpose unknown to the troops on the field, were prone to announce solemnly that the enemy had withdrawn, when in fact nothing of the sort had happened, as the troops being shot at by the ephemeral enemy knew only too well.

Butterfield Keeps Hooker Informed

At army headquarters in Falmouth Butterfield kept watch on Sedgwick's Sunday morning movements across the river in order to keep his boss at Chancellorsville informed of the progress of the left wing. Acutely conscious of the fact that Hooker at the other end of the battlefield was figuratively biting his finger nails, (but doing little else as he awaited the Sixth Corps' anticipated approach to attack Lee's rear), Butterfield started sending dispatches even before daylight, as the reports came in from Sedgwick. Between 5:30 and 9 A. M. Sunday, May 3, the following messages, sent off to Hooker, gave him a progressive bird's eye view of the fighting in and west of Fredericksburg:

5:45 A. M.: Heavy cannonading in Sedgwick's front for the last twenty minutes, apparently in front of Fredericksburg.

6:08 A. M.: Balloon reports enemy reappearing on heights in front of Sedgwick's crossing. Sedgwick, judging from the sound, is meeting with strong resistance.

6:20 A. M.: Sedgwick reports himself at Sumner's old battleground at 5:30 A. M., hotly engaged, and not sanguine of the result.

6:45 A. M.: Sedgwick's prospects here look unfavorable, from reports. He is not out of Fredericksburg.

7:05 A. M.: Sedgwick still in front of Fredericksburg, as far as I can judge. Trains were running up all night to vicinity of Hamilton's Crossing. It may be that the enemy were reenforced.

8:30 A. M.: Our skirmishers just occupied rebel rifle-pits on Hazel Run. Gibbon moving to right, with prospects of flanking the enemy. Enemy resist desperately.

8:45 A. M.: Sedgwick at 7:40 o'clock reports about making combined assault on their works; Gibbon on right; Newton center; Howe on left. If he fails, will try again.

Impatient at the delay, and apparently feeling that Sedgwick was dragging his heels against unimportant opposition, Hooker at 9:15 sent him the following message:

> You will hurry up your column. The enemy's right flank now rests near the Plank Road at Chancellorsville, all exposed. You will attack at once.

Sedgwick's thoughts have not been recorded, but he doubtless knew that Hooker had at Chancellorsville over twice as many men as Lee could muster, had committed only about half of them in action, and yet persisted in hounding Sedgwick to carry the major burden for the entire army.

Early had shifted his weight to the right when the bulk of Sedgwick's corps had crossed and driven the Confederate skirmishers back into the woods from the Bowling Green Road (Old Richmond Stage Road). Most of his own division was on the ridge below Fredericksburg, with the brigades of Barksdale and Hays holding the two-mile line from Taylor's Hill, at the river, through Marye's Heights, to the Howison House. Marye's Hill, the key position with the stone wall and sunken road at its base, which had proven to be Burnside's nemesis in December, was occupied by only two regiments supported by eight guns, from the Plank Road to Hazel Run.

Jubal Early with one division and a couple of brigades was making a noble effort to outsmart his West Point classmate, John Sedgwick, and succeeding rather well in upsetting the time schedule of still another classmate, Joe

Hooker. It would not be surprising if General Lee, with his vast stored-up knowledge of the characters of so many of the prewar West Pointers, had personally advised Stonewall Jackson to leave Early at Fredericksburg on the ground that he probably knew Sedgwick best and could deal with him more effectively for that reason.

MAJOR GENERAL JUBAL A. EARLY, C.S.A.

Sedgwick's movement by the flank in the direction of Fredericksburg was started soon after midnight May 2-3, Newton's division in the lead, followed by the Light Division and then Howe's division. Brook's division remained for the time being to protect the bridges at Deep Run and below. The Confederates contested the advance as they slowly fell back, but Sedgwick's column kept advancing and reached Fredericksburg at daylight. With the completion of a bridge opposite the Lacy House, Gibbon's division crossed over and took position on Sedgwick's right about seven o'clock Sunday morning.

Using the town as a base, Sedgwick launched repeated attacks on the Confederate position to the west. Between

MAP 24. THE SITUATION ON SEDGWICK'S FRONT ABOUT 7:30 A. M., MAY 3

During the early morning hours the VI Corps moved north from its bridges at Franklin's old crossing site, preparing to assault the Confederate works back of Fredericksburg. The bridges were then taken up and moved upstream, one to the old position below the ruined railway bridge, and the other near the Lacy house. Gibbon, who was to cross at the upper bridge, was delayed in getting across, but about 7:30 was in the north end of town, with advance detachments attempting to cross the canal and advance west in the Stansbury area. Newton's

8 and 10 A. M. Newton made the first attempt along Hazel Run and was repulsed. A second assault against Marye's Hill was also stopped cold. Gibbon's division then tried to get around Taylor's Hill to turn the Confederate left, but the heavy artillery fire that played on the canal prevented him from bridging it, and he too had to admit failure. Then Howe's division tried to turn the hill south of Hazel Run but met with no success. It was becoming rather plain that the Confederates were in strength and determined to keep the heights for themselves, concurrently making something of super-optimists out of both Butterfield and Hooker.

As Lee was to do at Gettysburg eight weeks later, Sedgwick had tried the enemy right and left and found them invulnerable. He now decided to make a direct frontal assault, putting out of his mind no doubt the terrible disaster to Burnside's divisions which resulted from the identical attempt over the same ground at the first Battle of Fredericksburg.

Sedgwick was a cautious and deliberate general both in planning and execution. He had missed the first battle of Fredericksburg in December while convalescing from the serious wounds received at Antietam, but he knew all about what Burnside had done and failed to do, particularly in front of the stone wall at the foot of Marye's Hill.

Sedgwick reasoned it all out. He was not going to be rushed into a premature attack, regardless of the continuous pressure from Hooker and Butterfield, until his plan had been perfected and fully explained to his officers and men. His efforts to flank the Confederate position at

---

division of the VI Corps led the advance into Fredericksburg, followed by Burnham's Light Division. Opposition was slight. Howe followed Newton as far as Hazel Run, and Brooks followed Howe as far as Deep Run when skirmishing in his rear caused him to halt and face west and southwest.

The Confederate fortifications on the heights were occupied by Early's Division, the brigades from right to left being Smith's, Gordon's, Hoke's, two regiments each from Hay's and Barksdale's; Barksdale's and Hays'. Wilcox came up to the vicinity of Taylor's Hill, having marched from the vicinity of Banks' Ford. He was just in time to stall Gibbon's advance.

either end of the line had fizzled, due partly to the fact that Gibbon's attempt to move around Taylor's Hill near the Rappahannock had been slow in getting underway. This had given the Confederates time to bring up enough guns on that flank to interdict the crossings over the canal, with such effect that Gibbon didn't even try to repair the bridges. A half hour earlier he could have achieved his purpose against negligible opposition, and Sedgwick's later frontal attack might conceivably have been avoided.

Sedgwick's deliberations, which led to the head-on charge against the stone wall and the heights above it, considered three major premises: Hooker's insistence that the Sixth Corps hasten to Chancellorsville by the most direct route; the failure of the attempts to outflank the ridge on right and left, which left only the alternatives of a frontal assault or nothing; and Burnside's ill-fated venture over the same ground in December, which had led to bloody failure and 6,300 casualties. Sedgwick's decision was a bold, calculated risk that laid his reputation as a field general on the line.

Recalling that every one of the six charges made in December had demonstrated the sacrificial courage of the men of Sumner's Right Grand Division, Sedgwick was confident that what they had done his soldiers of the Sixth Corps could certainly do. He reasoned that all previous attempts had failed because the attacking lines had halted and thrown themselves on the ground to load and fire as well as to escape the hail of bullets that hit them from the sunken road. The result, in Sedgwick's thinking, had been to cool their ardor and subject them to far greater punishment than they would have suffered had they kept moving. This time there would be no stopping to fire and re-load; but to make doubly certain he issued orders that the assault echelon should advance over the open field at the double with unloaded rifles, bayonets fixed, to give the enemy cold steel. And it worked!

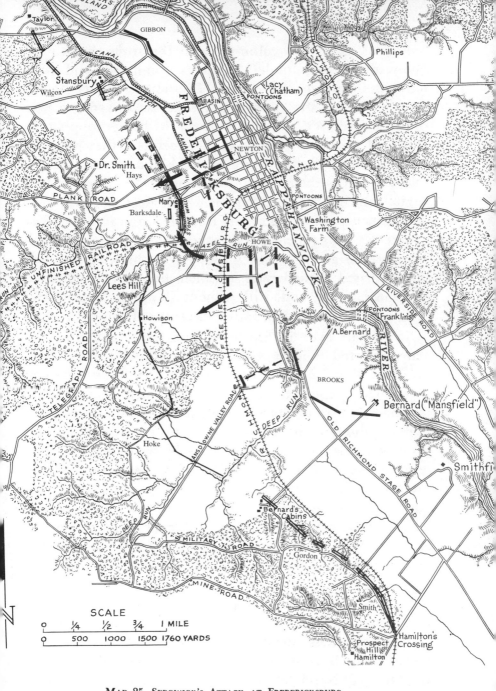

MAP 25. SEDGWICK'S ATTACK AT FREDERICKSBURG

This shows the actions of the VI Corps in capturing Marye's Heights between
10:30 A. M. and 11 A. M., May 3, 1863.

Advancing in two columns, with the strength of a re-enforced division, under Newton's command, and with Colonel Burnham of the Light Division in charge of the assault echelon, the Federals advanced with fixed bayonets on and alongside the Plank Road without stopping to load and fire their pieces. As in December, they were assailed by heavy artillery fire of grape and canister, which failed to stop them, and when within 25 yards of the stone wall, history repeated itself as a sheet of flame from the sunken road blasted their faces in a murderous fire of musketry. This time, however, the momentum of the Federals was so great that they swept over the wall, engaged the surprised Confederates in violent but short-lived hand-to-hand combat, and, still without stopping to load and fire, rushed up Marye's Hill and captured the crest.

It was all over in fifteen minutes from the time the charge started. The routed Confederates took to their heels in panic, throwing away guns, pistols, knapsacks—anything that might impede their flight. As the victorious Federals reached the top of Marye's Hill, it was a mighty pleasant sight, although one to which they were unaccustomed, to look across the broad plateau to the west and feast their eyes on the large number of fleeing Confederates, riderless horses, and artillery and wagon trains careening at a mad gallop across the fields to safety.

While Newton was capturing Marye's Hill, Howe's division carried the heights below the town, putting the entire ridge in Federal hands, and driving Early's troops in a rapid retreat by the Telegraph Road to the south.

The cost to Sedgwick's men was a heavy one, but the price was ridiculously cheap when compared with the previous fruitless attempt over the same ground in December. Then Burnside lost 6,300 men and accomplished nothing. This time Sedgwick, with a loss of only 1,500 killed and wounded, had broken the enemy resistance, captured a thousand prisoners, a handful of battle flags, and fifteen pieces of artillery (six of which were recovered when Early returned to Fredericksburg), and cleared the way for his advance on Chancellorsville. The defending Confederates had been split right down the middle, so that the divided segments were forced to escape in two directions. The opportunity for use of a cavalry regiment or two, to exploit the success, was one that the horse cavalry used to dream about, but there was no Federal cavalry at hand to make history.

The Significance of Banks' Ford

Banks' Ford on the Rappahannock River, about half-way between Falmouth and United States Mine Ford, the latter Hooker's lifeline for the movement of his army in both directions, was a valuable pawn in the hands of either Lee or Hooker. Both realized its importance and both utilized its facilities during the campaign.

Hooker's strategy had contemplated the uncovering of United States Mine Ford and Banks' Ford in succession, as his right wing swung around Lee's left on April 28-30 and came up on his rear at Chancellorsville. The first phase concluded, Meade's Fifth Corps was proceeding along the River Road to seal off Banks' Ford, the occupation of which would have immeasurably shortened the communications between Hooker's two wings, when Hooker inexplicably pulled the advancing divisions back in a foolish and unnecessary shift from the offensive to the defensive, even though there was at that time no enemy to defend against except Anderson's Division and a hand-ful of Stuart's cavalrymen.

The following day, May 1, Hooker had sent his Chief of Artillery, General Hunt, to take charge of the approaches to Banks' Ford on the left or north bank, to prevent the Confederates from crossing at that point in case they should take it into their heads to do so. Hunt reported that Engineer General Benham's 600 men were insufficient for the purpose, and requested that a full division be sent. The result was that 22 guns of the horse artillery and 2 batteries of Napoleons were ordered up from Sedgwick's wing, while Gibbon was concurrently instructed to detach one of his brigades from Falmouth to reenforce Benham.

Anderson's Confederate Division, after withdrawing from Chancellorsville on the approach of Hooker's three corps on April 30, had fallen back to the junction of Mine Road and Plank Road, where it spent the rest of the day digging entrenchments to strengthen the line from Banks' Ford on the right to the Plank Road. But when Jackson came up from Fredericksburg on the morning of May 1, he pulled Anderson off that job in order to advance with Jackson's Corps and McLaws' Division against Hooker's Chancellorsville hideout in the Wilderness. Upon Lee's arrival from Fredericksburg later in the day, however, he wisely disapproved of Jackson's decision to give up the position at Banks' Ford and directed Wilcox's Brigade of Anderson's Division to return and reoccupy the rifle pits covering the ford on the south side of the river. Whether Lee was then aware of the fact that Reynolds' corps was marching up from Fredericksburg is not known. If so it un-doubtedly influenced his decision. The Federals thought that was the reason when Hunt reported the reoccupation at 6:45 P.M. Whether Lee was smart or just lucky in acting when he did, the fact is that Reynolds would have crossed at Banks' Ford if the bridge had been laid and interesting tactical developments would certainly have followed.

Two pontoon bridges had been delivered at Banks' Ford by Benham's engineers May 1, but not laid. It was not until the afternoon of Sunday, May 3 that one of them was put down, between three and four o'clock, after Wilcox had left the position to reenforce Early's troops against Sedgwick's advance from Fredericksburg. It was also about that time that Hooker ordered the second bridge to be transferred to United States Mine Ford, providing three bridges at that place. Hooker was taking no chances on his own security and evidently getting ready, even then, to retreat from Chancellorsville. Apparently he was willing to weaken Sedgwick's auxiliary equipment even further than he had already, but Benham used his head, having already calculated the width of the river at both fords, and only sent half the second bridge to Hooker. It was a good thing that he did, as will be seen later.

Lee Makes Another Bold Decision

Shortly after 12 noon General Lee, resting in the vicinity of the Chancellor House as his hard-fighting Confederates reshuffled themselves after the tough but successful battle which gave them possession of all the important terrain features of the battlefield, was handed a bit of bad news. Hooker's left wing had captured Fredericksburg and driven Early's Confederates from their position on the heights where Longstreet's Corps had brought Burnside to disaster in December!

There was no time to savor the fruits of victory. Lee must immediately turn to meet the new threat from the east. But by this time he had taken the full measure of Joe Hooker and found him sadly wanting in enterprise. Lee did not hesitate. He would again take a calculated risk, divide his force once more in the face of the enemy, leave a holding force to occupy Hooker's attention and move with McLaws' Division and one of Anderson's brigades to oppose Sedgwick. Jackson's Corps, under Stuart, would remain in contact at Chancellorsville, while Lee in person would march with McLaws, back over the ground they had covered in their advance May 1, to engage Sedgwick as soon as the two forces should meet. Instead of attacking Lee's rear, as Hooker had planned, Sedgwick would be confronted, in a meeting engagement on even terms, by the confident general who had just proven his superiority over Hooker's much larger force, and in the process taken all the fight out of its commander.

Jackson's Corps, which had been fighting ever since five-thirty the previous evening, after its 12-mile march through the Wilderness, and had enjoyed very little rest during the night, was much reduced in strength by casualties and close to exhaustion by fatigue, hunger, and thirst. Withal it was preparing to renew the battle by moving on Hooker's last defense line with the object of forcing it back across the river.

General Colston, commanding one of Jackson's divisions, was designated to lead the attack. At one o'clock he was summoned to report to Lee who was standing in a small tent beside the road. In Colston's words:

> In low, quiet tones he said to me: General, I wish you to advance with your division on the United States Ford road. I expect you will meet with resistance before you come to the bend of the road. I do not want you to attack the enemy's positions, but only to feel them. Send your engineer officer with skirmishers to the front to reconnoitre and report. Don't engage seriously, but keep the enemy in check and prevent him from advancing. Move at once.

Colston adds that at the time he was not a little puzzled and wondered why the army was not to continue the advance and hurl Hooker into the river. He learned the reason later in the day, when the sounds of battle were heard from the direction of Fredericksburg, and it is quite likely that he reflected as well on the ability of his commanding general to keep his own counsel.

SALEM CHURCH

CHAPTER 17

THE BATTLE OF SALEM CHURCH

A LTHOUGH NOT exactly planned that way, the Battle of Salem Church was fought on terrain that was made to order for the Confederates, a wooded ridge line running north and south where the Orange Turnpike comes closer to the Rappahannock than at any other point between Chancellorsville and Fredericksburg. Anchored firmly at the river on the left and the Turnpike on the right, the position was a difficult one to overrun frontally, a necessity if Sedgwick were to make any speed in his march on Chancellorsville.

Much of the landscape east of the ridge was open, to afford the defenders a decidedly advantageous field of fire through which the Federals would have to advance on their march from Fredericksburg. It was fine maneuver country, and a pleasant change from the dense wilderness in the Chancellorsville area.

McLaws' Confederates had the longer distance to travel, approximately five miles from their position southeast of

[329]

Chancellorsville to Salem Church, but with no opposition to slow them down they reached their objective by three o'clock. Sedgwick on the other hand, moving against Wilcox's Confederate Brigade which fought the delaying action, necessarily made slower progress from the Fredericksburg heights, which his corps had captured at mid-day Sunday, May 3, to Salem Church, three to four miles distant.

Salem Church, picturesquely situated in a grove of trees just south of the Turnpike, one and a half miles east of the junction where the Plank Road rejoins the Pike, sits atop Salem Ridge and overlooks the battlefield. Covered with dense woods and underbrush, the ridge was a low water-shed whose spine runs in a northeasterly direction for slightly over a mile and a quarter, then dips down to the river near Banks' Ford, where the Rappahannock makes a sharp V-turn whose point aims south.

The country folk who lived in the area must have been devout churchgoers, for there were three houses of worship

SALEM CHURCH IN 1958

Note the present size of the oak tree on the right, as compared to the illustration at the head of the chapter.

within a few miles of one another: Tabernacle Church, on the Mine Road a short distance below the Plank Road near its junction with the Turnpike; Zoan (occasionally misspelled Zoar and Zion) Church, at the junction of the Mine Road and the Turnpike; and historic Salem Church, after which the battle was named, a solid, rectangular, red-brick Baptist edifice which was organized in 1840 but not built until 1844. Salem Church was a haven for refugees from Fredericksburg when Lee and Burnside fought the first Battle of Fredericksburg in December 1862. In an excellent state of repair despite its age, Salem Church is still standing but no longer in use. The original Zoan Church has been replaced.

Sedgwick Advances

After the fighting of Sunday morning, which resulted in the complete evacuation of Marye's Heights, Sedgwick pulled his divisions together and prepared for the march to Chancellorsville. Gibbon was directed to remain with his reduced division in Fredericksburg to prevent stray Confederate units from crossing to the north bank. Brooks' division, which had not moved from its crossing position at Deep Run, was placed at the head of the column, in extended order by column of brigades, with skirmishers to the front and flank and artillery on the road. Newton's division followed that of Brooks, marching in column along the Orange Plank Road. Howe's division and the Light Division brought up the rear.

Wilcox's Confederate Brigade, which had hastened from Banks' Ford to Early's support at Fredericksburg in the morning, provided the sole resistance as he withdrew slowly before Sedgwick's advancing troops. A section of horse artillery to the right of the Federals greatly hampered their advance by occupying each successive crest, firing as long as possible, and then displacing to the next crest.

Early's Confederate Division, after its defeat on the

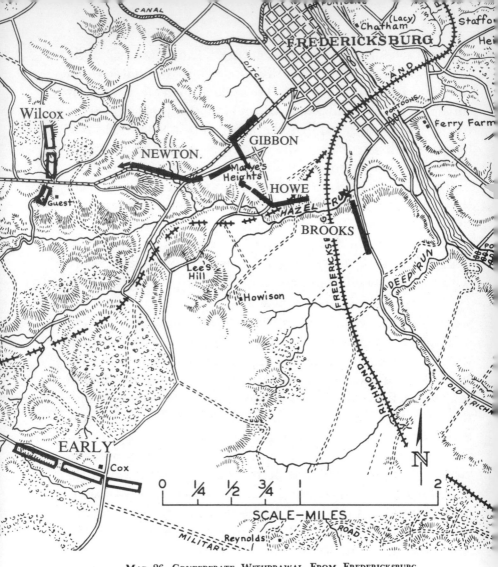

MAP 26. CONFEDERATE WITHDRAWAL FROM FREDERICKSBURG

This shows the situation about 1 P. M., May 3, 1863. Early's Division withdrew down the Telegraph Road and assembled near Cox's. Wilcox's Brigade marched west on the Plank Road and occupied a delaying position near Guest's.

Sedgwick moved out slowly on the Plank Road to join Hooker at Chancellorsville, as ordered. Gibbon moved through the town and occupied Marye's Heights. The leading division of the VI Corps, Newton's, delayed to allow Howe and Brooks to catch up. This allowed the Confederates time to reorganize, and permitted Lee to reinforce Wilcox.

heights, withdrew along the Telegraph Road to the southwest, but on finding that it was not being pursued, halted after covering about two miles. Remaining in the vicinity until Sedgwick had passed, Early returned on Monday morning, May 4, reoccupied his former position on the heights, and prepared to cut off Sedgwick's possible retreat to Fredericksburg.

By this maneuver the Confederates had again turned the tables on the Federals. Once more Hooker's plan had backfired; instead of pocketing Lee between wings of the Union army, Sedgwick now found himself in a comparable position, with Confederate troops on his front and rear.

As happened so frequently on the battlefields of 1861-1865, former West Point classmates who in many instances were good friends in their undergraduate and pre-Civil War years found themselves pitted against each other as division or corps commanders in the deadly game of killing as many of the other's men as they could. The Battle of Salem Church was no exception. Here the class of 1841 was represented by Federal Generals W. T. H. Brooks and Albion P. Howe, while graduates of the year 1842 who fought it out under Lee and Sedgwick included division commanders Lafayette McLaws and Richard H. Anderson for the Confederates and John Newton on the opposite side.

The Meeting Engagement

When Sedgwick's leading elements arrived within a mile of Salem Church, about 4 P. M., they were met by a handful of cavalry skirmishers and greeted with solid shot from two rifled guns posted near the church. The open space between was crossed by a small stream where hostile guns, firing steadily as long as their ammunition held out, definitely checked the Federal advance.

Brooks' division, already deployed, pressed forward as soon as the Confederate guns had retired, and after an

MAP 27. THE BATTLE OF SALEM CHURCH

This map also shows the position to which Hooker withdrew on May 3.

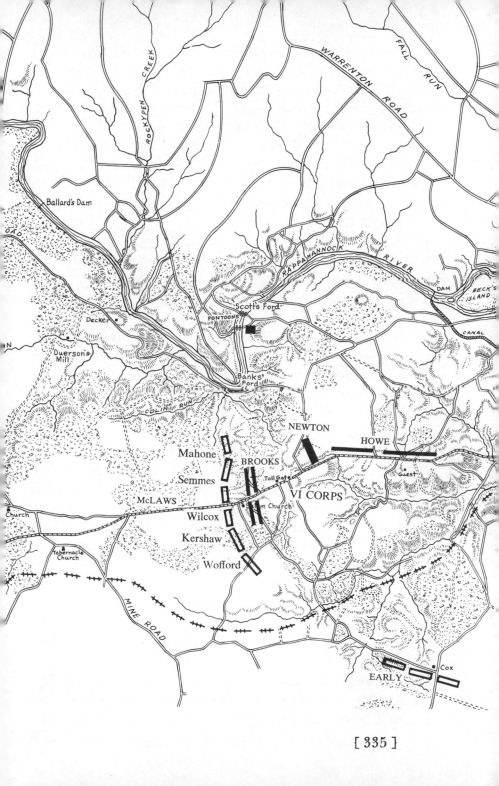

Ballard's Dam

ROCKYPEN CREEK

WARRENTON ROAD

FALL RUN

RAPPAHANNOCK RIVER

BECK'S ISLAND

DAM

CANAL

Scott's Ford

PONTOONS

Decker

Duerson's Mill

Banks' Ford

COLIN RUN

NEWTON

HOWE

Guest

Mahone

BROOKS

Toll Gate

Semmes

Church

VI CORPS

McLAWS

Wilcox

Church

Kershaw

Wofford

Tabernacle Church

MINE ROAD

EARLY

Cox

extended period of brisk fighting drove McLaws' defenders off the ridge. Newton's division, advancing in column on Brooks' right rear, was unable to develop battle formation promptly, whereupon Wilcox's Brigade, counterattacking, came in on Brooks' flank to force him in turn off the crest. Federal artillery, ably supporting the infantry, checked the counterattack, affording Newton the opportunity to move up to reenforce Brooks. A second time the Federals attacked and. again the Confederates were driven back in confusion. By that time the sun had set and darkness put an end to the seesaw battle for the day. The troops on both sides, remaining under arms, thereupon settled down until morning.

Critics of Sedgwick have charged that he was unconscionably and unnecessarily show in all his movements on May 2 and 3 and hence contributed substantially to the loss of the Chancellorsville campaign by the Union army. This amateur analyst doesn't subscribe to that theory in light of the facts. On the contrary, Sedgwick's tactics, considered in context with Hooker's lack of initiative and disjointed orders to him from the other side of the battlefield, were based on sound thinking and careful evaluation of all the factors present. Hooker's demands were unrealistic and can even be called hypocritical, for he assured Sedgwick that he would attack Lee in front as Sedgwick came up on his rear, when in fact he had no intention of doing so. If he had, Lee could not successfully have detached the divisions of McLaws and Anderson; Sedgwick *would* have marched on to Chancellorsville unopposed except by Wilcox's retiring Brigade, and Lee *would* have been caught in a vise between Hooker and Sedgwick, from which even that redoubtable leader could have extricated himself only by superhuman efforts.

As it was, with Hooker content to allow Lee complete freedom of action at both ends of the field, Sedgwick, with a 2 to 1 advantage over Early, accomplished the first half of his mission almost as soon as it was possible, even though hours later than Hooker's logistical, impracticable table of time-and-space factors had stipulated. By midafternoon, however, when he reached Salem Church, the situation was entirely different than he had been led by Hooker to believe. Lee was there, halfway between Chancellorsville and Fredericksburg, facing him with perhaps 6,000 men, increased to 10,000 a few hours later when Anderson came up; and Early stood at his rear with another 8,000 to 9,000, his original strength less losses incurred in the Sunday morning battle at Fredericksburg. The opposing forces at Salem Church could therefore be considered approximately equal, but with the odds in Lee's favor because Sedgwick was now faced with a fight in two directions.

Given the advance knowledge that Hooker intended that Sedgwick should be left to fight Lee without help from the main army, and that McLaws was marching east to meet him, there is little doubt that Sedgwick would have adopted for the march a formation of two divisions abreast and one in reserve, even though that would probably have lost another hour. Nevertheless, he could then have developed in sufficient strength to launch a coordinated assault against McLaws with a 2 to 1 superiority, with every chance of success. Instead of which his three divisions, strung out in column, were perforce thrown into the attack piecemeal and inconclusively.

It was no wonder the greatly disturbed Sedgwick slept fitfully the night of May 3. With little knowledge of what Hooker had been doing or intended, he knew he was behind schedule, that the Confederates had blocked him, and, it was rumored, had even reoccupied the heights at his rear. It has been said that every so often during the night he threw off his blanket, rose from the damp grass, walked a few paces and listened carefully; then returned, threw himself on the ground and tried vainly to sleep. On the other hand General Lee, who believed that Sedgwick still had two corps at his disposal instead of only one, may safely be said to have slept soundly, as was his custom, to awake refreshed, alert, and ready to finish the task of driving Sedgwick into the river regardless of numbers.

In the course of the afternoon, the Confederates who had remained to guard Banks' Ford were pulled away to join the battle over by the Turnpike, whereupon General Benham quickly laid his bridge. Early the next morning, May 4, the report reached Sedgwick that 15,000 of the enemy, moving from the direction of Richmond, had occupied the heights at Fredericksburg and cut his communications with the town and Gibbon's division. That would be Jubal Early, retracing his steps and resuming his former position, his strength exaggerated approximately one hundred percent.

Sedgwick Boxed In

Sedgwick's official report indicates that he anticipated some such eventuality, and in order to protect his rear and prevent the Confederates from cutting him off from Banks' Ford as well, Howe's division, in the rear, early in the morning was formed in line of battle facing east, extended to the left to rest his flank on the river and secure the ford. Thus Sedgwick repeated Hancock's tactics of the previous day at Chancellorsville and had his divisions facing in two directions against the aggressive Confederate brigades, a type of maneuver that is not considered in the best military families to be overly conducive to high morale on the part of the participants. Nevertheless, General Howe's men performed their task in splendid fashion, repelling an effort by the Confederates to achieve the very result that Sedgwick was guarding against, and in their success taking 200 prisoners and a battle flag.

During the night, General Gouverneur G. Warren, of Hooker's staff, who had joined Sedgwick at Fredericksburg to observe his advance and guide the column, returned to army headquarters by way of Banks' Ford and United States Mine Ford and reported the day's action in person to the army commander. Shortly after midnight he was directed to send a dispatch to Sedgwick, the significance of which has to be read in context to be appreciated:

> I find everything snug here. We contracted the line a little, and repulsed the last assault with ease. General Hooker wishes them to attack him tomorrow, if they will. He does not desire you to attack again in force unless he attacks him at the same time. He says you are too far away for him to direct. Look well to the safety of your corps, and keep up communication with General Benham, at Banks' Ford and Fredericksburg. You can go to either place, if you think best. To cross at Banks' Ford would bring you in supporting distance of the main body, and would be better than falling back to Fredericksburg.

The above message, delayed in transmission, did not reach Sedgwick till late in the forenoon of May 4, by which time he was boxed in, could not have reached Fredericksburg if he had wanted to, and was in no shape to retire safely by Banks' Ford, either. His east flank rested on the river about halfway between Banks' Ford and Fredericksburg; the line extended south across the Turnpike, then west at right angles for two miles, where it again turned north across the road and anchored part way to the river. Hence his west flank rested on no natural obstacle. The three-sided line, covering a distance of at least five miles, could not readily be contracted without inviting attack while moving into a new position.

Sedgwick's decision was to stand fast and await attack, possibly from three directions; then, after dark, to fall back on Banks' Ford. In view of Hooker's above quoted order he had little choice, and by this time had no doubt come to the same conclusion as the corps commanders with Hooker, that the general was a defeated man, devoid of initiative, incapable of attacking, and thinking only of safety and any excuse to get his army away from it all at the earliest opportunity. Hooker's unwarranted superiority complex was likewise revealed in that sentence which implied that because Sedgwick was too far away for Hooker to lead him by the hand and personally guide his actions, the only course open to Sedgwick was to retreat. A strange man, Joe Hooker, who seemingly had no confidence in the abilities of any one but himself, and even that satisfaction had been denied him as a result of his disgraceful timidity in this campaign.

Lee's discovery that the Union army had materially strengthened its fortifications on the new defense line convinced him that it would be folly to attack Hooker at Chancellorsville with only a part of his force, while engaged with the remainder at Salem Church. His revised strategy was to detach Anderson's three remaining brigades from Stuart, leaving only Jackson's three reduced divisions to contain Hooker; bring Anderson to strengthen McLaws and Early on the perimeter of Sedgwick's position; and drive the latter out.

Lee was satisfied by this time that Hooker had no intention of coming to Sedgwick's aid by moving troops over the River Road and thence down the Mine Road to connect up with Sedgwick between the river and the Turnpike. That possibility had been on his mind the preceding afternoon when he had sent McLaws from Chancellorsville to Salem Church and shifted Anderson, less the brigade with McLaws, to take position astride the River Road opposite Hooker's left flank, for the dual purpose of frightening his opponent with the possibility that his communications across the Rappahannock were being threatened, and concurrently to guard against a surprise Federal attack on McLaws' left rear.

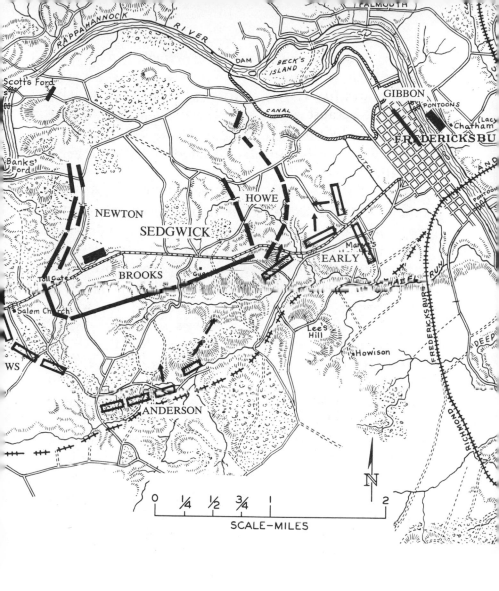

MAP. 28. THE ATTACK ON SEDGWICK ON MAY 4, 1863

Anderson has marched from his position shown on Map 27 to Salem Church, and from there is moving to participate with Early in the attack on Sedgwick's left flank. Barksdale and Smith have reoccupied Marye's Heights and Gibbon has withdrawn to his bridge.

Lee's plan of action for the afternoon of May 4 was for Anderson to move around Sedgwick's left, join Early west of the Fredericksburg heights, form a continuous line and, with McLaws forming the pivot opposite Sedgwick's center, launch a converging attack calculated to drive the Federals into the river.

Although Anderson reached the field about noon, much time was lost in disposing the troops for the attack. It was six o'clock before the combined forces of Anderson and Early were ready to push off. The first part of the plan worked beautifully; Sedgwick's troops were forced back across the Turnpike in the direction of the river, but it was growing dark and McLaws failed to see what was transpiring on the right until it was too late to make his contribution to speed the Federal withdrawal.

Howe's division, facing Fredericksburg, with the Light Division on his left, again bore the brunt of the Confederate attack. Strong artillery support enabled the Federals to contest the enemy advance, which came to a halt when a dense river fog settled over the field, making it difficult to distinguish friend from foe. The Confederates had to pay for their impetuous attack, however, losing heavily in killed, wounded, and captured. Among the several hundred Confederates taken prisoner were a number of officers, including one general (allegedly), but the attack served its purpose, for as soon as it was dark the divisions of Newton and Brooks, with the Light Division, were directed to retire rapidly to the river. There they took position in a contracted, protective semicircle on the heights near Banks' Ford and in the rifle pits that had been constructed by the Confederates, while Howe's division was left as rear guard until the others had completed the movement, when it too pulled back and formed on Newton's right.

Never before had Lee ordered a night attack, but this time he did so in the fear that otherwise Sedgwick would

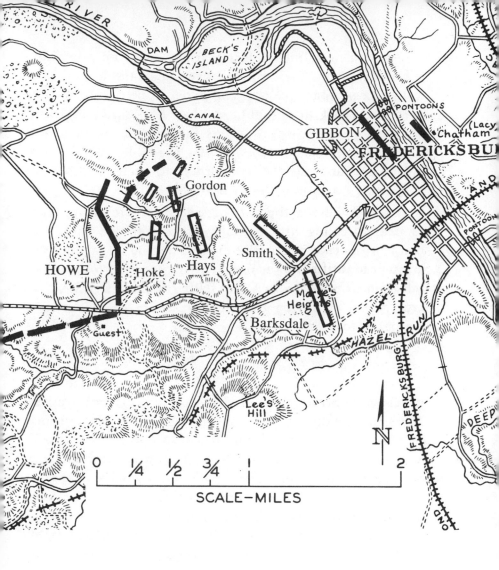

MAP 29. THE ATTACK ON HOWE

The Confederate attack made during the afternoon of May 4 was easily repulsed, mainly with artillery. This map shows the situation on the left flank at about sunset. Dense fog brought the fighting to an end, and after dark Sedgwick withdrew to the vicinity of Banks' Ford, covered by Howe's division.

construct a new line of fortifications and force the Confederates to fight the battle all over again the next day. It was to Lee imperative that the Federals be driven into or over the river that night, so that he could return to Chancellorsville to continue his interrupted attack to put the final quietus on Hooker. All available artillery was moved forward rapidly with orders to shell Bank's Ford and make it as unhealthy as possible.

Sedgwick during the evening received a telegram from Hooker directing him to hold his position on the south bank till morning. But the order-changing department at army headquarters soon justified its existence, for another telegram arrived, at 2 A.M., telling Sedgwick instead to cross the river during the night, take up the bridge, and cover the ford.

The Sixth Corps Withdraws

Old soldier that he was, Sedgwick stood not on the order of his going, lest "the old man" change his mind again. Benham's headwork now paid off. During the afternoon of May 4 he had thrown the second bridge at Scott's Ford, part of the time under long-range Confederate shelling, whereupon the troops moved with alacrity to put the river between them and the enemy. Within an hour, between 2 and 3 A.M. May 5, Sedgwick's entire corps, including his trains and 55 guns, crossed on the two bridges (probably at the double); after which the bridges were taken up and the battle of Salem Church passed into history.

That is, all but the anticlimax. For as the rear element of the Sixth Corps was on the bridge, still another dispatch was received from Hooker countermanding the order to withdraw. This was "change-order No. 4," which Sedgwick properly and understandably ignored, going instead into bivouac and sending a detachment to cover the ford.

News of Sedgwick's recrossing having been sent to Gibbon, who still held Fredericksburg, orders were at once issued to Hall's brigade to relinquish its hold on the town, retire to the north bank and take up the bridge, all of which was accomplished under cover of darkness and with only mild interference from the Confederates.

Sedgwick's casualties at the battle of Salem Church amounted to almost 3,000 of a total of 4,600 for the Sixth Corps during the entire campaign. Confederate casualty records are less dependable than the Federal, but it would seem reasonable to conclude that Lee took at least equal losses, in percentage of troops engaged, at Salem Church, where together with the Marye's Hill engagement the Sixth Corps captured 15 guns, 5 battle flags, and 1,400 prisoners.

On the morning of the 5th, having effectively disposed of the threat to his rear, but conscious of the fact that Sedgwick was quite capable of recrossing at Banks' Ford, Lee ordered Early and Barksdale to return and resume their watch on the Fredericksburg heights, while McLaws and Anderson once again retraced their steps to Chancellorsville.

The returning divisions of McLaws and Anderson reached their old positions at Chancellorsville during the afternoon of Tuesday, May 5, in the midst of a violent storm which practically guaranteed that there would be no active fighting until morning. Now that Sedgwick had been disposed of and Lee's separated forces were again united General Lee felt confident that one more blow would be sufficient to drive Hooker back across the Rappahannock.

Hooker's Council of War

The decision "to cross or not to cross" the Rappahannock at Banks' Ford had not yet been resolved for Sedgwick when Hooker decided to call a council of war at midnight, May 4-5. This was the army commander's first and only full-fledged council of the campaign, for which a number of possible reasons suggest themselves. It must be remembered that not only was Hooker supremely confident, in the early stages, in his self-assurance that his plans were perfect, but he then disdained advice or counsel from his subordinates and members of his official and personal staff, who were not even informed as to his intentions. Now however he had been so badly shown up by his own deficiencies and the superior performance of General Lee that his own confidence in Joe Hooker had evaporated. This self-assurance was to be replaced, temporarily at least, by sufficient humility to prompt him to consult his corps commanders in what appeared on the face of it to promise an open discussion as to what the next move should be.

The suspicion cannot be ruled out, however, that the retreat of the Army of the Potomac across the Rappahannock, opposed by less than half as many men in Lee's Army of Northern Virginia, was already a fait accompli in Hooker's mind; had been in fact, if only subconsciously, for two days. If true, the council would be a mere rubber stamp. Whatever censure should descend on Hooker from the Administration and the public would then be shared by his corps commanders, fellow architects of the withdrawal blueprint.

Shortly after midnight the generals arrived at Hooker's tent; corps commanders Couch (second in command), Meade, Sickles, Howard, and Reynolds. Chief of Staff Butterfield and Chief Engineer Warren were also present. Sedgwick had other things on his mind at Banks' Ford, and Stoneman was miles away in the direction of Richmond. Slocum, the only other corps commander on the field, had some distance to travel. He only arrived after the conference had broken up.

Hooker opened the meeting with a few remarks to set the tone, emphasizing that his instructions compelled him to cover Washington, and conveying by implication the thought that that was the most important thing, to which the mere defeat or even the destruction of Lee's army was secondary. He then added a gratuitous and uncalled-for insult to the soldierly character of the men of his army who, with the exception of elements of the Eleventh Corps and several renegade regimental and brigade commanders in the fighting of May 3, had demonstrated the greatest courage and fighting ability throughout. Contrary to the evidence, Hooker expressed apprehension of what he termed the want of steadiness in some of the troops, as exemplified by unnecessary firing along some parts of the line, as though the act of showing an interest in offensive measures deserved condemnation. In any event, he presented that weak argument to the council as one basis for determining the question of advancing or retiring. After further pointing out the obvious fact that if his own army were destroyed it could not protect Washington, a form of logical but specious reasoning that was nothing but camouflage in support of his own thesis, Hooker with Butterfield left the generals to consult among themselves.

Just as at courts-martial, where opinions are expressed by the individual members of the court, commencing with the junior and running up the scale to the ranking senior, so it was at councils of war. Dan Sickles took the lead in speaking his piece, which was in favor of withdrawing the army. This was patently in support of what were obviously Hooker's sentiments. Butterfield and Sickles were two of Hooker's intimate cronies, in spite of which Sickles ventured to criticize his superior for seeming to place on the corps commanders the responsibility for deciding to fight or quit, and also for his negligence in not insisting that their opinions be reduced to writing. On that score he need not have worried, for as a meeting to guide the army commander the council was to prove a sheer waste of time.

Sickles, a politician, admitted that he knew more about that subject than the other generals, while conceding with a rare show of modesty that his colleagues of the professional army were probably more expert in matters of military strategy. He then went on to comment on the gains made by the Northern Peace Party in the recent election, pointing out the dire political results that could stem from a clear cut defeat of the Union army. On that premise he primarily rested his argument in favor of retiring.

Meade, Reynolds, and Howard were more brief in their remarks, all voting to stay and fight it out. There was, however, a subsequent difference of opinion between Hooker and Meade as to what position Meade had taken at the council. The argument became so heated that Meade exchanged letters on the subject with Reynolds, Sickles, Howard, and Warren several weeks after the battle. All four generals confirmed the fact that Meade wanted Hooker to attack, but Sickles' letter added that at the close of the discussion, when Hooker announced his decision to recross the river, Meade's "original preferences appeared to have been surrendered to the clear conviction of the commanding general of the necessity which dictated his return to the north bank of the Rappahannock, and his unhesitating confidence in the practicability of withdrawing his army, without loss of men or material."

Couch was a bit reticent when it came his turn to speak, possibly because he was thoroughly disgusted with Hooker and his bungling, and feared he might say things that would be harmful to the cause of the army by airing dirty linen. His vote was in favor of retirement, which he afterwards explained simply gave expression to his conviction that the Army of the Potomac did not deserve to be further sacrificed under Hooker's incompetent leadership. But in his written account, printed in the *Philadelphia Times* after the war and reprinted in *Battles and Leaders,* Couch says that he expressed a doubt similar to Meade's whether the army could successfully get their guns safely away, and stated that he would favor an advance if he were permitted to designate the point of attack.

With the majority three to two in favor of going over to the offensive, Hooker and his Chief of Staff returned to the tent and called on each of the five corps commanders to indicate plainly whether or not they recommended an advance. Meade, Reynolds, and Howard categorically voted in favor, Couch and Sickles just as categorically against. Whereupon Hooker, in spite of the majority vote, announced that he would take upon himself the responsibility of ordering the retirement.

After Hooker had left, Reynolds followed Couch out of the tent with the remark, clearly echoing the sentiments of the group: "What was the use of calling us together at this time of night when he intended to retreat anyhow?"

There would be another, later, council of war in a small white farmhouse just over the crest of Cemetery Ridge, Gettysburg, on the night of July 2, 1863, after two days of bitter fighting between these same two armies. There would be a striking similarity between the two councils, except that at the second council Meade would be sitting in the place of Hooker as the army commander. At Gettysburg the same question would be voted on and the result of the ballot would again be to stay and fight it out. It is a certainty that memories of Chancellorsville would be in Meade's mind; for at Gettysburg he would accept the recommendation of the corps commanders, stand fast on the famous ridge, and watch Lee lose his first great battle as Pickett's charge shattered itself against the rock of Union determination.

Final Act of the Drama

During what remained of the rest of that night and through Tuesday morning, May 5, the troops of each corps labored to cut new roads, several as long as three miles, from their positions to United States Mine Ford, where three bridges awaited the retrograde movement. The idea was that Lee was not to be afforded the opportunity of interfering with the withdrawal, which he might very well do if the entire army were to converge on the single road that provided the only avenue of approach to the ford after the last road junction had been passed.

In the afternoon a heavy rainstorm churned the newly cut roads into mud, as the Rappahannock rose rapidly until it lapped at the bridges, still usable but in danger of being washed away if the waters should rise much further. Sometime during the day Hooker in person crossed the river, leaving orders that indicated the hour at which each corps should move during the night. The corps commanders were not advised that the commanding general had left the field, which in effect was an act of abdication, however unofficial.

About midnight General Couch received a note from Meade advising that Hooker had in fact crossed, that the river was now over the bridges, communication had been severed with the north shore, and that General Hunt had expressed his fear that the bridges would be lost. Couch immediately rode over to army headquarters and conferred with Meade, who agreed that the former was now in command of the army. Couch thereupon announced that the crossing orders were suspended and the army would stay where it was and fight it out.

Nature had come to the welcome aid of the Army of the Potomac by a pretty slim margin, but apparently in time to restore the self-respect of the tens of thousands who made up its ranks. Then by a quirk of fate the river crested and started to recede, uncovering the bridges, and restoring communication. Couch received a sharp message from Hooker at 2 A. M. directing him to execute the original evacuation order and by nine o'clock in the morning all troops and trains had safely effected the crossing, Meade's corps acting as rear guard. The bridges were

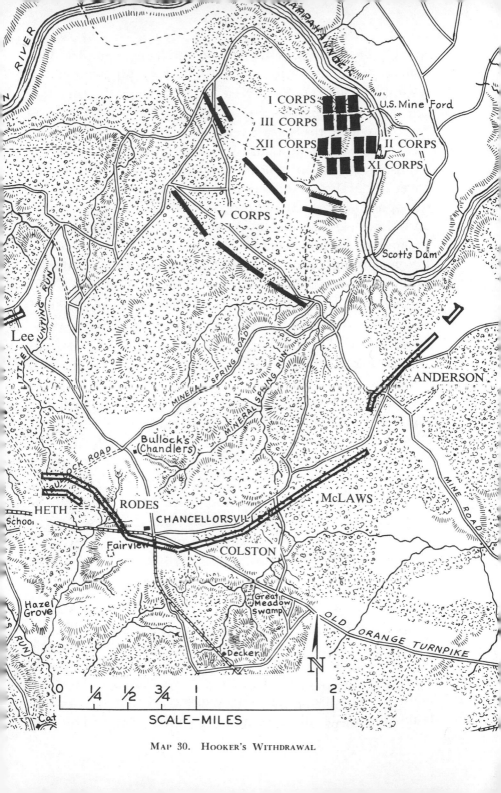

RIVER

I CORPS

III CORPS

XII CORPS

II CORPS

V CORPS

XI CORPS

U.S. Mine Ford

Scott's Dam

Lee

ANDERSON

Bullock's
(Chandlers)

HETH

RODES

McLAWS

School

CHANCELLORSVILE

Fairview

COLSTON

Hazel
Grove

Great
Meadow
Swamp

Decker

OLD ORANGE TURNPIKE

MINE ROAD

MINERAL SPRING RUN

N

Cat

0   ¼   ½   ¾   1   2

SCALE—MILES

Map 30. Hooker's Withdrawal

quickly taken up and the entire operation completed in a matter of hours without the Confederates making the slightest move to interfere.

For that last phase of the campaign it was First Fredericksburg all over again. In each instance the stormy weather was officially blamed for the failure of Lee's army to discover that the Union army was withdrawing under cover of darkness. General Lee made no effort to hide his disappointment on the two occasions, December 15, 1862, and May 5, 1863, when Burnside and Hooker respectively, without punishment, extricated the powerful Army of the Potomac from the much smaller but tenacious Confederate bulldog.

To cross a river in a retrograde movement on a limited number of pontoon bridges is an extremely vulnerable operation for a retreating army. Lee knew this full well. But he also understood human nature; his divisions had fought magnificently against odds both at Fredericksburg and Chancellorsville, and had to rest sometimes. Just the same, it was a bitter experience, after defeating Hooker at Chancellorsville and Sedgwick at Salem Church, for Lee to return to Chancellorsville only to find, on the morning of May 6, that the large bird had duplicated the action of the smaller at Banks' Ford and flown across the Rappahannock at United States Mine Ford; but it was even more disappointing that not a single Confederate of Stuart's three divisions had discovered that 75,000 Blue infantry, with their artillery, were moving in a steady procession across a swollen river in their very presence.

It was young Dorsey Pender, brigade commander in A. P. Hill's Light Division, who at an early hour galloped up to Lee's tent to bring him the news. Pender's skirmishers had moved forward to gain contact with the Federals behind their strong entrenchments, preparatory to the launching of the planned general attack, only to find the lines empty, with no sign of a single Union soldier anywhere.

"Why, General Pender!" remarked Lee in a surprised tone. "That is the way you young men always do. You allow those people to get away. I tell you what to do, but you don't do it. Go after them, and damage them all you can."

Lincoln Receives the News

At 11 A. M. May 5, by Hooker's direction, Butterfield had wired the President the bad news, the gist of which was as follows:

> The cavalry have failed in executing their orders. Averell's Division returned; nothing done; loss of 2 or 3 men. Buford's regulars not heard from.
>
> General Sedgwick failed in the execution of his orders, and was compelled to retire, and crossed the river at Bank's Ford last night; his losses not known.
>
> The First, Third, Fifth, Eleventh, Twelfth, and two divisions of Second Corps are now on south bank of Rappahannock, intrenched between Hunting Run and Scott's Dam, Trains and Artillery Reserves on north bank of Rappahannock. Position is strong, but circumstances, which in time will be fully explained, make it expedient, in the general's judgment, that he should retire from this position to the north bank of the Rappahannock for his defensible position. Among these is danger to his communication by possibility of enemy crossing river on our right flank and imperiling this army, with present departure of two-years and three-months' (nine-months') troops constantly weakening him. The nature of the country in which we are prevents moving in such a way as to find or judge position or movements of enemy. He may cross tonight, but hopes to be attacked in his position.

At 1 P.M., May 6, Butterfield advised Lincoln that the army had recrossed and been given orders to return to camp. At 4:30 P.M., same day, Hooker wired the President that he had withdrawn because the army had none of its trains of supplies with it and he saw no prospect of success from a general battle with the enemy in that area. Moreover, that no more than three of his corps had been engaged and he thought there was a better place nearer at hand to fight the whole army.

Lincoln was sunk! Overcome with shocked disappointment, all he could say to his intimates was "My God! What will the country say? What will the country say?"

Hooker's Fate is Decided

Impatient to learn firsthand what had happened and to size up once more what manner of general he had placed in command of the army, the President set out at once for Falmouth in company with General Halleck. Lincoln remained with Hooker for a short time only, but left Halleck with instructions to "remain till he knew everything." Halleck was a keen lawyer, who knew how to cross-examine witnesses. He had no love for Hooker, who had ignored him and reported direct to the President ever since his appointment. Smarting under such a humiliating situation, Halleck could be counted on to get the full story and report to Lincoln everything that he could extract from the corps commanders, however reluctant they might be to volunteer information that would reflect unfavorably on the reputation of their army commander.

While no record is available to give a blow-by-blow account of Halleck's unofficial "court of inquiry," on his return to Washington the President, Secretary of War Stanton, and the General-in-Chief went into a huddle, from which emerged the unanimous conclusion that both the defeat at Chancellorsville and the retreat were inexcusable and it would be unsafe to entrust to General Hooker the conduct of another battle. Hooker had told Halleck at the conference that he could resign the command without embarrassment, since he had never sought it in the first place (tongue-in-cheek, no doubt), and that he would be happy to do so if he could be restored to the command of his old division.

The Treasury faction headed by Secretary Chase had become a political force to be reckoned with. That group still backed Hooker, otherwise he would almost certainly have been removed from command right after Chancellorsville. Politics or no politics, however, the die had been cast and Hooker as army commander was on the skids. Nevertheless it took Lee's invasion of Maryland and Pennsylvania, a few weeks later, to provide the necessary grease. The administration was able to just barely needle Hooker into resigning in the nick of time, and to supplant him with General Meade less than three days before the Battle of Gettysburg.

A Striking Contrast

The fighting over, it was expected of army commanders that they issue a communique to their officers and men, expressing satisfaction with their efforts, pin-pointing their accomplishments, and in a general way commenting on the results achieved.

Lee's task was the easier of the two. He had fought the greatest battle of his career, had worsted his opponent in every phase, and finally forced him, with twice his own strength, to retreat ignominiously across the river, swallowing his own flamboyant boasts as he left the field *ahead of his own troops.*

Lee's modest character, self-effacement, typical readiness to give credit to his subordinates, and thanks to the Almighty for his victories, are revealed in the general order which he published after the battle.

HDQRS., ARMY OF NORTHERN VIRGINIA
May 7, 1863

GENERAL ORDERS
No. 59
With heartfelt gratification the general commanding expresses to the army his sense of the heroic conduct

AFTERMATH
The dead in the Wilderness near Chancellorsville, still unburied after
several years.

displayed by officers and men during the arduous operations in which they have just been engaged. Under
trying vicissitudes of heat and storm, you attacked
the enemy, strongly intrenched in the depths of a
tangled wilderness, and again on the hills of Fredericksburg, 15 miles distant, and by the valor that
has triumphed on so many fields, forced him once
more to seek safety beyond the Rappahannock. While
this glorious victory entitles you to the praise and
gratitude of the nation, we are especially called upon
to return our grateful thanks to the only Giver of
victory for the signal deliverance He has wrought. It
is, therefore, earnestly recommended that the troops
unite on Sunday next in ascribing to the Lord of Hosts
the glory due unto His name.

Let us not forget in our rejoicing the brave soldiers
who have fallen in defense of their country; and, while
we mourn their loss, let us resolve to emulate their
noble example.

[356]

The army and the country alike lament the absence for a time of one to whose bravery, energy, and skill they are so much indebted for success (Stonewall Jackson).

(The order then quotes a brief letter of appreciation and congratulation to the army from President Jefferson Davis).

R. E. LEE,
General.

Hooker's general order similarly mirrors the character of the man, but the contrast is a striking one. In his distorted statements, Hooker seems to be whistling in the dark, trying almost pathetically to convince his men that they had done a noble thing by choosing not to fight what he euphemistically termed a "general engagement." It is doubtful that General Orders No. 49, published only six days after General Orders No. 47 (see page 146), fooled anybody but Joe Hooker; but let the order speak for itself.

HEADQUARTERS ARMY
OF THE POTOMAC
Camp near Falmouth, Va.
May 6, 1863.

GENERAL ORDERS
No. 49

The major-general commanding tenders to this army his congratulations on its achievements of the last seven days. If it has not accomplished all that was expected, the reasons are well known to the army. It is sufficient to say they were of a character not to be foreseen or prevented by human sagacity or resource.

In withdrawing from the south bank of the Rappahannock before delivering a general battle to our adversaries, the army has given renewed evidence of its confidence in itself, and its fidelity to the principles it represents. In fighting at a disadvantage, we would have been recreant to our trust, to ourselves, our cause, and our country.

Profoundly loyal, and conscious of its strength, the Army of the Potomac will give or decline battle whenever its interest or honor may demand. It will also be the guardian of its own history and its own fame.

By our celerity and secrecy of movement, our advance and passage of the rivers were undisputed, and on our withdrawal not a rebel ventured to follow.

The events of the last week may swell with pride the heart of every officer and soldier of this army. We have added new luster to its former renown. We have made long marches, crossed rivers, surprised the enemy in his intrenchments, and whenever we have fought we have inflicted heavier blows than we have received.

We have taken from the enemy 5000 prisoners; captured and brought off seven pieces of artillery, fifteen colors; placed *hors de combat* 18,000 of his chosen troops; destroyed his depots filled with vast amounts of stores; deranged his communications; captured prisoners within the fortifications of his capital and filled his country with fear and consternation.

We have no other regret than that caused by the loss of our brave companions, and in this we are consoled by the conviction that they have fallen in the holiest cause ever submitted to the arbitrament of battle.

By Command of Major-General Hooker,

S. WILLIAMS,
Assistant Adjutant General

FEDERAL WITHDRAWAL AT U.S. MINE FORD

CHAPTER 18

AN EVALUATION OF THE CAMPAIGN

THE Chancellorsville campaign, which started out so
auspiciously and ended so disastrously for the cause
of the Union, affords material for speculation and evaluation that approaches, if indeed it does not equal, the
interest aroused by the Gettysburg campaign that followed
in a matter of weeks. There is even basis for a legitimate
difference of opinion as to which of the two campaigns
marked the crest in the high tide of the Confederacy.

The magnificent victory which Lee won at Chancellorsville, and it *was* magnificent in all its aspects, raised Southern enthusiasm almost to fever pitch, while the stunning
blow to its hopes dropped the morale of the North to a
correspondingly low level. So much faith had been placed
in "Fighting" Joe Hooker, following the long series of
defeats which culminated in the first battle of Fredericksburg, that the almost unbelievable anticlimax to the Chan-

cellorsville campaign made the situation for the North appear a great deal worse than it actually was.

On the political front the effect was foreshadowed by Lincoln's gloomy rhetorical question: "What will the country say?" Perhaps the Administration at Washington was fortunate that popular polls were not in fashion at the time, for the voices of those who had been articulate in urging peace without union were now raised even louder in support of the thesis that the Confederacy had proven itself too strong to be defeated on the battlefield. The time had come, therefore, to face the political and military facts of life and throw in the sponge.

The weeks following Chancellorsville were about as grim as could be for the Union. The possibility that England and France would decide to recognize the Confederate States as an independent government now became a probability in the view of many in the South, and in the North as well. The Army of the Potomac, visibly disheartened by its most recent experience, may have lost some measure of confidence in itself as well as in its commanding general.

After Fredericksburg, the army and the North had needed nothing so badly as a resounding victory. After Chancellorsville the need became almost desperate. But General Hooker remained in command, as the men in the ranks prayed for the return of George B. McClellan. The lines in Abraham Lincoln's sad face were becoming more deeply etched as he wrestled with the seemingly insoluble problem of where to find a general capable of winning a battle.

South of the Rappahannock the realistic Robert E. Lee faced an entirely different situation. A very human person as well as a proven genius in war, he was naturally gratified in the military sense by his Fredericksburg and Chancellorsville victories. Neither singly nor in combination, however, did they succeed in blinding him to the heavy burdens which still rested on the people of the Confederate

States, nor to the fact, which he recognized, that both had been inconclusive victories. His army had suffered combat losses aggregating more than 18,000 in the two most recent battles, a depletion in fighting manpower that would require Herculean efforts to replace. His supply problem was growing increasingly difficult; food for the army was hard to come by, and horse replacements for his cavalry and artillery were by now almost nonexistent. True, he had twice driven his opponent back across the Rappahannock barrier and prevented him from investing Richmond, but nothing of lasting consequence had been gained, and he knew it. The Army of the Potomac, with vast reserves of active and potential manpower and resources, had been humiliated twice within six months. But both times it had escaped destruction, bounced back stronger than ever, and even now was occupying the same Virginia soil from which it had launched its offensives in December and April.

At Chancellorsville Lee fought his greatest battle. There he carved out a glorious victory against heavier odds than he had faced in any previous campaign. He had been confronted by a reorganized, reinvigorated, and confident Union army which outnumbered his own more than 2 to 1. He lacked the support of his number one corps commander, General Longstreet, and two of the latter's divisions. He had the assistance only of a greatly weakened cavalry force in place of the powerful aggregation of superbly mounted brigades that had served him in earlier campaigns. Yet in spite of all those handicaps Lee managed to outguess, outmaneuver, and outfight his opponent at every turn after Hooker's initial success in placing his right wing on Lee's rear in a surprise march at the very start of the campaign.

The fifth major attempt by Northern armies to take Richmond had failed as had all the others. It began to appear that the Confederates might be right in their conviction that they were invincible. The combination of Lee and his corps commanders was one that no Union leader had yet been able to solve, but it must be remembered that the Army of Northern Virginia, man for man no better than those in the ranks of the Army of the Potomac, had won their major battles on their own soil. It remained to be seen whether offensive operations in hostile territory would yield comparable results.

In appraising Chancellorsville, and with full credit to the superior quality of Lee's leadership and the aggressive manner in which he conducted the operations against Hooker, the real story of the battle is to be found in the surprisingly large number of errors, both of omission and commission, for which Hooker was responsible during the period of actual fighting, May 1 through 5.

The first error was in calling a halt to the steady advance of his right wing when the three corps reached Chancellorsville on the early afternoon of April 30. The inevitable result was an important loss of momentum and resulting confusion in the minds of the corps and division commanders, who were impatient to keep rolling in order to get clear of the dense wilderness into open and maneuverable country.

That initial check, while frustrating and unwise, need not have been fatal. The second was. Hooker's unaccountable changeover on the following day from the offensive to the defensive. just at the moment when his advancing Fifth and Twelfth Corps under Meade and Slocum had advanced to within a stone's throw of the Salem Church position, cannot be explained on rational grounds. If Hooker had only thought to take a couple quick drinks of his favorite whisky and gone to sleep for a few hours that morning, the story of Chancellorsville might have been a very different one. If Meade and Slocum had been permitted to move out at daylight, before Jackson's Corps had come up from Fredericksburg, Banks' Ford would have been uncovered, communication between the two wings of the Union army shortened, Lee's retreat route to Gordonsville closed; and Hooker's army out of the Wilderness in a position where his powerful artillery could have made its strength felt. None of that happened only because Hooker had lost his nerve.

Whether Hooker lacked confidence in his wing and corps commanders, or simply had such a high opinion of his own ability that he couldn't bear to share responsibility with them, his method of issuing combat orders was fundamentally unsound. At no time during the campaign did he issue a directive or even a plan of operations for a *combined* movement. The natural result was that the left hand never knew what the right was expected to do, or vice versa. It was consequently impossible for his major subordinates to do their best work as part of a team, as did the Confederates. Strict secrecy as to his plans may have been a good idea at the start, although that too is open to question. But when Hooker kept on playing his cards so close to his chest that none of his generals, except possibly his second-in-command, General Couch, had any idea what his next move was to be, cooperation and coordination between the right and left wings and even between corps and divisions on the same battlefield, became mere words without meaning.

There are times when oral and fragmentary orders to certain elements of a command are essential in order to meet a crisis or exploit a fleeting opportunity where time is everything. But even then the wise commander or a member of his staff (if he is fortunate to have a well-trained staff), takes pains to inform contiguous elements in order to assure intelligent cooperation. Hooker's failure to transmit at any time any sort of a combined attack order was not due to lack of time or opportunity and therefore must have been a calculated policy.

Consider also the smug complacency which prompted Hooker's flamboyant boasts about what he would do to Lee unless the latter followed Hooker's blueprint, calling for him either to "ingloriously fly or come out from behind his intrenchments, where certain destruction awaited him." As it happened, Lee chose the latter alternative, but was unwilling to agree with Hooker about the "certain destruction" portion of the prophecy.

Hooker displayed almost criminal military negligence in failing to take the most fundamental precautions to secure his right flank in the Wilderness Church area. This in turn lulled corps commander Howard and his subordinates into a sense of false security, which nevertheless does not relieve them of equal culpability. Furthermore, Hooker's inaction in marking time all of Saturday, May 2, which gave Lee the entire day to move into position for the overthrow and rout of Howard's Eleventh Corps, coupled with his obsession in interpreting Jackson's flank march by the Brock Road as evidence that Lee was retreating on Gordonsville, combined to set the stage for a neat and effective Confederate tactical maneuver. The result was that Lee paid in his own coin the Union general whose own successful initial strategy had taken the form of a giant turning movement that placed three corps on Lee's left rear.

As if his lack of initiative on the two preceding days were not sufficient, Hooker's ineffective redispositions and timid defensive psychology on Sunday morning, May 3, caused him to tamely hand over to the Confederates the indispensable key position at Hazel Grove. This in turn naturally led to the successive pinching off of the Union salient at Fairview and the prompt Confederate seizure of the Chancellor House.

In yielding the initiative to Lee on April 30, although he did so from strength and not from weakness as is normally the case, Hooker doomed the Army of the Potomac to a passive role where neither its superior strength nor its guns could be effectively employed. The result of permitting Lee to call the shots was that Hooker was kept busy attempting to parry his opponent's blows instead of delivering his own. The superiority complex with which Hooker had started out had been strangely transformed into a mental state which could have been a fear psychosis of some sort, although that is something for the psychiatrists to explain.

Hooker's dogged unwillingness to send supporting troops where they were most needed during the actual fighting was illustrated in the case of Sykes' division on the morning of May 1, Sickles' corps at Hazel Grove on the night of May 2, and Slocum's corps at Fairview on the morning of May 3. In the same category was his failure to employ to advantage two full corps, Meade's and Reynolds', a total of six divisions aggregating more than 30,000 men, which he held in defensive idleness Sunday and Monday, May 3-4. Meanwhile Lee scored a triumph over the remainder of Hooker's augmented right wing and then, accompanied by two-fifths of his victorious regiments, left the Chancellorsville battlefield and defeated Sedgwick's Sixth Corps at Salem Church.

Depressing as were all of the foregoing evidences of Hooker's weakness, none of them quite equalled his complete abdication of responsible leadership in ordering Sedgwick to attack Lee's rear with his lone corps, on the promise that Hooker would simultaneously engage him in front, and then calmly abandon Sedgwick to his fate. It is an understatement to use the term reprehensible— a more appropriate description would be moral cowardice. At best it is a sad commentary upon "Fighting" Joe's reputation that he huddled supinely behind his constricted forest fortifications without lifting a finger to send aid to the embattled Sedgwick, who was fighting a forlorn battle six miles to the east, or without even staging a diversionary show to engage Stuart's much smaller contingent.

Finally, his serious error of strategic judgment in sending the major portion of his large cavalry corps under

Stoneman on a poorly conceived raid far to the rear of Lee's army and completely out of touch with his own, made an important contribution to Lee's success. Stoneman's brigades accomplished nothing of lasting value, failed to have any psychological or practical effect on Lee's operations, and deprived Hooker of the very troops that would otherwise have been on hand to carry out essential security, screening, and reconnaissance missions on either flank. Had several cavalry divisions been operating beyond Hooker's right, west and south of Chancellorsville, Fitzhugh Lee would not have discovered that Howard's flank was in the air, because it would not have been; nor is it likely that the risk inherent in Jackson's flank march would under those circumstances have been taken by the careful Lee. Thus, without the "eyes of the army" Hooker suffered all through the battle from self-inflicted blindness.

A careful study of relative combat strengths throughout the various stages of the battles at Chancellorsville and Salem Church leads to the reasonable conclusion that there was not a single moment, from the beginning to the end, when the Union army as a whole was decisively beaten. There was no time, after the right wing crossed the Rapidan and until both wings had recrossed the Rappahannock, when a vigorous, combined assault by Hooker's army could not have succeeded in defeating Lee. During all of Saturday, May 2, as Jackson executed his flank march, Lee with 16,000 men held Hooker's 50,000 in position. Again from Sunday afternoon, May 3, until Monday midnight, when Lee was operating against Sedgwick's equal force, Stuart's 25,000 thoroughly tired soldiers pinned down Hooker's 86,000, almost half of whom had not fired a shot.

An army is not defeated so long as there remain unused reserves. Even as late as the morning of May 6, after Hooker had given orders the night before to recross the Rappahannock, and his divisions were streaming over the almost submerged pontoon bridges at United States Mine Ford, the Army of the Potomac had ample strength to turn defeat into victory, but only under a leader other than Hooker. Lee was at that time preparing to launch 40,000 men, who had been marching and fighting for seven days, in a converging attack against the entire Union army of 100,000 or more, counting Sedgwick's corps, which was only a short march from United States Mine Ford and could have brought no less than 15,000 men into action in a short time. It was the opinion of at least one Confederate general, artilleryman Alexander, that Hooker's decision to withdraw "was the mistake of his life."

General Hooker rather than the Army of the Potomac was defeated at Chancellorsville. The army as a whole was never given the opportunity to win. Worse than that, every effort that individual corps and division commanders made on particular areas of the battlefield to gain an advantage or demonstrate an offensive attitude was as abruptly discouraged or terminated by Hooker's actions and orders as though he were working for Lee rather than the Union.

Subordinate officers, whether they be corps, division, regimental, or lesser commanders, or members of the commander's staff, have a right to expect from their army commander the qualities of leadership and judgment which are assumed to be his when he is elevated to that exalted rank. Hooker's fighting reputation as a division and corps commander had been such that the army had been encouraged to believe that the monotonous succession of defeats, due largely to unaggressive or incompetent army commanders, would now be a thing of the past. Hooker's energetic measures during the period of reorganization and rehabilitation after Fredericksburg supported that view, as did the first phase of the Chancellorsville campaign, when his beautifully conceived and executed plan had surprised his experienced opponent and gained a tremendous initial advantage for the Army of the Potomac.

It was consequently that much more of a letdown when all semblance of moral courage and even of ordinary good judgment suddenly faded as the army commander was transformed from a swashbuckling d'Artagnan into a timid milquetoast almost before a single shot had been fired. With all his faults, Burnside had the moral courage and the instincts of a gentleman when after Fredericksburg he assumed full responsibility for that debacle. Not so Joseph Hooker, who at first took the position that he had done the wise thing in engaging less than half his army and then completely disengaging in order to be free to fight again under more favorable circumstances. In later years, however, when the full facts had been thoroughly aired and the responsibility for the historic defeat laid squarely on his own doorstep, Hooker openly blamed Howard and Sedgwick for the failure of his plans. The closest that he ever came to an admission of personal responsibility was a letter to an acquaintance, years afterwards, in which he stated at Chancellorsville for the first time in his life he had lost confidence in Joe Hooker.

Clausewitz lists the chief moral powers that exert a decisive influence in war as "the talents of the commander, the military virtue of the army, its national feeling." And it was Baron Jomini, who was more responsible than any other single individual for interpreting that great master of war, Napoleon Bonaparte, and in making his influence felt in the development of modern warfare, who gives first place among the most essential qualities for a general to "a high moral courage, capable of great resolution," with "physical courage, which takes no account of danger" taking second place.

Granting the reasonable assumption that neither of the armies at Chancellorsville held a monopoly on either military virtue or national feeling, the competition narrows down to the relative quality of the talents and of the moral courage displayed by each of the opposing commanders. Examined in that light, it becomes a more simple matter to evaluate the battle of Chancellorsville. The great disparity in numbers and equipment, the stamina, courage, and capabilities of the officers and the men in the ranks, matters of supply, logistics, marching ability, tactics, and all the other factors that are present on every battlefield— all of these were of minor importance in relation to the talents and moral courage of Hooker and Lee.

General Lee's qualities were demonstrated in almost his every word and action during this campaign, while moral courage on the part of General Hooker was conspicuously absent in virtually every one of *his* words and actions. In fact, Lee was so vastly superior to Hooker in every category that he could afford to violate fundamental military principles at frequent intervals during the campaign, and did so, each time with impunity because of the marked deficiency of his opponent.

For example, it is considered a cardinal strategical sin for a commander to divide his forces in the presence of the enemy and thus risk the danger of being defeated in detail. Lee did just that not once, but four distinct and separate times, even to the extent of subdividing an already divided army when he left Early's Division to hold Sedgwick at Fredericksburg while he moved with the rest of the army to confront Hooker at Chancellorsville. Again he risked disaster by sending Jackson's Corps around the Union right flank, and finally, as the crowning gesture, turned his back on the crouching Federal giant and headed back with a portion of his army to deal with a threatening Sedgwick.

The young officer at a military finishing school who is studying how to become a general receives a very low mark if he is so brash, in a map problem, as to march his outfit across the front of an enemy already in position.

Lee knew that it was a risky procedure to do that when he dispatched Jackson through the forest, but he also knew that great results do not reward the leader who fears to dare greatly, no matter what the book says. And so he cheerfully allowed Jackson to march his corps across the front of Hooker's army, while with a superb display of moral courage he himself remained with only 16,000 men to oppose a Union army which at that moment outnumbered him more than five to one.

The so-called principles of war, a distillation of the successful actions of the great captains over the centuries, have by trial and error come to be accepted as valid, basic guides in practising the art of war. Hence it is possible, and rewarding, in appraising the commander's conduct of a battle, to use those timeless principles in measuring the extent to which he has or has not demonstrated his qualifications for the great responsibility his government has reposed in him. There are but nine principles, which can be briefly summarized as follows:

1. *The Objective:*		The designation of a specific plan leading to the achievement of victory on the battlefield.
2. *The Offensive:*		The only way by which a decision is gained, through exercise of the initiative.
3. *Mass:*		The ability to exert sufficient force at the right time and place.
4. *Economy of Force:*		Use of the means at hand to gain the ascendancy without undue waste of manpower and material.
5. *Movement:*		The skillful employment of troops by the use of maneuver.

6. *Surprise:*	The employment of secrecy and rapidity to attain maximum effect with minimum loss.
7. *Security:*	To take all measures to secure against observation and surprise, and to maintain freedom of action.
8. *Simplicity:*	Avoidance of complicated movements and the use of direct, unambiguous orders.
9. *Cooperation:*	Team work through coordination.

The military student will find pleasure and profit in determining for himself the manner in which Lee and Hooker applied each of the nine principles in the Chancellorsville campaign. For the general reader it is sufficient to note the interesting and significant fact that Lee scored a perfect mark, while Hooker grossly violated or ignored seven of them, and negated the other two merely by his failure to follow through. On the other hand, Hooker's plan of campaign, had he carried it through with resolution, could and almost certainly would have assured compliance with all of the principles except, possibly, number 4—*Economy of Force.* But his abrupt decision to halt his army and go over to the defensive muddied the waters so thoroughly that thereafter everything went wrong.

The final act in the Chancellorsville campaign was interestingly concluded by an operation that was identical to the denouement of the battle of Fredericksburg almost five months earlier. Substitute Burnside for Hooker and in all other respects the ending was the same, even to the weather. In both instances the heavy fighting had terminated and the two armies, virtually locked in each other's embrace, were standing to arms, eyeing one another warily, but motivated by diametrically opposed tactical intentions.

Both Burnside and Hooker had started out offensively and then shifted to the defensive, the latter, however, much sooner than his predecessor. The major difference was that at Fredericksburg Lee couldn't believe Burnside would quit without further offensive effort, so he bided his time and the quarry escaped across the river. At Chancellorsville, Lee was going great guns, giving Hooker no peace, and after disposing of Sedgwick he came rapidly back to the major battlefield with the full intention of bringing the battle to a victorious conclusion by delivering a knockout punch on the morning of May 6.

Again there was a violent rainstorm and Lee's dog-tired men, as soldiers will always do, took advantage of the lull to do a little bunk fatigue—even the pickets failed to show their customary alertness. So once again the Army of the Potomac got clean away, over the same river, while the disappointed Lee no doubt reflected sadly on the weakness of human nature.

APPENDIX

TABLE I—SUMMARY OF STRENGTHS[1] AND CASUALTIES[2] DURING THE CHANCELLORSVILLE CAMPAIGN

ARMY OF THE POTOMAC

Organization	Present for Duty	Killed and Wounded		Killed, Wounded and Captured or Missing	
		Number	Percent	Number	Percent
General & Staff	60	0	0	0	0
First Corps	16,908	245	1	299	2
Second "	16,893	1,193	7	1,925	11
Third "	18,721	3,023	16	4,119	22
Fifth " , ...	15,824	541	3	700	4
Sixth "	23,667	3,145	13	4,610	19
Eleventh "	12,977	1,618	12	2,412	19
Twelfth "	13,450	1,703	13	2,824	21
General Art. Reserve	1,610	0	0	0	0
Engineers and Signal Corps	800*	9	1	9	1
Cavalry Corps	11,541	81	1	389	4
Provost Guard	2,217	0	0	0	0
Army Total	134,668	11,558	9	17,287	13

* Approximated.

ARMY OF NORTHERN VIRGINIA

Organization	Present for Duty	Killed and Wounded		Killed, Wounded and Captured or Missing	
		Number	Percent	Number	Percent
Anderson's Division ......·	8,370	1,189	14	1,445	17
McLaws' "	8,665	1,395	16	1,775	20
Corps Artillery	720	52	7	106	15
Total First Corps ..	17,755	2,636	14	3,326	19
A. P. Hill's Division	11,751	2,616	23	2,940	26
Rodes' "	10,063	2,228	22	2,937	29
Early's "	8,596	846	10	1,346	16
Colston's "	6,989	1,870	27	2,078	30
Corps Artillery	800	69	9	80	10
Total Second Corps	38,199	7,629	18	9,381	25
General Arty. Reserve	480	3	1	3	1
Cavalry	2,500	25	1	111	4
[3] Army Total	58,934	10,293	17	12,821	22

[1] Based on Bigelow, op. cit., and *Official Records,* Vol. XXV, Part II.
[2] Based on *Battles and Leaders* III.
[3] Based on return for March 31. Recruits received in April probably brought the total to some 61,500.

TABLE II—ORGANIZATION, COMMANDERS, AND APPROXIMATE TIMES OF ARRIVAL ON BATTLEFIELD

ARMY OF THE POTOMAC

Unit	Commanding General	Rank	Arrived on Chancellorsville Battlefield
ARMY	Joseph Hooker	Major General	Apr. 30—night
First Corps	John F. Reynolds	Major General	May 2—6:00 P. M.
1st Div.	Jas. S. Wadsworth	Brig. General	" 3—3:00 A. M.
2nd "	John C. Robinson	" "	" 2—7:00 P. M.
3rd "	Abner Doubleday	Major General	" "—7:30 P. M.
Second Corps	Darius N. Couch	Major General	Apr. 30—night
1st Div.	Winfield S. Hancock	" "	Apr. 30—night
2nd "	John Gibbon	Brig. General	*
3rd "	Wm. H. French	Major General	Apr. 30—night
Third Corps	Daniel E. Sickles	Major General	May 1—A. M.
1st Div.	David B. Birney	Brig. General	May 1 "
2nd "	Hiram G. Berry	Major General	" "
3rd "	Amiel W. Whipple	" "	" "
Fifth Corps	George G. Meade	Major General	Apr. 30—noon
1st Div.	Chas. Griffin	Brig. General	" "—11 A. M.
2nd "	George Sykes	Major General	" "—12 noon
3rd "	Andrew A. Humphreys	Brig. General	" "—night
Sixth Corps	John Sedgwick	Major General	*
1st Div.	Wm. T. H. Brooks	Brig. General	*
2nd "	Albion P. Howe	" "	*
3rd "	John Newton	Major General	*
Light "	Hiram Burnham	Colonel	*
Eleventh Corps	Oliver O. Howard	Major General	Apr. 30—2 P. M.
1st Div.	Charles Devens, Jr.	Brig. General	" "—2 P. M.
2nd "	Adolph von Steinwehr	" "	" "—2:30 P. M.
3rd "	Carl Schurz	Major General	" "—3:00 P. M.
Twelfth Corps	Henry W. Slocum	Major General	Apr. 30—1 P. M.
1st Div.	Alpheus S. Williams	Brig. General	" "—1 P. M.
2nd "	John W. Geary	Brig. General	" "—1:30 P. M.
Cavalry Corps	George Stoneman	Brig. General	(a)
1st Div.	Alfred Pleasonton	" "	Apr. 30—10:30 A. M.
2nd "	William W. Averell	" "	(b)
3rd "	David McM. Gregg	" "	(a)
Reserve Brigade	John Buford	" "	(a)
Artillery	Henry J. Hunt	" "	Apr. 30—May 1

* Engaged at Fredericksburg and in Battle of Salem Church.

Strength		Losses	
Infantry	111,000	Killed	1,606
Cavalry	11,500	Wounded	9,762
Artillery	8,000	Missing	5,919
Special Troops	3,000 (approx.)		————
	————		17,287
Total	133,500	Present—404 guns	

(a) Engaged in raid on rear of Lee's army.
(b) At Rapidan Station; reached Ely's Ford on evening of May 2.

Army of Northern Virginia

Unit	Commanding General	Rank	Arrived on Chancellorsville Battlefield
ARMY	Robert E. Lee	General	May 1—afternoon
First Corps	James Longstreet	Lt. General	Not present
McLaw's Div.	Lafayette McLaws	Major General	May 1—6:00 A. M.
Anderson's "	Richard H. Anderson	Major General	Apr. 29
Art. Reserve	E. P. Alexander	Colonel	May 1
Second Corps	Thos. J. Jackson	Lt. General	May 1—8 A. M.
Light Div.	Ambrose P. Hill	Major General	" 1—8-10 A. M.
D. H. Hill's Div.	Robert E. Rodes	Brig. General	" 1—8-10 A. M.
Early's Div.	Jubal A. Early	Maj. General	*
Trimble's Div.	R. E. Colston	Brig. General	May 1—8-10 A. M.
Art. Reserve	S. Crutchfield	Colonel	" " "
Reserve Art.	Wm. H. Pendleton	Brig. General	May 1
Cavalry Div.	James E. B. Stuart	Major General	April 30
Second Brig.	Fitzhugh Lee	Brig. General	April 30
Third "	W. H. F. Lee	" "	**
Horse Art.	R. F. Beckham	Major	April 30

Strength		Losses	
Approximately 61,000		Killed	1,649
170 guns		Wounded	9,106
		Missing	1,708
			12,463

* Engaged at Fredericksburg and in Battle of Salem Church.
** Observing Averell's division at Rapidan Station.

PARTIAL BIBLIOGRAPHY

An English Combatant. *Battlefields of the South*. New York: John Bradburn, 1864.

Battles and Leaders of the Civil War. New York: Century Co., 1884.

Bigelow, Maj. John. *The Campaign of Chancellorsville*. New Haven and London: Yale University Press, 1910.

Blackford, Lt. Col. W. W., C.S.A. *War Years With Jeb Stuart*. New York: 1945.

Caldwell, J. F. *The History of a Brigade of South Carolinians Known as "Gregg's," and Subsequently as "McGowan's Brigade."* Philadelphia: King and Baird, 1886.

Clark, Walter, ed. *Histories of the Several Regiments and Battalions From North Carolina in the Great War, 1861-65*. Raleigh: State of North Carolina, 1911.

Command and General Staff College. Chancellorsville Source Book. C&GSC, Fort Leavenworth, Kansas.

Comte de Paris. *History of the Civil War in America*. Philadelphia: The John C. Winston Co., 1907.

Confederate Veteran. A periodical.

Cox, Maj. Gen. Jacob D. *Military Reminiscences of the Civil War*. New York: Charles Scribner's Sons, 1900.

De Chanel, General. *The American Army in the War of Secession*. Leavenworth, Kansas: Geo. Spooner, 1894. A portion of an official French observer's report to his government. Covers organization, services, supply, combat arms, personnel, and numerous other subjects. Very valuable but readable compilation.

Downey, Fairfax, *Sound of the Guns, The Story of the American Artillery*. David McKay Co., N. Y., 1955.

Early, Gen. J. B. *Autobiography. Philadelphia;* J. B. Lippincott, 1912.

Freeman, Douglas Southall. *R. E. Lee*, and *Lee's Lieutenants*. New York: Charles Scribner's Sons, 1935 and 1944.

Gough, Col. J. E. *Fredericksburg and Chancellorsville*. London, 1913.

Henderson, Col. G. F. R. *Stonewall Jackson and the American Civil War*. London, 1927.

Herr, Maj. Gen. John K, and Wallace, Edward S. *The Story of the U. S. Cavalry*. Boston, 1953.

Hotchkiss, Jed, and Allan, William. *The Battlefields of Virginia—Chancellorsville*. New York: D. Van Nostrand, 1867.

Lindsley, John Berrien, ed. *The Military Annals of Tennessee—Confederate*. Lindsley and Co., Nashville, 1886.

Livermore, Thomas L. *Numbers and Losses in the Civil War*. Bloomington: Indiana University Press, 1957.

McClellan, H. B. *Major-General J. E. B. Stuart*. Boston; Houghton, Mifflin, and Co., 1885.

Shannon, Fred A. *Organization and Administration of the Union Army*. Cleveland. Arthur H. Clark, 1928.

Sorrel, Moxley G. *Recollections of a Confederate Staff Officer*. New York: Neale Publishing Co., 1905.

Southern Historical Society Papers.

Steele, Mathew Forney. *American Campaigns*. Harrisburg. The Telegraph Press, 1927.

Thomason, Maj. John. *Jeb Stuart*. New York, 1934.

Walker, Gen. Francis A. *Great Commanders: General Hancock*. New York, 1897.

War of the Rebellion. Official Records of the Union and Confederate Armies.

Wilson, Gen. James H. *The Campaign of Chancellorsville: A Critical Review*.

COMMENTARY

by D. Scott Hartwig

No event of our nation's history, except perhaps the Vietnam War, is the source of such intense debate and study as the Civil War. Being a purely American affair with a multitude of colorful and controversial personalities, it has captured the imagination of the American people as no other period of our history has. Battles and campaigns have been scrutinized with a critical eye and hotly debated again and again with as many variations in interpretation and opinion as there are autumn colors.

When General Stackpole wrote *Chancellorsville: Lee's Greatest Battle*, the book represented the interpretations and opinions he had developed through his research and his personal experience as a professional soldier who had served in both world wars. Other distinguished historians of the time differed in their conclusions on certain points. And in the 30 years since General Stackpole published his work, additional conclusions have been drawn through further study of this fascinating campaign.

A Closer Look at General Joseph Hooker

General Stackpole was decidedly anti–Joe Hooker. Indeed, there is little in Hooker's management of the battle at Chancellorsville that deserves praise. Aside from Burnside's defeat at Fredericksburg, Chancellorsville was probably the most poorly managed battle, at the army command level, in which the Army of the Potomac engaged during the entire war. Although Hooker certainly lacked the moral courage of a great commander and fought the battle badly, his admirable qualities and accomplishments related to his command of the Army of the Potomac have been largely eclipsed by his dismal performance during the Battle of Chancellorsville.

General Stackpole (p. 171) relates a story told by Brigadier General James Wilson concerning the Battle of Antietam. If taken at face value, Wilson's account is most damaging to Hooker's character and reflects harshly upon his bravery as a soldier. Some scholars, however, believe the story was a deliberate distortion of the facts by an officer who was an enemy of Hooker's and who sought to further damage his reputation by questioning his soldierly courage.

In the first place, Wilson was not a personal observer of the incident he described. Although he was present at the Battle of Antietam as a lieutenant on the headquarters staff of army commander George B. McClellan, he did not accompany Hooker's 1st Corps in their attack and was therefore not a witness to anything he described. The source of his story may have been nothing more than army gossip or his own version of that gossip, for his story bears no resemblance to the record. It is doubtful that anyone on Hooker's staff would have told Wilson such a story.

The record indicates that Hooker exhibited great moral and personal courage during the Battle of Antietam. He opened the battle by attacking with his unsupported corps, and he sustained the fight for nearly an hour and a half before the 12th Corps came to his support. Throughout the battle, he was conspicuous for his personal exposure to enemy fire. At about 9:00 A.M., three hours after the battle opened, Hooker received the "slight wound" in the foot that Wilson described. It was serious enough that he nearly fainted from loss of blood and was carried from the field in a semiconscious state, hardly a condition in which to return to the field on a stretcher for the purpose of "restoring the shattered morale of his troops and encouraging them to renewed efforts" (p. 171).

Actually, although the 1st Corps had suffered heavy losses, by the time Hooker was wounded the battle was swinging to the advantage of the federals, and Hooker left the field believing that . . . "we had everything in our own hands" (*Report of the Joint Committee*, 1865:582). Contrary to Wilson's accusation, there is no reliable evidence that anyone urged the woozy

Hooker to return to the battlefield. Even if Hooker had returned, he would have fallen under the orders of Major General Edwin V. Sumner, the senior officer who had led the 2nd Corps onto the field.

Indeed, Hooker's combat record on the Peninsula, at Antietam, at 2nd Manassas, and at Fredericksburg was what won him command of the Army of the Potomac. The difference between Hooker in the earlier battles and Hooker at Chancellorsville was that he was not in command of the Army of the Potomac in the former battles. It was under the burden of command that Joe Hooker apparently faltered. Kenneth Williams (Volume 2:604) believed that "heavy responsibility, fatigue, and nervous exhaustion had stripped away the mask of personal bravery, ready confidence, and boastfulness which he had always worn, and had left the real Joe Hooker. . . ."

Hooker's most conspicuous contribution to the Army of the Potomac was not in *fighting* in the Chancellorsville campaign but in reorganizing and refitting the army before it embarked to fight. "He received the Army of the Potomac, rent by internal jealousies, discontented, discouraged, and humiliated under the stigma of defeat," wrote Lieutenant Colonel Rufus Dawes, who served under Hooker. "With indefatigable zeal he addressed himself to the task of its reorganization and, if I may so express it, re-inspiration. It was for Hooker to arouse the drooping spirits of the grand army and he accomplished the task. He had the true Napoleonic idea of the power of an 'Esprit de Corps.' It was he who first devised the beautiful and, to the soldiers, inspiring system of corps badges" (Dawes, 1890:132).

The Union cavalry that performed so well in the Gettysburg Campaign had much for which to thank Hooker. He organized them into a cavalry corps that, with superior numbers and weapons, could finally meet Stuart's cavalry on a more equal footing. Hooker also made more aggressive use of his cavalry than any previous commander had. He may not have employed it wisely during the Chancellorsville Campaign, but the experience gained there helped mold the fine cavalry corps of the Gettysburg Campaign.

Hooker also displayed progressive thinking in his creation of a military intelligence agency. The only other general who had seen the need for a separate intelligence-gathering organization had been McClellan, who had employed private detective Allan Pinkerton with uneven results. Hooker placed his intelligence collection in the hands of the military, who handled intelligence gathering in a more systematic, professional manner and brought far more accurate information to Hooker than any commander of the Army of the Potomac had ever enjoyed. This unique military agency was the first of its kind in either the Union or Confederate army during the war.

General Robert E. Lee and His Staff

General Stackpole praises General Lee for his work in creating a staff system for his army, writing, "The evolution of the Confederacy toward the substance of a general staff system made greater progress than was the case with the armies of the North. Probably the genius of General Lee was as much responsible as any other single factor, his personality and perception in dealing with the authorities at Richmond making the difference" (p. 72). Other historians have noted exactly the opposite situation: the Union armies developed a more professional staff organization, while the Confederates maintained a primitive one throughout the war. It should be noted that it was George McClellan who saw the need at the earliest moment in the war for an army chief of staff with rank commensurate with duties, and it was Hooker who created a military intelligence agency. Lee did advocate to President Davis the formation of a "corps of officers to teach others their duty, see to the observance of orders, and to the regularity and precision of all movements" (O.R., Series IV, Volume 2:447–48). In essence, Lee was seeking to create a primitive staff and command college. But Davis never acted upon Lee's advice, and southern army staffs were never particularly distinguished throughout the war.

Despite Lee's apparently "modern" idea of creating a pool of professionally trained staff officers, one of his biographers and admirers, Clifford Dowdey (1965:272) believed that Lee "never

[380]

had any advanced ideas on staff." In discussing Lee's preparations for the Gettysburg Campaign, Kenneth Williams (Volume 2:617) wrote, "Apparently Lee was completely unaware of the inadequacy of his staff for an operation such as he was beginning. Above everything else he needed a good chief of staff with sufficient ability and rank to command respect and to handle the multitudinous details that were certain to arise. At his headquarters were little more than high-ranking clerks and letter writers."

Lee never had any officers of rank on his staff, and his staff rarely took part in the planning of operations. Only Lee, in consultation with his corps commanders, Longstreet and Jackson, was responsible for planning. This helps explain one of the reasons Lee missed Jackson so much after his death. "Unless God in his mercy will raise us up one [Jackson]," he wrote to "Jeb" Stuart, "I do not know what we shall do" (O.R., Volume 25:821). The loss of Jackson, coupled with an inadequate staff, would be felt severely in the three days at Gettysburg, where clumsy marching and abysmal attack coordination crippled Lee's offensive efforts.

In contrast, at the beginning of the Gettysburg Campaign, the Army of the Potomac had a major general as chief of staff, a brigadier general as adjutant, a brigadier general as chief engineer, and a quartermaster who would soon be a brigadier general.

Lee's staff played a relatively limited role in the Battle of Chancellorsville. Lee and Jackson planned the flank attack alone, although Jackson's staff assisted with details of its execution. Colonel R. H. Chilton, Lee's chief of staff, nearly caused a disaster when he confused a verbal order Lee had given him to deliver to Early (p. 284). Hooker, on the other hand, made more active use of his staff; for instance, he utilized his chief of staff, Butterfield, to maintain communications between the separated wings of his army. And he employed Chief Engineer Gouverneur K. Warren to act as the "eyes" of headquarters by accompanying the advance of Sedgwick's 6th Corps from Fredericksburg.

Although he was not present during the Battle of Chancellorsville, Lee's 1st Corps commander, Lieutenant General James Longstreet, is sharply criticized by General Stackpole (p. 131) for not moving the divisions of Hood and Pickett more promptly to Lee's assistance. General Longstreet received his orders to join Lee without delay late on April 30. At that time, Longstreet's command was occupied keeping nearly 25,000 Union troops around Suffolk contained, and his trains were scattered about gathering food and forage desperately needed by the Army of Northern Virginia. The Georgian issued the necessary orders for his brigades to break contact with the enemy and to prepare to march for Petersburg. It would take time to assemble his trains, though, and Longstreet questioned Secretary of War James Seddon as to whether he should abandon them. Seddon advised him not to leave them but to proceed with all possible speed to complete the movement.

Disengaging from an enemy force known to be in considerable strength was no simple matter. However, Adjutant General Samuel Cooper notified Lee that although Longstreet would be delayed, his divisions would be in Richmond by May 2. This correspondence has probably influenced writers to believe that Longstreet's failure to reach Richmond by the second was deliberate, and it has added further confirmation to their contention that he was unwilling to cooperate with Lee. Such a rapid movement on the part of Longstreet's command was simply impossible in the face of the enemy, the marching distance, and the lack of sufficient rail transportation. He did not arrive in Richmond until May 6.

Donald B. Sanger, one of Longstreet's more able biographers, believed that Lee did not expect Longstreet to be able to join him before he would be forced to engage Hooker. "Lee's letter of May 7 (Lee to Longstreet, May 7, 1863, O.R. XVIII, p. 1049) contains no intimation that he expected Longstreet to be with him at Chancellorsville," Sanger wrote. "He stated his message to Longstreet on May 1 was meant solely to be informative of intended movement and contained the wish rather than the expectation that one of Longstreet's divisions could have co-operated" (Hay and Sanger, 1952:149).

In Defense of Major General John Sedgwick

Another officer who became embroiled in Chancellorsville's many controversies was Major General John Sedgwick, commander of Hooker's 6th Army Corps. Any student of the Chancellorsville Campaign knows that Sedgwick was one of the tragic figures of the campaign. Confused by conflicting orders, he was given the impossible assignment of relieving the mass of the army at Chancellorsville by fighting his way through Lee's rear with one corps.

General Stackpole largely sympathizes with Sedgwick's plight. However, he takes Sedgwick to task on pages 187, 217, and 284, for a lack of initiative and "for not stirring himself more energetically" (p. 217). The general's criticism stems from Hooker's May 1, 11:30 A.M. orders to Sedgwick to "threaten an attack at full force at 1 o'clock, and to continue that attitude until further orders" (p. 187). The general felt that Sedgwick, having crossed the Rappahannock, had not exerted himself to determine "what was before him. . . . With a bit more aggressiveness, Sedgwick should have ascertained that only 10,000 men, not 40,000, were now occupying a thinly held seven-mile front on the heights west of Fredericksburg" (p. 187).

For Sedgwick to have determined that the Confederates had withdrawn sizable numbers of troops from their Fredericksburg defenses, he would have had to probe Early's line, which would have required a reconnaissance in some force and might have drawn him into a full-fledged battle. Sedgwick's orders called for a demonstration, not a reconnaissance.

Actually, the entire incident is a moot point, for Hooker's 11:30 A.M. order was not telegraphed to Butterfield until 5:05 P.M. Butterfield received it at 4:55 P.M., due to a failure to synchronize watches between headquarters. In the meantime, Butterfield had passed on a 2:00 P.M. order from Hooker to Sedgwick directing the 6th Corps commander "to keep a sharp lookout and attack if can succeed" (O.R., Volume 25:326). Hooker's command to make a demonstration came on the heels of this order.

Sedgwick had not attacked, apparently in the belief that the enemy in his front had not reduced its forces sufficiently to hazard what would likely have to be a frontal assault. In fact, as of 12:30 P.M., Butterfield did not think the Confederates had detached 10,000–15,000 men from Sedgwick's front, which meant, in the eyes of the federals, that the southerners still held their defenses in considerable strength. Sedgwick had decided to make a demonstration and was proceeding with his preparations when the order was countermanded by Hooker.

What of General Stackpole's contention (p. 217) that on May 2 Sedgwick had little reason "for not stirring himself more energetically" when Hooker ordered him at 4:10 P.M. to cross the river "as soon as indications will permit; capture Fredericksburg with everything in it, and vigerously [sic] pursue the enemy"?

This order was not transmitted to Sedgwick until 5:50 P.M., and at 6:30 P.M., it was apparently superseded by orders to "pursue" the enemy on the Bowling Green Road, which meant moving away from Fredericksburg. Furthermore, the enemy had to be retreating to be "pursued," and the Confederates in front of Sedgwick displayed no signs that they were retreating. "I had been informed repeatedly by Major-General Butterfield, chief of staff, that the force in front of me was very small," wrote Sedgwick, "and the whole tenor of his many dispatches would have created the impression that the enemy had abandoned my front and retired from the city and its defenses had there not been more tangible evidence than the dispatches in question that the chief of staff was misinformed" (O.R., Volume 25:558). It was the old story of headquarters presuming the presence of an entirely different situation at the front than the one that really existed. If anything, Sedgwick deserves praise for keeping his head despite conflicting orders and for refusing to be prodded into something foolish or rash by a headquarters that was out of touch with the actual situation.

[384]

Another question of Sedgwick's conduct during his operations is, why did he not capitalize upon the staffwork blunder (p. 284) that led to the withdrawal of nearly all of the Confederate defenders in Sedgwick's front? "It would almost seem that Hooker's lack of initiative at Chancellorsville had infected his left wing commander at Fredericksburg," writes General Stackpole (p. 284). Was it a case of low initiative that caused Sedgwick to be unaware of Early's temporary withdrawal? A study of the record would seem to indicate it was not.

Because the morning of May 2 was quite windy, Professor T. S. C. Lowe was unable to get his balloon up to observe Confederate activity at Fredericksburg until between 2:00 and 3:00 P.M., and he was not able to attain the altitude he desired. Lowe did observe Early pulling elements of his division out of the line, but he was not able to report positively until 5:30 P.M. that the enemy earthworks were largely abandoned.

Early did not pull out the brigade of Brigadier General Harry Hays, whose skirmishers confronted Sedgwick's near the mouth of Deep Run. Therefore, Sedgwick's skirmish line, which was in contact with the enemy, did not observe anything unusual on the Confederate lines, and Sedgwick was probably skeptical of one more report from headquarters telling him only a thin force was in his front. The strength of the Confederate position had been established during the Battle of Fredericksburg, and if Sedgwick erred on the side of caution in the face of those solid entrenchments, he can hardly be criticized. As General Stackpole himself states (p. 336), "On the contrary, Sedgwick's tactics, considered in context with Hooker's lack of initiative and disjointed orders to him from the other side of the battlefield, were based on sound thinking and careful evaluation of all the factors present."

Speculation about a Counterattack against Jackson's Troops

Superficial overviews and histories of the Battle of Chancellorsville have frequently painted the result of "Stonewall" Jackson's flank attack as an unqualified success; they have assumed that the battle was won on the night of May 2 and that Lee had only to mop up the debris of the federal army. General Stackpole, like other more serious students of the battle, depicts Jackson's attack as a brilliant success, but one that was far from decisive, since it left the well-concentrated Union army interposed between the divided wings of Lee's army. Jackson's command was disorganized; units were intermingled and exhausted after the fighting in the tangled wilderness. The general speculated that had Union generals Slocum and Sickles organized a coordinated counterattack, Jackson's troops, demoralized by the loss of Jackson and A. P. Hill, and disorganized by their attack and the terrain, might have been routed like the Union 11th Corps.

With the exception of several men who served as litter bearers, Jackson's command passed the night of the second not knowing that he or Hill had been wounded. In fact, the news of Jackson's being wounded was deliberately withheld from the men "for fear of disheartening them, in view of the serious work ahead of [them] in the morning" (Freeman, 1946:574). In the ranks of Jackson's command, morale was certainly still quite high as a result of the crushing victory over the 11th Corps.

If Slocum and Sickles had launched a coordinated attack, the success of the attack would have depended upon what hour of the night it was launched. An attack at the time of Jackson's wounding would undoubtedly have achieved some success, since the Confederate command structure would have been in chaos and the Confederate front line was in the process of being relieved. Realistically, the possibility that Slocum and Sickles could have organized a successful attack against Jackson that night is slim.

In the first place, the attack would have probably needed some overall direction and support from army headquarters, which it certainly would not have received. Secondly, even in the daylight the terrain was a nightmare. The difficulties a large attack might have encountered at night can only be imagined. Brigadier General Alpheus Williams (1959:190) of the 12th Corps wrote that "the underbrush was densely thick, almost impenetrable to man, and I had the greatest difficulty in finding a place to crowd my horse through." Thirdly, there was considerable disorganization within the Union lines, and they were not in a good position to launch an attack that night. If they had attacked after Hill's division had taken over Jackson's front line, it certainly would have been repulsed the way the night attack was that Sickles did launch. The wilderness was no place for night fighting.

When the morning of May 3 broke, there is little dispute that Jackson's corps, now under "Jeb" Stuart, was confronted with a potentially dangerous situation. Its flanks were exposed and Hooker had the fresh 1st and 5th Corps, plus the largely intact 3rd and 12th Corps, upwards of 50,000 men, with which to counterattack. General Stackpole (p. 294) believed that if Hooker had roused himself from his defensive-minded stupor and had launched these four corps in a coordinated attack, "it cannot be doubted that Stuart could have been overrun and possibly decimated. . . ."

To have accomplished such an attack would have required considerable energy on Hooker's part during the night of the second, for the 12th Corps would have had to have been relieved of its portion of the line to change its facing to the west in order to take part in the attack. Presumably, the 2nd Corps would have taken over the 12th Corps line to resist the efforts of Lee's forces to effect a junction with Stuart. Given the conditions within the Union perimeter the night of the second, and given the nature of the terrain, it would have been nearly impossible for the 3rd and 12th Corps to have been in position by daylight to launch an attack. One of the advantages Jackson's attack had given the Confederates was that it had restricted the room in which the federals had to maneuver.

What of the 5th and 1st Corps? Could they have rolled up Stuart's left? If these two corps had attacked, they probably would have checked Stuart's assault or caused him to shift considerable reserves from his attack upon the Union U-shaped perimeter. The problem with attacking in the wilderness was that if the attacking force did not have something substantial to guide upon (for instance, Stuart had the turnpike to guide his attack upon), attacks ended up getting disoriented and drifting astray. Meade might have guided the left of his corps attack upon the Bullock Road, but there was no landmark for his center and right. Reynolds's entire corps had no substantial terrain feature upon which to guide its attacks. One year later, during the Battle of the Wilderness, the federals would experience just how difficult it was to conduct offensive operations in the tangled Virginia forest.

The point is that a coordinated attack by the 3rd, 12th, 1st, and 5th Corps against Jackson's exposed corps would have been extremely difficult to have organized and to have executed before Stuart himself attacked. Would Hooker's forces have easily overrun and decimated Stuart's corps? Probably not. The terrain greatly favored the defender, and Stuart's corps was far from demoralized after its heady victory of the evening before. However, a counterattack by the 1st and 5th Corps would have spelled trouble for Stuart's attack, no matter how misguided it might have been. Some 30,000 federal troops thrashing about on Stuart's flank would have been something to be concerned about.

The Assumption that Lee Intended to Attack Hooker's Retreating Army

What of the possibility that Lee, after disposing of Sedgwick at Salem Church, could have attacked Hooker's retreating army on May 6 and inflicted a crippling defeat? Some writers have advanced this theory. General Stackpole writes that Lee returned from Salem Church "with the full intention of bringing the battle to a victorious conclusion by delivering a knockout punch on the morning of May 6" (p. 372), and that he was greatly disappointed to learn that Hooker had escaped during the night. Did Lee intend to deliver a knockout punch on May 6, and would he have been capable of inflicting a knockout blow?

Actually, the federal army had not escaped during the night. At daylight, six corps remained on the south bank of the Rappahannock River waiting for the passage of the artillery before they could cross; and the 5th Corps still held its strong defensive position to cover the withdrawal. Both flanks of this corps were anchored upon the river, and any attackers would have had to approach head-on — a costly affair in that rugged terrain. John Bigelow, a painstaking scholar of the battle and author of *The Campaign of Chancellorsville*, expressed the view that had Lee attacked on the morning of May 6, it might have been *his* army that suffered the knockout punch. Bigelow believed that casualties among Lee's already worn-out and depleted divisions would certainly have been heavy and might have been severe enough to have prevented the Virginian from embarking upon his ambitious Gettysburg Campaign several weeks later (Bigelow, 1910).

But this is presuming Lee intended to attack Hooker on the morning of the sixth. The evidence indicates he did not. In a letter written to Secretary of War Seddon on the sixth, Lee wrote that Hooker had retreated to a strong position in front of the United States Ford, "where he is now fortifying himself, with a view, I presume, of holding a position this side of the Rappahannock" (O.R., Volume 25:779). Indeed, at that moment Hooker was retreating across the river.

The idea that Lee intended to attack Hooker early in the morning is presumably drawn from his report, written in September 1863, which states, "Preparations were made to assail the enemy's works at daylight on the 6th, but on advancing our skirmishers, it was found that under cover of the storm and darkness of the night he had retreated over the river" (O.R., Volume 25:802). The aggressive Lee probably would have attacked Hooker if elements of his army had lingered for long south of the Rappahannock. But, there were no preparations made or orders transmitted on the night of the fifth for a daylight attack on the sixth.

Despite its various differences with opinions and interpretations expressed in other works and by other scholars, General Stackpole's *Chancellorsville* has merit. It is the only work published on the campaign and battle since John Bigelow's classic *The Campaign of Chancellorsville*, which was published in 1910. Few of the post–Civil War studies, such as Samuel Bates's or Abner Doubleday's, provide a balanced account of the campaign. With its superb maps and its general study and overview of the campaign and battle, *Chancellorsville* offers the reader an appreciation and understanding of this largely neglected campaign, and it provides a fine starting point for those with a thirst to learn more.

D. Scott Hartwig is the Supervisory Park Ranger at Gettysburg National Military Park, Gettysburg, Pennsylvania.

Bibliography

Bates, Samuel P. *The Battle of Chancellorsville.* Meadville: Pennsylvania, 1882.
Battles and Leaders of The Civil War. Edited by R. U. Johnson and C. C. Buel. New York: Century Company, 1887–88.
Bigelow, John. *The Campaign of Chancellorsville.* New Haven and London: Yale University Press, 1910.
Catton, Bruce. *Terrible Swift Sword.* Garden City: New Jersey, 1963.
Chambers, Lenoir. *Stonewall Jackson.* New York: Wm. Morrow & Co., 1959.
Dawes, Rufus R. *Service with The Sixth Wisconsin Volunteers.* Marietta: Ohio, 1890.
Doubleday, Abner. *Chancellorsville and Gettysburg.* New York: C. Scribner's Sons, 1882.
Dowdey, Clifford. *Lee.* New York: Bonanza Books, 1965.
Freeman, Douglas S. *Lee's Lieutenants, Vol. 2.* New York: C. Scribner's Sons, 1946.
Hay, Thomas R. and Donald B. Sanger. *James Longstreet.* Baton Rouge: Louisiana State University Press, 1952.
McPherson, James M. *Battle Cry of Freedom.* New York: Oxford University Press, 1988.
Report of the Joint Committee on the Conduct of the War at the Second Session, Thirty-Eighth Congress. Volume 1. Washington, D.C.: United States Congress, 1865. (*Supplemental Report.* Volume 2. 1866.)
The War of the Rebellion: A Compilation of the Official Records (O.R.) of the Union and Confederate Armies. Washington, D.C.: U.S. Government Printing Office, 1880–1901.
Williams, Alpheus. *From the Cannon's Mouth: The Civil War Letters of General Alpheus S. Williams.* Edited by Milo M. Quaife. Detroit: Wayne State University Press, 1959.
Williams, Kenneth P. *Lincoln Finds a General.* New York: Macmillan, 1949–59.

INDEX

A

Aldie, Va., 58

Alsop's farm, cavalry fight, 161

Anderson, Gen. Richard H., 73, 76, 130, 135, 138, 142, 154, 155, 175, 178, 179, 191, 206, 210, 216, 227, 247, 294, 324, 326, 333, 336, 337, 339, 342, 345

Antietam, Battle of, 6, 8, 26, 80, 86, 106, 132, 167, 171, 204, 270, 272, 321

Appomattox, 81

Aquia and Richmond R.R., 109

Aquia Creek Landing, 2, 18, 87

Archer, Gen. James J., 217, 288

Arms and equipment (see also Ordnance), 21, 27

Army of Northern Virginia (see also Lee, R. E.; Operations; and Confederate), absentees, 68; advance on May 1, 179; artillery, 69, 75; contact on May 1, 184; defensive position, 76, 88; discipline and morale, 67, 68, 284; mentioned, 26; ordnance, 70, 71; organizational improvements, 69, 71; promotion, 72; staff, 71-3; strength and composition, 32, 73, 77; supply bases, 88

Army of the Potomac (see also Hooker; Operations; and Federal), able and willing to fight, 279; concentration at Chancellorsville, 141, 173; conditions improved, 13 ff; contact on May 1, 184; corps insignia adopted, 14; crosses Rappahannock, 117, 124; crosses Rapidan, 124; desertions, 14; did not panic, 248; discipline and morale, 14, 31, 284; dispositions, May 1, 197; health, 14-15; intelligence agency, 15; lost opportunity, 268; mentioned, 17, 18, 26, 33, 38, 17, 85; moves up for jumpoff, 113; President's visit, 1-15; retreat, 350; staff deficiencies, 34-5

Arrowsmith, Capt. Charles, 251

Artillery, Confederate, 27-9, 70-1, 75, 191, 209, 290, 295, 297, 324; Federal, 26-9, 32, 135, 193, 245, 252-4, 261-2, 290, 325-6, 342

Ashby, Col. Turner, 56

Averell, Gen. William W., 25, 46, 47-55, 74, 112, 267 69, 289, 353

B

Balloon observation, 163, 175, 217, 305, 316

Ball's Bluff, Battle of, 35

Baltimore and Ohio R.R., 32, 61

Banks' Ford, 64, 76-7, 96, 98, 113-16, 128, 130, 134, 138-9, 142-3, 148, 150, 155-6, 164, 178-80, 186, 189, 192, 277, 290, 324, 326, 330-1, 337-9, 345, 352-3, 362

Banks, Gen. N. P., 67

Barksdale, Gen. William, 155, 309, 318, 345

Barlow, Gen. Francis C., 223

Beauregard, Gen. P.T.G., 90

Benham, Gen. Henry W., 96, 127-8, 139, 164, 326-7, 337, 339, 344

Berry, Gen. Hiram, 245, 263, 265, 288, 290, 292-4, 299

Best, Col. Emory F., 216

Beverly Ford, 106

Birney, Gen. David A., 200, 210-11, 216-7, 249, 263, 265

Black, Dr. Harvey, 262

Blakely guns, 70

Boswell, Capt., 273

Bowling Green Road, 318

Brandy Station, Va., 50, 156, 267

Brentsville, Va., 48

Brigades, divisions, corps (see respective commanders)

Brock Road, 184, 206, 233

Brooks, Noah, 7

Brooks, Gen. W.T.H., 307, 309, 319, 331, 333, 336, 342

Buford, Gen. John, 23, 25, 112, 353

Bullock's (Chandler's), 147, 200, 245, 258, 266, 274, 280, 290

Bull Run, First Battle of, 122

Bull Run Mountains, Va., 58

Burnham, Col. Hiram, 307, 324

Burnside, Gen. Ambrose E., 1, 2, 8, 9, 15, 18, 20, 26, 28, 29, 30, 31, 36, 62, 67, 74, 83, 90, 91, 132, 308, 322, 324

Burton's farm, 233, 235

Butterfield, Gen. Daniel E., 2, 21, 117, 145, 163-4, 187, 189, 202, 217, 309-17 321, 346-7, 353

C

Caldwell, Gen. John C., 300

[391]

[397]